People, Poverty, and Politics

People, Poverty, and Politics

Pennsylvanians during the Great Depression

Thomas H. Coode
John F. Bauman

Contributors:
Ernest B. Fricke
Donald D. Housley
W. Wayne Smith

Lewisburg
Bucknell University Press
London and Toronto: Associated University Presses

Associated University Presses, Inc.
4 Cornwall Drive
East Brunswick, New Jersey 08816

Associated University Presses
69 Fleet Street
London EC4Y IEU, England

Associated University Presses
Toronto M5E 1A7, Canada

Library of Congress Cataloging in Publication Data

Coode, Thomas H 1931-
People, poverty, and politics.

Bibliography: p.
Includes index.
1. Depressions--1929--Pennsylvania. 2. Pennsylvania--Economic conditions. 3. Pennsylvania--Politics and government--1865-1950. I. Bauman, John F., 1938- joint author. II. Title.
HC107.P4C66 338.5′42 78-75198
ISBN 0-8387-2320-9

Printed in the United States of America

For Liz and Barb

Contents

Acknowledgments

Several years ago the authors conceived the idea for a book which would attempt to illuminate the broad impact of the Great Depression on the social, political, and economic life of Pennsylvania. Since then, numerous people and institutions have supported us in many ways toward transforming that idea into this book. Our indebtedness is considerable. California State College, California, Pennsylvania, availed us of both time and travel funds. The authors owe special gratitude to our collaborators, Professors Smith, Housley, and Fricke, whose contributions to this history of Pennsylvania during the Great Depression not only strengthen its conceptual framework, but also enlarge the book's dimension.

But our gratitude extends to many others. The authors are grateful to the staffs of the Urban Archives of Temple University, the National Archives, the Library of Congress, the Historical Society of Pennsylvania, the Pennsylvania Historical and Museum Commission, the Free Library of Philadelphia, the Archives of Industrial Society of the Hillman Library at the University of Pittsburg, the California State College Library, and the Franklin D. Roosevelt Library. The staffs of these institutions cheerfully and efficiently facilitated our search for materials. We are especially grateful to the students of California State College who conducted numerous interviews cited in the text.

Many people have contributed extensively to the preparation of the manuscript. Professors H. Viscount Nelson of Dartmouth College, Thomas A. Bryson of West Georgia College, and Ron Forsythe of California State College read portions of the work and offered invaluable suggestions for its improvement. And without Liz Coode's yeoman service at the typewriter and her vigilant questioning of spelling and the use of commas this manuscript would never have reached the publisher's desk.

For all this aforementioned help and the dedicated and cheerful support of many friends and colleagues we are sincerely grateful. While months of proofreading, coffee conferences, and editorial sessions have hopefully tightened and strengthened the manuscript, weaknesses doubtless remain; alas, for these the authors alone are responsible.

T. H. C.

J. F. B.

California, Pennsylvania

Introduction

Most studies of the Great Depression and the New Deal have focused on the nation, and not on states, cities, or small towns. Of course, the decade has invited macroscopic inspection, since in the1930s the entire nation seemingly floundered in an economic abyss. The jobless numbered in the millions, and the enormity of the recovery problem begged bold and national solutions from Republicans such as Herbert Hoover, as well from Democrats such as Franklin Delano Roosevelt. Moreover, the latter's New Deal spurred unprecedented federal intervention replete with experiments in national planning and broad-scaled public works.

Historians have explored the social, political, and economic issues raised by the crash of the American economy, and have speculated endlessly on the ideological, administrative, and political ramifications of the New Deal. Social historians, probing the consequences of the Great Depression, have described the "poverty of abundance," the collapse of voluntarism, and the emergence of modern social work. Scholars have investigated topics ranging from the New Deal and the problem of monopoly, to New Dealers themselves, such as Rexford Tugwell, Harry Hopkins and Marriner Eccles, among many others.[1]

While these studies on a national scope have enlivened the historiographical debate over the 1930s as a "watershed," or the New Deal as "revolutionary," they have added minimally to an understanding of the effect of the depression and the New Deal on the social processes involving particular groups and communities. In fact, few historians have examined how the era altered the social relationships binding individuals and groups to their communities and the nation. While a few macroscopic studies have dealt with the centralizing tendencies of the New Deal, they have contributed little toward understanding the decade of the 1930s as an episode in the process of modernization. Such a task awaits more microscopic expositions on how the events of the decade shaped individual and community attitudes and how the centralization of social, political, and economic functions influenced events on a local or regional scale.[2]

The ten chapters which comprise *People, Poverty, and Politics* offer a modest attempt to address some of these locality-relevant issues. These studies of Pennsylvania in the 1930s examine the impact of the Great Depression and the New Deal in places such as company-owned mining villages, city textile districts, and farming communities. Each of the studies focuses on either a city or a region of Pennsylvania, and each seeks to discover how events of the decade affected people's lives and therefore altered basic social and political institutions. The studies also speculate on the extent to which New Deal programs may have been influenced by local forces.

Not that all of the recent histories of the 1930s have ignored the cities or the states. James T. Patterson's seminal study of *The New Deal and the States* explores the political impact of the "new federalism" which was created by the proliferation of federal welfare programs. And in volume 2 of *The New Deal,* John Braeman, Robert H. Bremner, and David Brody have edited a collection of articles which investigates the impact of the New Deal on various states. Such studies as Bruce Stave's *The New Deal and the Last Hurrah* have helped illuminate the effect of the New Deal on local machine politics.[3]

However,most studies of the New Deal have underplayed the element of social and political change wrought by a decade-long output of extensive federal labor and welfare legislation. Instead, histories of the period have stressed the themes of consensus and continuity. The above studies are no exception. Patterson, for example, observes that state houses generally remained as conservative and socially unenlightened in the 1930s as they were in the 1920s. He argues that only a few states such as Pennsylvania, where the New Deal generated "political competition," experienced their own "little New Deals." And even in this handful of states Patterson detects little more than a modicum of progressivism, which produced ephemeral results at that.

Whether dealing with the nation, cities, or states, most historians of the depression years have focused on the political aspects of the era and have questioned the extent to which the Great Depression and the New Deal disturbed the ideological roots of America's social and political institutions. Admittedly, none of the chapters in this volume proposes that anything other than the "American Way" prevailed in the 1930s; that is, the New Deal did not undermine America's basic beliefs regarding the good to be gained from hard work and the evil which was inherent in the dole.[4] On the other hand, these examinations of local and regional events in Pennsylvania attempt to uncover crucial insights into the spirit of America in the 1930s. They suggest that the decade wrought major changes in the social and political configurations of local communities, and that these changes resulted in a significant leavening of fresh hopes and aspirations, especially among immigrants, blacks, and organized labor.

In many ways Pennsylvania affords an excellent vantage point from which to observe the grass roots impact of the Great Depression and the New Deal. The state embraced a variety of "new" and "old" ethnic groups, a diversity of industry, and large regions of agricultural production. In addition, the Appalachian mountain chain created a natural cleavage between the eastern and western regions of the state. Therefore, in the 1920s, Pennsylvania encapsulated a near microcosm of the United States, rendering the state somewhat representative of national trends. Although intraparty factionalism within Pennsylvania's sovereign Republican party enabled Governor Gifford Pinchot (1923-27, 1931-35) to keep a flicker of liberal activity alive, the business ideal in Pennsylvania, as in other states, easily eclipsed the glimmer of progressivism. During the

1920s, Pennsylvania legislators openly proclaimed obeisance to the sanctity of protection and the open shop. For example, industrialist-politicians such as Bucks County textile magnate Joseph Grundy anticipated a glorious "New Era" of prosperity founded upon industrial paternalism, trade associationalism, and the benevolence of government toward business.

Nevertheless, despite Pennsylvania's macrocosmic features, it would be a mistake to treat the state's history as typical, especially after the events of the 1920s yielded to the depression1930s. Although the Keystone State had sizable regions of farming and timber culture, Pennsylvania boasted an enormous urban population, making it among the nation's top centers of manufacturing. On the eve of the Great Depression only New York state's plethora of small plants and loft industries outnumbered Pennsylvania's 17,314 industrial establishments. Other industrial states such as Illinois, Ohio, Michigan, and Massachussets housed fewer than 15,000 manufacturing plants and factories. While Pennsylvania's $6.5-billion output of bridge steel, locomotives, oil products, carpets, hosiery, and other manufacturers was only 70 percent of New York's overall production, the state's output of manufacturers still ranked far above other rival industrial states such as Ohio, Michigan and Illinois. Significantly in 1927 Pennsylvania employed almost a million workers in manufacturing alone, only 85,000 fewer than New York. Not surprising, then, that when the nation's economy collapsed in 1929, the effect on Pennsylvania's economy was catastrophic.[5]

The index of manufacturing activity vividly recorded the state's economic plunge during the depression years. Between 1927 and 1933 Pennsylvania lost over 5,000 manufacturing establishments; only New York lost more. The value of the state's industrial production plummeted 50 percent from $7 billion in 1927 to slightly over $3 billion in 1933. Worsening economic conditions exacted a costly human toll. In 1933 the state employed 270,000 fewer laborers in manufacturing than in 1927. Industrial employment in New York dropped by 339,000 in the same period; and in Illinois, which endured its own share of economic losses, the number of manufacturing jobs fell by 203,000.[6]

Understandably, throughout the Great Depression, Pennsylvania sheltered one of America's largest relief populations. In 1930, in fact, with over 200,000 jobless Pennsylvanians searching for work, the state had the third highest unemployment total in America. Only New York with 350,000 out of work and Illinois with 227,000 looking for jobs exceeded Pennsylvania's jobless rate. Nevertheless, in 1932 state relief administrators complained that Pennsylvania bore the nation's heaviest welfare burden. Over 324,000 families, or close to 2 million people jammed Pennsylvania's relief rolls, compared to the 312,000 dependent families in New York, the 234,000 in Illinois and the 203,000 jobless families seeking assistance in Ohio.[7]

Pennsylvania's relief burden never lightened. By 1934 the state's case load of dependent families rose to 441,000. As in other states, many of the needy lived in cities. Over 11 percent of the families in Philadelphia, and 18 percent of those in Pittsburgh were on relief in 1933. At the same time, in many of the state's rural and semi-rural towns and hamelts joblessness and grinding poverty were equally endemic. Thirty-seven percent of the work force in rural Fayette County was unemployed in 1934. After touring Pennsylvania in the fall of 1933 Lorena Hickok, a roving reporter for New Deal relief administrator Harry Hopkins, reported ruefully that, between the plagues of labor strife and serious unemployment, Pennsylvania could experience a "good deal of disorder in the next few months." "Relief," surmised Hickok, "now entered the picture as a stabilizing influence."[8]

The following chapters hopefully fathom some of the despair that Hickok found among Pennsylvania's jobless, and afford at least faint insight into her perhaps sardonic reference to relief as a "stabilizing influence." Focusing on several major regions of the state and a number of important communities such as Philadelphia and Allentown, the studies explore a number of major topics, including the collapse of voluntarism, the bureaucratization of social welfare, the New Deal and the triumph of organized labor, and the role of ethnic and racial groups in the whirligig of depression politics in Pennsylvania.

Chapter 1 describes the gnawing poverty which characterized the lives of coal miners in the bituminous fields of southwestern Pennsylvania even before the Great Depression brought economic hardship to millions of other Americans over the country. The next two chapters look at the attempts of the state's jobless to cope with the sociopsychological malaise of unemployment and poverty. For example, chapter 2 investigates the jobless marches and demonstrations which pierced the depression gloom overhanging the mill districts of Philadelphia. The next chapter employs the theme of modernization in relating the depression and the New Deal to the emergence of bureaucratic relief in rural Snyder County.

Chapter 4 deals with the thrift garden projects, cooperative stores, and other self-help activities which physically and emotionally sustained the unemployed of Allentown, Pennsylvania. Politics dominate chapter 5, which examines the role of Indiana County labor and ethnic groups in promoting the Democratic party in the critical election of 1934. However, relief competed for importance with big labor in contemporary politics. Chapter 6 thus describes how the Great Depression and the New Deal helped make the United Mine Workers of America a powerful social and political force in Pennsylvania. The next chapter uses southwestern Pennsylvania to illustrate the crucial role of federal relief in restructuring the region's social and political institutions.

Two following chapters utilize the community base to explore the role and effect of New Deal work projects and housing programs. Shifting the focus again to Philadelphia, chapter 8 looks at the entrenched conservative opposition which the Works Progress Administration confronted in that city. Still concerned with Philadelphia, chapter 9 addresses the problem that housing reformers experienced in shaping the federal housing program to accommodate the city's growing black population. The concluding chapter views Pennsylvania panoramically and attempts to summarize the New Deal's effect on the politics of the state in the 1930s.

One of the particular themes explored throughout these studies concerns the role of the Great Depression and the New Deal in breeching the isolation which kept rural, ethnic, racial, and such occupational groups as miners and textile workers out of the mainstream of modernizing trends in America. In their studies of the social changes affecting Middletown, U. S. A., in the 1920s and1930s, Robert and Helen Lynd assigned considerable importance to modern industrialism, the automobile revolution, and the bureaucratization of society. However, many other sociologists and political scientists have observed that the building of the "mass society" was far from completed by the eve of World War II. Moreover, by 1930, the small town still dominated much of American life. In effect, the flapper and tin-lizzy mobility popularized by F. Scott Fitzgerald and the slick magazines, while portentous, touched only the veneer, and not the corpus of society. Large segments of American society barely glimpsed the trappings of modernism advertised so lavishly in magazines such as *Better Homes and Gardens, Life,* and others. Automobiles and radios were luxuries inaccessible to most miners, steelworkers and textile workers in the 1920s and 1930s. Rural roads were typically unpaved and impassible in rain or snow.

Undoubtedly, however, the psychological dimensions of isolation outweighed the physical constraints of both distance and technological backwardness. Arthur J. Vidich and Joseph Bensam, Robert K. Merton, and Roland Warren have all described in one way or another the social-psychological barriers which as late as the 1960s still separated numerous small-town and neighborhood populations from the cosmopolitan or decision-making sectors of society. Warren posits the situation diagrammatically by constructing a model in which community-based institutions are located along a horizontal plane. He hypothesizes that as the modernizing forces of urbanization and bureaucratization engulf the locality, institutional ties become vertically extended, penetrating further and further into the more impersonal, cosmopolitan realm of the "extra-community." In such a way local school boards become linked to state and nationally based school-board associations, small town Veterans of Foreign Wars receive leadership from

Washington, D.C. headquarters, and United Mine Workers' locals implement policy hammered out in national offices.

Ultimately, as Vidich and Bensam detail in *Small Town in a Mass Society: Class Power and Religion in a Rural Community,* local organizations rooted in a provincial orientation inexorably become integrated into the expanding orbit of the "mass" or urbanizing society.[9]

These chapters deal extensively with the nationalizing forces at work expanding the extraterritorial linkages in American communities in the 1930s. Undoubtedly, the Great Depression and the New Deal accelerated these centralizing tendencies informing the modern urban-industrial society. Although historians have traced an undercurrent of decentralist opinion through the labyrinth of New Deal thought, for many millions of Americans the Roosevelt administration made Washington, D.C., the main street of America. Under various banners — the Blue Eagle, the PWA, WPA, FSA, FDIC — the New Deal experimented with a national economics, a national welfare system, national planning, and, according to Jane DeHart Mathews, even a national theater and a national art. Under the aegis of the New Deal, organized labor grew from a feeble starveling, waging losing wars in one organizational battleground after another, to the young giant of the late 1930s. In this line, several chapters in this book pose the question as to what degree big labor, nurtured by the New Deal, broadened the purview of young steelworkers, miners, and textile workers, beyond locally derived concerns and aspirations and into the nation. Therefore, by focusing on the impact of the New Deal on local populations and organizations these chapters investigate the degree to which the events of the 1930s broke the crust of isolation and hastened the modernization of society.

Finally, while this volume is not authentic "history from the bottom up," it does attempt to peer beneath the exterior of major social and political institutions and glimpse the human strivings and tribulations. Accordingly, although several of the chapters discuss labor unions, they never overlook the miners, loom fixers, or machinists who belonged to the unions. Nor do the discussions of relief foresake concern for the unemployed, or the examinations of politics abjure interest in Italian, Hungarian, or Slovak voters. In effect, then, this work seeks to grapple with grass roots' topics, and offers at least some insight into the relationship between FDR's "bold, persistent experimentation," social insolation, and modernization among the people, their politics and poverty in Pennsylvania.

NOTES

1. Albert Romasco, *The Poverty of Abundance: Hoover, the Nation and the Depression* (New York, 1965); Roy Lubove, *The Professional Altruist: The Emergence of Social Work as a Career, 1880-1930* (Cambridge, Mass., 1965); Ellis W. Hawley, *The New Deal and the Problem of Monopoly: A Study of Economic Ambivalence* (Princeton, N.J., 1966); Bernard Sternsher, *Rexford Tugwell and the New Deal* (New Brunswick, N.J., 1964).

2. James T. Patterson, *The New Deal and the States: Federalism in Transition* (Princeton, N.J., 1969).

3. Ibid.; John Braeman, Robert H. Bremmer, David Brody, eds., *The New Deal: The State and Local Levels* (Columbus, Ohio, 1975); Bruce Stave, *The New Deal and the Last Hurrah: Pittsburgh Machine Politics* (Pittsburgh, 1970).

4. William W. Bremer, "Along the American Way: The New Deal's Work Relief Program for the Unemployed," *Journal of American History* 52, no. 3 (December 1975), pp. 636-49.

5. U. S. Department of Commerce, *Bureau of the Census, Biennial Census of Manufacturers*, 1927, 1931, 1933 (Washington, D.C.).

6. Ibid.

7. U. S. Department of Commerce, *Fifteenth Census of the U. S., 1930, U. S. Survey of Unemployment* (Washington, D.C., 1931); U. S. Federal Emergency Relief Administration, *Unemployment Relief Census, U. S. Summary* (Washington, 1934); U. S. Emergency Relief Administration, *Statistical Summary of Emergency Relief Activities, January 1933-December 1935* (Washington, D.C., 1937).

8. U. S. Federal Emergency Relief Administration, *Statistical Summary of Emergency Relief Activities, January 1933-December 1935* (Washington, 1937); Field Report of Lorena Hickok, August 7-12, 1933, in Harry L. Hopkins Papers, Franklin D. Roosevelt Library, Hyde Park, New York.

9. Arthur J. Vidich and Joseph Bensam, *Small Town in a Mass Society: Class Power and Religion in a Rural Community* (Princeton, N.J., 1968); Robert K. Merton, *Social Theory and Social Structure*, (Glencoe, Ill., 1957); Roland Warren, *The Community in America*, 2nd ed. (New York, 1972).

People, Poverty, and Politics

[1]
The Long Depression of Southwestern Pennsylvania Coal Miners

During World War I southwestern Pennsylvania coal miners shared in the prosperity that the war brought to the coal industry. As the nation mobilized for war, hundreds of new shafts were dug and many old ones reopened. By the end of the war 9,000 mines were operating over the country – three times the number of thirty years before. In the bituminous fields, the value of output increased fivefold and employment tripled. To both operators and miners alike the coal industry "looked robust indeed."[1]

In a wartime effort to stabilize coal production, the Wilson administration sponsored the Washington Agreement (1917), which provided for union recognition and wage increases. The miners welcomed the higher wage scale, even though they believed it inadequate compensation for a wartime inflation that increased almost 50 percent between 1917 and 1919 and another 30 percent the following year. Thus, the war's end found miners chafing at the bit for wage adjustments, and a brief strike in 1919 did in fact result in an industry-wide general wage increase. The United Mine Workers of America (UMWA) claimed miners had won a great victory. It would be their last one for almost fifteen years.

In 1920 the output of bituminous coal reached an all-time peak of 568 million tons, and the number of employed miners soared to 640,000. Over a half-million of these miners belonged to the UMWA, which had won for most of its members a basic daily wage of $7.50. However, within ten years, overcapacity would cause chaos in the fields and nearly bankrupt the coal industry. During the war, high prices for coal caused new mines to open in the South, where coal operators capitalized on newer machinery and cheaper labor. Postwar competition from oil, gas, and electricity as well as increased efficiency in coal use led to widespread mine closings. New and more efficient mining machinery replaced many coal miners. One study showed that, if mechanical miners were to operate full time, they would leave work for only 150,000 to 250,000 of the industry's 700,000 men. By 1926, bituminous capacity surpassed one billion tons; demand equaled half that. Prices plunged, and operators cut costs, increased hours, and ignored safety standards even more than before. Stockpiled coal lay in unused heaps. Unemployment rose, mines closed, wages fell. Finally, a series of disastrous strikes all but destroyed the United Mine Workers, creating what labor historians came to call the Lean Years.[2]

In 1922, with unemployment in the coal fields at a record high and the bituminous industry already reeling from economic imbalance, operators in southwestern Pennsylvania demanded wage cuts from 25 to 30 percent. At the same time, the UMWA insisted that its members needed a wage boost. Both sides failed to budge, and on April 1, the miners struck. Anthracite miners from eastern Pennsylvania joined the strike, as did the 70,000 miners in the Connellsville coke region who had neither belonged to a union nor participated in a major strike in thirty years. In southwestern Pennsylvania, John Brophy, president of District 2 of the UMWA issued a clarion calling for nonunion to join the union's effort:

STRIKE CALL
TO NON-UNION MEN

> Miners of Non-Union Fields of Pennsylvania:—
> Fellow Workers:—
> RISE!
> STRIKE!
> This is your fight.

You have had wage cuts in the last year.
Do you want another?
You'll get it if the Union gets its.
QUIT WORK APRIL 1ST.
Join our fight.
You will get
A checkweighman.
Correct Weight.
Decent Wages.
Your independence as free men and miners.
DROP YOUR TOOLS!
LEAVE THE MINE!
The Union welcomes you.
600,000 miners are out to maintain wages for all miners.
Miners united win.
Miners divided lose.
Don't scab on Men Who Are Fighting Your Fights.
Your only reward for scabbing will be
Short weight.
More Wage Cuts.
REFUSE TO BE ROBBED!
COME OUT APRIL 1ST!
STRIKE!

Over 600,000 miners left the pits in what was called a classic labor struggle of equal parts.[3]

Nonetheless, the strike was no contest. The miners lost at every turn, and in southwestern Pennsylvania the owners developed the method they would employ successfully against miners — on strike or not — throughout the decade before the New Deal.

In both commercial and "captive" mines, operators moved ruthlessly to break the strike and destroy the miners' union, importing Negroes from the South by the trainload, especially into Fayette County. These scabs, also called "cotton pickers" by some of the strikers, were paid low wages. Also, according to the strikers, they mined very little coal. White strikebreakers were also brought in and, along with the Negroes, were escorted to and from work by company and county police and deputies. They were housed in segregated barracks and company houses (to this day a few coal patches still contain a "scab hill"). Strikers attempting to get at the scabs often battled the police who stood between them and the strikebreakers.[4]

Both sides were guilty of violence. In taverns in California, Pennsylvania, scabs were beaten by strikers; in nearby Crescent Heights, where a number of black strikebreakers were housed, a Negro was shot, his body concealed in a hayloft, and the hayloft burned. The operators employed spies among the strikers and circulated blacklists through the coal fields. The companies virtually owned the county sheriffs and deputies they ordered to disperse all gatherings and carry out thousands of evictions. The police used whips to intimidate the strikers and pickets, and patrolled the area around the tent camps erected by evicted miners. One former president of a local union was rousted from his tent at two o'clock in the morning and accused of dynamiting a company building. He was taken to a police headquarters located in the company store, where "they beat hell out of (him)." He was finally released, along with his fourteen-year-old brother, who had also been arrested.[5]

During 1922, more than 380,000 miners participated in strikes in southwestern Pennsylvania. Lost wages totalled over $208 million. In the Uniontown area of Fayette County, where the strike was especially bitter, looting, dynamiting, train derailment, and even murder were common. Compounding the grim statistics was the miners' realization that the mine towns were shut off from the rest of Pennsylvania and the nation. As one mine leader later wrote:

> One would find it hard to prove that [southwestern Pennsylvania] was under the jurisdiction of the United States Constitution during 1922. The Commonwealth of Pennsylvania was no more interested than the federal government in the rights and welfare of the coal diggers. State Policemen and militia were as eager as county and private police to do the bidding of the operators.[6]

Matters remained that way for a decade or more. A terrible depression persisted in the coal counties of southwestern Pennsylvania for years before the great crash of 1929 brought economic deprivation to millions of other Americans. Only later did outside forces reach into the state's isolated coal fields to bring some measure of well-being to the miners.

The company-owned coal patches of southwestern Pennsylvania were one of the last remnants of feudalism in America. When the coal companies opened new territories in the late 1800s, they provided homes for their miners simply because nobody else would. Even if they could have afforded them, miners were unwilling to purchase homes before they knew how long a mine would remain open. Further, homebuilders were reluctant to erect houses in potential ghost towns. Consequently, the companies built their own villages, closed them to the public, and ran them as they saw fit. As one student of the coal fields has written, "The miners in the patch houses were much farther from town than the actual miles that separated them". They "lived on feudal islands in the country," but were "not of it." This tenant system stultified ambition and depressed the lives of the miners and their families in almost every possible way.[7]

The patch houses where the miners and their families lived stood in rows of identical eight-room, double structures, four rooms to a side. They were usually painted a dull and ugly red. Some of the patches contained four, five, or even more rows of houses. In larger patches as many as 400 families existed at the sufferance of the companies. In "scab hill" locales, the rows of houses isolated above the mine tipple were occupied by black miners and their families. A few elderly coal miners have recalled that the patch houses were kept in good repair, but in fact most companies paid more attention to their police and store activities than to miners' dwellings, and allowed them to go without paint or repairs for years. In the early days windows were left unscreened, and coal dust invaded the houses in summer, covering everything. Most houses — those at the Pittsburgh Coal Company's patch at Arnold City in Fayette County were typical — were "cheaply constructed, ramshackle affairs" that provided "ample protection against the elements," but were "devoid of even the most elementary comforts and conveniences." The houses contained no inside utilities, and each family had to draw its own water from street-corner pumps. The houses were lighted by kerosene lamps and heated by coal stoves which also cooked the family's meals.[8]

Inside the houses the kitchen was the family center. Often

furnished with no more than a stove and a table (the latter often made from old packing boxes), the kitchen dominated the dusty household. One visitor to a Washington County patch described a typical kitchen containing "a wide plank over two saw horses" for a table, two chairs, a carbide light, a shaving set for the men, and a stove "over which hung a gaudy calendar provided by the local grocery man." Many kitchens featured Slovak or Italian "God Bless our Home" wall plaques and tablecloths, pathetic testimony to the faith of the inhabitants. Later, many miners decorated their walls with framed newspaper or magazine pictures of President Franklin D. Roosevelt.[9]

The other rooms were crowded with beds to accommodate the miners' large families. A few battered tables and chairs and a chest of drawers were sometimes arranged among beds furnished with mattresses stuffed with straw. Furniture tended to be secondhand, usually purchased piecemeal on the installment plan. Upstairs, an old pedal sewing machine patched and sewed the family's meager clothing. Clothes were hung on hooks or nails. Often, an old box served as a trunk for the family's few special-day clothes.[10]

Patch houses had small front yards. The slightly larger back yard was often occupied by a garden. Coal shanties and outhouses, located at the rear of the back yard, lined the alleys. Many Old Country people crowded their small yards with grape arbors, chicken coops, and pig sties, often leaving only room enough for a wash line, an outdoor oven, and few rows of tomatoes and beans. The younger families grew vegetable gardens. Since work in the mines was insecure and work weeks frequently short, most mining families took advantage of the summer to grow as many vegetables as the yard could produce. These gardens were necessities; a failed garden meant a winter of black bread and beans. Even the most wretched miners used the ground; a social worker in 1933 found families who had to live in the abandoned coke ovens around Latrobe growing "pathetic little patches of tomatoes and cabbages."[11]

Looming above the miners' houses were the more substantial frame or brick homes of mine officials. The superintendant lived in the best house, followed by the mine foremen, a few of the fire bosses, and so on down the line. These homes usually included inside baths and toilets, luxuries not available to patch residents. At the Crucible Steel Company mine in Greene County the superintendant resided in a sturdy fourteen-room frame home complete with swimming pool and tennis court. A miner's promotion to face boss or foreman brought not only increased income but a change in life style. Living quarters in the patch depended upon one's rank in the mine.[12]

The Coal and Iron Police, whose presence, one officer claimed, had a "clean, moral effect upon our employees, which gives them a feeling of security," controlled the patch. Despite this flattering description, few police forces were ever so widely hated and denounced.[13]

Established by statute in 1866, the Coal and Iron Police were no more than loosely organized feudal retainers who imposed the operators' private laws on the patch. Appointments under the Coal and Iron Police Act required only a petition to the governor requesting a commission. The coal and steel corporations made their requests; state officials made no attempt to determine the fitness or character of the applicant. Indeed, evidence shows that the state attempted to learn no more about the applicants than their names. The corporations and the state thus cooperated in a system whereby police power was farmed out to industry. State regulation, supervision, or responsibility was nonexistent. The patches became "islands of police power . . . free to float as the employers saw fit." By allowing these private armies to exist, the state further isolated patch residents from the legitimate police power of Pennsylvania.[14]

Officially, the coal police stamped out gambling, narcotics, and prostitution in the patch, stopped fights, uncovered and destroyed stills and moonshine, and investigated murders, stabbings, and other crimes. Further, it was their duty to "expedite the production of coal and maintain a peaceful community." (Old miners recall that they seemed to be everywhere.) The police protected payrolls, guarded company property, and, during times of particular strife, "met all trains, streetcars and busses entering (mine) properties, furnishing information and ascertaining the business of all strangers."[15]

One superintendent remarked that the coal policeman was "respected by the employees of the company for the authority he represents and exercises, thereby simplifying the preservation of law and order." Officers and patrolmen were impressed with the necessity of familiarizing themselves "in a detached way" with each employee in the patch, obtaining thereby "first hand knowledge of the man's efficiency and value to the company, his home surroundings and whether he is devoted to family life."[16]

The miners, on the other hand, despised and distrusted the police, calling them "Cossacks" or "Yellow Dogs." Not surprisingly, they believed them to be paid tools of the company. The police were especially active during strikes, breaking up meetings, protecting scabs, accompanying strikebreakers to and from the pits, evicting strikers from company property, watching over all social events, paying "special attention to strangers and the passage of literature" (sic) at such gatherings. Many old diggers still display scars from police-inflicted wounds, grim reminders of preunion years.[17]

Before 1933 miners had also to contend with the state militia (often called in to protect company property and to disperse gatherings of miners) and county sheriffs. The latter, especially in southwestern Pennsylvania, were notoriously anti-union, repeatedly serving as strikebreakers. Old coal miners particularly remember the "deputies" commissioned by county sheriffs to do the companies' bidding. Sheriffs entered into individual contracts with coal companies, charging them so much per day for each deputy and paying the deputies. The state exercised no control over this system, and the deal allowed for widespread fee-grabbing by county sheriffs. The deputies were not police by training or temperament; those not chosen by the sheriff himself (usually as a political favor) were selected from lists provided by detective agencies.[18]

Operators also used the company store to control the miner's life. Retired miners may disagree on store policies and prices, but they agree unanimously that the ubiquitous company store helped to isolate them from the outside world.

Items purchased in the company stores might have been

"generally of the highest quality" (as one student has contended), but prices were for the most part higher there than in the other area stores. The operators argued higher prices were necessary; it cost more to ship goods to these isolated areas than elsewhere, and the miners' reliance on credit buying increased expenses. Of course, isolation and credit buying reinforced company control of the patch. Company stores could charge higher prices without fear of losing business. Some operators even claimed that they made more money from their stores than from selling coal. Some miners called these commissaries "pluck-me" stores; price lists were called "plucks."[19]

In many patches a variety of pressures forced miners to buy all their goods at company stores. Miners who bought on credit were seldom given that courtesy by local entrepeneurs. In some patches, buying at the stores was a condition of employment, especially in bad times. In others, miners were not forced to buy at the company store, but if they did not, they were the first to be laid off.[20]

Miners not only bought their working tools at the company store, they paid their rent and other bills there as well. Many of the companies, such as the Jones and Laughlin Steel Corporation at the Vesta mines in Washington County, deducted the miner's store bill from his pay. Often, the bill equaled the miner's entire salary. Sometimes an X was drawn on the miner's statement to indicate that his bill was the same as or greater than his pay. The red line often substituted for the X was called a "snake." Miners called these no-pay statements "roosters."[21]

Some older miners insist that the stores were "good to people," that the prices were fair, that a miner was not forced to deal there, and that the merchandise was of excellent quality. A few even claim that the company store kept them going during hard times and that in their area, at least, "nobody went hungry, because of the store." Others believe that miners took unfair advantage of the company store, rather than the other way around. Nonetheless, as one old-timer put it, the company store held "a life mortgage on the men."[22]

In a few patches, scrip was used as currency. In the Frick patches, scrip bills looked like government greenbacks except that, instead of the usual political face adorning one side, a group of coal miners with picks gazed out at the holder. Crude scrip coins made of aluminum or cardboard were called "chicken feed," "stickers," "flickers," and "drag." By issuing scrip, the operator gained the advantage of conducting his business without cash and was assured of his miners doing business at the commissary — in most cases the only place where the scrip was honored. A few miners remember "scrip books." In some places where miners were paid in currency, those who owed excessive amounts to the store were paid only in scrip until their bills were paid. However, the entire system came to an end when the state outlawed the use of scrip.[23]

After the 1922 coal strikes and during the hard times that followed, companies used more stringent store operations as a means of strictly supervising the miner's lives. Labor strife, depression and unemployment, fear of theft and break-ins brought in the Coal and Iron Police as store guards. Further, the police were ordered to keep close surveillance over debtors, so that they "may not move out owing the Company for either furniture or merchandise." The police refused "to permit anyone to move who (did) not have permission of the Superintendent and the Manager of Stores." At the Bethlehem Steel mine at Mather in Greene County, miners were compelled in early 1933 to buy from the company store, or were fired for not doing so. Abuses in the company-store system made the miner more than ready for the union when the new call came in1933.[24]

When a miner worked the day shift, he awoke in the darkness at five o'clock, hurriedly dressed, ate breakfast, grabbed his lunch bucket, joined his fellows waiting for him outside, walked down the hill or over the ridge past the powerhouse and coal washer, and then descended into the mine, where he lived on the edge of disaster. He had to make sure that he made the "man-trip," or he would miss an entire day's work.[25]

The man-trip's descent sometimes took from forty-five minutes to an hour or more — time for which miners were not paid until the resurgence of the union. The conversations during the trip were often a polyglot of languages, animated by an occasional jerk of the hands or head, reflecting the ethnic origins of the Pennsylvania miners. Most were first- or second-generation Americans, and frequently their last names were difficult for their Anglo-Saxon bosses. The Jones and Laughlin Vesta 4 mine in Washington County employed 450 men, who lived in the Daisytown-Richeyville patch. Of this number, more than a hundred were classified on J & L's rolls as "American" – presumably English, Irish, and Scotch-Irish. Seventeen were listed as "German," two as "Finns," and the remainder were of southern and eastern European extraction. There were 33 Italians, 62 Hungarians, 3 Croatians, 5 Lithuanians, 35 Russians, 38 Poles, and 95 were tabbed "Slovak."[26]

The mines were pitch black, and the oil lamps attached to the miners' caps allowed them to see for only about five feet. All was darkness except for the flashing patches of light that glowed eerily along the walls of black. Wriggling through the narrow, black tunnels carved from coal, the man-trip took the men to the "face." Here the coal was shot, cut, and loaded into wagons, which, in the 1920s and 1930s, often were still pulled by mules and horses. The miners were dropped off at the "entries" and "rooms" to dig at the walls. In many mines the ventilation was poor, and the chilly, damp rooms reeked of coal.[27]

There were very few black miners in southwestern Pennsylvania before World War I, but during the war large numbers of Southern blacks moved into the area, lured by labor agents sent south by the coal companies. After the war many came as strikebreakers, creating a racial animosity that persists to the present. Often their reception in southwestern Pennsylvania was as cruel as their treatment in the South had been. Blacks who were not strikebreakers sometimes found "No Colored" signs at mine portals; some others, however, were hired before whites by operators who considered them more docile than the eastern Europeans. But large numbers of black miners were always good union men; indeed, records kept by company spies and the Coal and Iron Police suggest that, by the time of the New Deal, a significant number of blacks had become officers in local unions.[28]

The coal operators seldom missed an opportunity to harrass and demean the miners. The checkweighmen consistently cheated the loaders; bosses frequently drew a chalk line across a coal car – for whatever reasons they wanted – and the miner who loaded it would receive only half-pay for that car. The companies also laid off miners for loading "dirty coal." Many times the bosses would allow their friends or the most submissive miners to take over a spot just after the "dead work" had been completed so that their favorites could "hog the coal and get the good money." Often, too, the companies would work at the best spots those miners who owed the most money to the company stores. Companies pressured miners to join the company unions, forced miners to work evenings even after they had been in the pits all day, and bullied miners into voting the way the companies dictated. When a miner returned to work after supporting a strike, he was given the spots at the face with the most slate and the deepest water, further, he was often victimized by blacklists, which, many veteran miners insist, followed a man even after the union returned.[29]

Much of what the coal miner did was called "dead work" – tasks that did not directly involve the loading of coal and for which there was no pay. Miners who worked in the older mines often had to cut, load, and remove seven or eight feet of slate for no pay. Moreover, miners earned nothing for the hours it took to roof and timber. When the coal carts moved too slowly, a miner could work a shift and a half and never get credit for a wagon. If he moved rock all day, he had nothing to show for it except frustration and fatigue.[30]

Invariably, families were large in the coal fields; perhaps of all the industrial workers in the years between World War I and World War II, miners had the largest families. Veteran miners of that era insist that the isolation of the fields, the harshness of life, the omnipresent oppressors—by they the mine officials, the Coal and Iron Police, the county sheriffs – tended to pull the family together. Many also claim that it was the family, even more than the union, which enabled them to persevere and survive these brutal years. Generally the sons of this century's first generation of coal miners had large families themselves; however, unlike their fathers, they did everything possible to see that their sons did not follow them into the pits.[31]

To the coal miners of the pre-New Deal days, their women were truly special people. When old miners who lived through those years speak of their wives, their recollections are proud, even touching. Although women never went into the coal mines, their lives of course were woven inextricably into those of their men. Wives and older daughters rose in the mornings with the family's breadwinner, prepared his breakfast, packed his lunch bucket, and sent him on his way. Besides caring for her children, the wife's routine included washing on old scrub boards, baking bread, mending, making clothes from gunny and flour sacks and old sheets, and working in the gardens in the warm months. Women ironed their clothes with flat irons heated on the stove, and wringer washers did not appear in the patch until the late 1930s and early 1940s. Each fall they helped butcher the hog if the family was fortunate enough to have one, which many families raised to make the sausage which helped carry the family through the winter. Muriel Earley Sheppard, a historian of the coke and coal fields, has written that the bosses "could hardly keep them (women) out of the coke-yards, they were so eager to help their men." She observed that even "when they were six or seven months pregnant they would snatch a coke fork and start shovelling."[32]

The wives, constantly called upon to sacrifice and skimp, were present at many picket lines alongisde their men. Indeed, one official of the United Mine Workers has claimed that "the real heroes of the union were the wives, the women." Old miners recall in awe that "some women were better fighters (for the union) than the men." Others claim that "a woman's smile went a long way in making the union." In fact, the entire family often became involved in union activities because, after awhile, most came to believe that the union was the miners' only salvation. Through the years the deputies and the Coal and Iron Police tried to keep women and children from the pickets, but they continued to show up. For instance, at Calumet in Westmoreland County during the 1922 strike, a company spy recorded that a woman had been jailed "for threatening to scald a man that (sic) went to work."[33]

The children shared the hard times with their parents. Of course, having scant knowledge of any better world outside, children had little with which to compare their lives; and they could not possibly have felt the same despair that often overcame their parents, especially in the bleakest years. Like rural youngsters elsewhere, the children of the patch fished in nearby streams and played ball on the local lots and school grounds. They would chase their skinny dogs up the hills and through the gullies and over the cinder paths that divided the hovels they lived in. In winter they climbed the ugly slag heaps to search for coal. When they were not helping in the gardens during the summer or standing guard to keep the chickens out, the boys would wrestle or play marbles in the spaces between the houses or romp in the mud around the water pumps that stood at the end of each row of houses.

However, reporters and reformers who came to the coal fields in the early 1930s often noticed the sickly complexion of the children, how undernourished they seemed to be, and how old they looked. One writer came to know a little girl who claimed to be ten years old; but "from the pallid line of her face," the visitor later wrote, "I had judged her to be nearer fifteen." These children with bony arms and purple with cold, wearing shoes much too large, were often yellow with jaundice and other ills. One miner's wife who grew up in the Frick patch at Grindstone in Fayette County best remembers the chicken pox, the whooping cough, the pneumonia, and the sad notices of "SCARLET FEVER" nailed to patch doors.[34]

Although Pennsylvania required every child to attend school until the age of sixteen, the isolation of the patch and the attitudes of parents and school officials precluded steady school attendance. Many children, with the approval of their parents, dropped out of school after seven or eight years; and school boards – often made up of small-businessmen, mine officials, and sometimes miners – rarely forced the students back to school. With only scant formal schooling themselves, miners saw little value in education beyond the elementary level. Since fathers were eager for their sons to begin work as soon as possible, and because employers generally did not demand proof of age, twelve-year-old boys went to work in mines all over southwestern Pennsylvania.[35]

Although women were not allowed in the mines, there were

many days and nights when the shrill whistle announcing an accident summoned them to the shafts to await anxiously the return of their men trapped in the pits below. Thousands never made it to the surface again. From 1906 through 1938, over 35,000 men perished in mine accidents across the nation. In the decade which ended with December 31, 1929, there were over 22,000 fatal accidents, and at least a million and a half nonfatal injuries serious enough to compel a loss of working time. Every sixth coal miner was injured on the job annually, and over 2,000 were permanently disabled each year. From 1915 to 1929, six disasters killed 100 or more miners, and 25 accidents killed 25 or more miners. At a Westmoreland County mine in 1908, 239 men perished in a fire. At Mather in Greene County twenty years later, 195 miners were killed in an explosion.[36]

Although these disasters commanded the headlines, many times more lives were lost in accidents claiming one, two, or three victims. One in six deaths in the 1920s came from men crushed between the underground trains and the tunnel walls. Electrical accidents of various kinds killed 80 to 100 miners each year. More deaths resulted from slate and roof falls than from any other source; 77 percent of all mine fatalities were the result of roof falls. In time, some progress was made in preventing explosions, but there was little the miners could do about roof falls except to erect timber as close to the mine face as possible and "to listen to the top talking," as they used to say.[37]

Although most accidents occurred underground, even surface workers had their hazards from railway and mine cars, from machinery and electricity, from powder and boiler explosions, or from falls. In fact, the fatal accident rate among the surface miners was higher than that of railroad workers and steel workers.

In 1934 the frequency of accidents in the bituminous coal fields was three times that of industry in general, and working time lost because of accidents was over six times greater. Standards were not only lax in those days but also were rarely enforced. The coal companies did not stress safety, and the states did not enforce many safety rules for fear of losing tax revenues should the companies move elsewhere. Besides, safety standards in those mines with power lines, motor haulage, and machinery,were expensive and difficult to maintain technically. The operators' concern for output and profits in such a chaotic industry as coal precluded extensive safety maintenance. And the miners themselves, not being paid for "dead work" and often driven by desperation to load as much coal as possible, did only the minimum of propping. Ironically, while the miners could discern those cracking sounds that usually preceded a fall, the introduction of more and more machinery drowned out those warning signals. By 1940, coal mining was killing only about half as many men as at the turn of the century. But that improvement did not bring back all those who had perished, because the state of Pennsylvania seemed little concerned about those miners and their families who were isolated from the rest of the state in the feudal existence of the coal patch.[38]

The recreational and social activities of the miners took place amidst this isolation and in the shadow of the mine and its dangers. Even then the miner faced an unhappy dilemma: when plenty of work was available, the miners worked long hours with little time for recreation; when there was little work — which was often during the interwar years — their spirits and funds were so low that they had little enthusiasm for fun.

Most of those miners who were fortunate enough to have regular work stayed in the pits from dawn to dusk. After such a long day even the younger miners would virtually collapse. After eating, they rolled a bit of "cutty pipe," sank into wash tubs to wash the coal dust away so their families could recognize them, and relaxed on the porch until bedtime. "After you loaded a cut of coal all day," as one old-timer put it, "you were usually too tired to do anything."[39]

Although "in the patch you made your own fun," as one miner recalled, the company occasionally sponsored activities. Almost all of the coal towns had baseball teams, and in the summer there would be two or three games a week, often at night or in late afternoon. The company allowed the good ball players to leave the pits early before games, and they were offered other gratuities as part of the company's paternalism.[40]

Despite hard times, miners entertained themselves in a variety of ways. There were chicken fights in some of the patches. Some miners played bocci, and others played cards, especially rummy. Boxing was also popular in that era, and southwestern Pennsylvania and the Pittsburgh district produced many a champion in the 1920s and 1930s. Younger men spent time in the poolrooms or watched semi-pro and high-school football on fall evenings. The great boxing and football traditions of southwestern Pennsylvania originated in these activities.

Ethnic clubs were often located just off company property, or adjacent to the patch, or in the little villages that surrounded the commercial mines. There the coal miners conversed in their mother tongues over beer, bocci, and cards. Sometimes they drank beer in the local hotels, and the story is that on Saturday nights many a miner would fill his miner's bucket with beer for only pennies, take it home, and drink it along with his cheese and crackers as part of his Saturday night "out." There were picnics, of course, especially when the union organizers returned to the area and provided plenty of beer and whiskey to the hundreds who came to these outings. Even union meetings could become a social event, sometimes lasting all day as one group battled another for the control of union affairs.[41]

In some of the patches the companies built churches for their employees. At others, old buildings were used for multidenominational services. In most areas, the miners and their families had to travel to attend church. Since few had cars, most miners went by train to churches in Uniontown, Washington, Fredericktown, Carmichaels, or other coal towns.[42]

But in their social and fraternal lives, the miners remained isolated in the coal fields. Few newspapers or magazines were featured at the company stores, and there were not many radios in the patch. Whenever one was available, small crowds would gather on the porch, and miners remember that as children they would listen outside the "Super's" window to the noise coming from his crystal set.

Although the miner enjoyed some recreational activities, he was usually restricted to his immediate area. With the return of the union in 1933 and with higher wages, fewer hours, and automobiles, the miners could go outside the patch for recreation. Besides, paternalistic activities supported by the companies declined after the union came, and, before too many years had passed, most of these activities became part of the miners' new and more abundant life.

But that largesse came later. The years following the strikes of 1922–1923 witnessed a sad and precipitous decline in the material fortunes of the miners of southwestern Pennsylvania. New machines were replacing men and increasing production, and coal and steel companies were buying new mining properties in nonunion areas. For instance, in 1924 the United States Steel Corporation purchased 100,000 acres in West Virginia and Kentucky. This purchase supplied more coal for the steel mills but further eroded the weakening position of the United Mine Workers.

Faced with the gravest crisis in its thirty-five-year history, the UMWA negotiated with union operators the Jacksonville Agreement of 1924. By this agreement the operators in the Central Competitive Field (Western Pennsylvania, Ohio, Indiana, Illinois) agreed on a $7.50-per-day rate through March 31, 1927. Secretary of Commerce Herbert Hoover, who aided the negotiations, called the settlement "the most constructive development in the bituminous industry for years."[43]

Nevertheless, the industry continued to deteriorate. Faced with these harsh economic realities, many operators asked the UMWA for wage reductions. When the union refused, these operators instituted reductions anyway, and then set out not only to reduce wages further but also to destroy the union at the same time.

The leader in this movement was the Pittsburgh Coal Company, controlled by the Mellon banking interests. Pittsburgh Coal, the largest bituminous coal producer in the nation and the key to the Central Competitive Field, had had a contract with the miners for over thirty years and was signatory to the Jacksonville Agreement. Late in 1924, the company shut down, leaving most of its almost 20,000 employees to fend for themselves. On August10, 1925, Pittsburgh Coal reopened its mines and posted notice that all wages would be reduced by 33

1/3 percent and that it would operate nonunion. Obviously in violation of the Jacksonville Agreement, the company argued that it had agreed to a wage scale only so long as it operated under union conditions, which it no longer did.

In western Pennsylvania, the Rockfeller-owned Consolidation Coal Company, the Bethlehem Mines Corporation, and almost 100 other operators – including the interests of Governor John S. Fisher – followed suit. Some of the companies lived up to the Jacksonville Agreement until its expiration on March 31,1927. They then opened their pits with wage reductions and without union recognition. Other companies simply closed down rather than face the competition.[44]

The UMWA fought back, and from 1925 through 1928 there were hundreds of strikes in western Pennsylvania. These conflicts were accompanied by wholesale destruction of property, a widespread denial of human and civil rights, and massive suffering and misery for miners and their families.

When all the trouble began, the companies used the same methods they had used before to defeat the miners. However, as the strike continued into 1926, southwestern Pennsylvania operators added the Coal and Iron Police to the arsenal of oppression. During the strikes of 1922-1923, there had been very few of these police in the bituminous fields. Then in 1926 the Pittsburgh Coal Company organized a police department under Captain John Searsh of the Pennsylvania Railroad Police. Searsh "was an able and scrupulous officer," an early student of the private police system has written, and "whatever discredit was later to develop" did not grow from Searsh's activity. The police force grew rapidly and by November 1927 numbered over 3,000. H. C. Frick, Pittsburgh Coal, and the Hudson Coal Company each had over 200 police operating in southwestern Pennsylvania; Bethlehem Mines and the Pittsburgh Terminal Coal Company employed almost that many. These figures do not include other private police who worked for the companies or the sheriffs and deputies who served the companies' interests.[45]

During the strikes, lockouts, and general disorder of the mid- and late 1920s, the police served their employers in a number of ways. While their major function was "to protect property," the police also helped to import and protect strikebreakers, most of whom were floaters from Northern cities and Negroes from the South. The police escorted these scabs to and from the pits, protecting them from angry strikers and their families. Union miners believed that the importation of Southern Blacks was designed to "break their hearts" by showing them that "even niggers" could do their work. Miners felt that the companies wanted to humiliate them further by evicting them so that Negroes could occupy the houses they once knew as home. Miners also understood that the Negroes were cheap labor and were not organized. In many mines, these Negroes received only "chocker" money, or scrip to be used at the company store, where they had to purchase everything. In fact, the scabs were less free than the medieval serf; the police would not allow them to leave company property, according to many who witnessed these years.[46]

Company police were very active. They evicted from company houses thousands of strikers who were forced to erect barracks and set up tent colonies to protect their families. Police on horseback routed miners on parade, even when the latter had a permit from local officials to march. Police tossed tear gas at miners' wives who threatened scabs, shot into crowds and into meeting halls, arrested thousands of strikers for "inciting to riot," and made sure no one entered or left company property without having been properly investigated.[47]

Coal and Iron Police also served as spies. At a union meeting in Slickville in 1928, a "Patrolman Bryant in plain clothes had no difficulty in getting in" and duly reported back to his chief. In California, Pennsylvania, whenever the miners met at Saeli's Garage, labor spies were able to give their superiors at Jones and Laughlin full reports even before the miners reached home. Sometimes the miners caught up with a spy. In 1927, one "Mike Kelly, age 31," who was "utilized by Bethlehem Mines in uncovering several union agitators among our employees," was shot by an enraged miner at Ellsworth.[48]

Miners fought back by attacking trucks hauling strikebreakers and by continuing to picket on and off company property. They held union meetings, collected funds to care for strikers' families, and paraded through mining villages to enlist support. They also hurled explosives into the homes of scabs, met trains to fight the police who were there to escort strikebreakers, and fired rifles from nearby hills into mine tipples and fire houses.

For awhile the mine war in Pennsylvania drew national attention. After a visit into the state, one reporter wrote from the safety of his New York office:

> I have seen horrible things there, things which I almost hesitate to enumerate and describe. I can scarcely expect my story to be believed. I did not believe it myself when the situation was first outlined to me. Then I went into the coal camps of western and central Pennsylvania and I saw for myself.
>
> . . . Many times it seemed impossible to think that we were in a modern, civilized America.
>
> We saw thousands of women and children, literally starving to death. We found hundreds of destitute families living in crudely constructed bare-board shacks. They had been evicted from their homes by the coal companies. We unearthed a system of despotic tyranny reminiscent of Czar-ridden Siberia at its worst. We found police brutality and industrial slavery. We discovered the weirdest flock of injunctions that ever emanated from American temples of justice.
>
> We unearthed evidence of terrorism and counterterrorism; of mob beatings and near lynchings; of dishonesty, graft, and heartlessness. . . .
>
> The mine fields are a bubbling caldron of trouble. If it boils over—and it threatens to do so—blood must flow freely and many lives pay the forfeit.[49]

In 1928, a special committee of the United States Senate investigated conditions in the bituminous fields. More than 3,400 pages of evidence and sworn testimony from coal operators' police, miners, union officials, and interested citizens revealed the sad conditions in the coal areas. The brutality of the Coal and Iron Police shocked the group, as did the volume of words testifying to the amount of moonshine, prostitution, and general lawlessness prevalent in one demoralized patch after another. One witness from "Mexico," a section of the patch at Cecil in Washington County, told the committee of the "houses of ill fame" that prospered there. The committee spoke with many people who had been beaten and mauled by company police, heard labor spies admit to being paid for firing into the homes of strikers, were told of "Blacks who were allowed to carry concealed weapons for protection," learned of the wholesale firings and evictions, and listened to the recitations of the perpetrators and the victims of hundreds of crimes of violence. One senator told Charles M. Schwab, chairman of the Bethlehem Steel Company:

> I want to say to you, Mr. Schwab, that I was in China this past year, and I thought I had seen the worst kind of degradation and misery that I had ever witnessed, but I have never seen it equaled in any place in the world unless it was up here in some of these hovels where we see women and children, 10 and 12 of them, huddled into a little miserable shack.

How many lives were wrecked and lost will never be known; the cost of the filth, disease, and poverty cannot be measured in human terms.[50]

Eventually, the combination of armed force and starvation crushed the miners and ended the strike. Although the coal companies hardly secured record outputs under these conditions, they did win their major objective — the virtual destruction of the union. Union men did not cease fully their attempts to frighten scabs or to prevent union miners from going back to work. UMWA officials still organized meetings and spoke to the miners; but fewer and fewer came, and parades and demonstrations became fewer, too. By 1929, company police were able to report "only a few major depredations that could be attributed to union activities." The UMWA, once a proud union of 450,000 members, was down to 150,000 men. Bargaining for only 20 percent of the nation's coal miners, the union was strong only in Illinois (50,000 members), the anthracite region in Pennsylvania (its largest membership), and among the employees of the Rocky Mountain Fuel Company. In southwestern Pennsylvania, union cards were hard to find, and even these were held by hands which had become toughened by hard times, but not from mining coal. For the coal miners who had come to test the promise of American life, a sort of democratic and perverse equity had arrived. As one old miner put it: "We were all equal; nobody had nothing."[51]

NOTES

1. W. Fisher and A. Bezanson, *Wage Rates and Working Time in the Bituminous Coal Industry, 1921-1922* (Philadelphia, 1932), pp. 5-6; Morton S. Baratz, *The Union and the Coal Industry* (New Haven, 1955), p. 47.

2. John S. Smith, "Organized Labor and Government in the Wilson Era, 1913-1921: Some Conclusions," *Labor History* 3, no. 3 (Fall 1962), p. 273; Bituminous Coal Institute, *Bituminous Coal, Facts and Figures, 1948.* (Washington, 1948), n.p.; Irving Bernstein, *The Lean Years: A History of The American Worker, 1920-1933* (Boston, 1960), pp. 127-28.

3. John Brophy, *A Miner's Life* (Madison, Wisc., 1964), pp. 181-82.

4. Interviews with Anthony P., Wyano, 13 April 1974; John P., Monongahela, 20 August 1974; Earl J., Uniontown, 5 August 1974; Van N., Melrose, 16 August 1974; Margaret S., Larimer, 30 July 1974; George G., Charleroi, 1 December 1974; LeRoy J., Herminie, 29 April, 1977. These interviews are part of the California Oral History Collection, an ongoing project involving both faculty and students which numbers over 400 taped interviews to date. In the interest of space, only a few of the interviews will be cited in these notes, although numerous others could be included. The places where the interviews were conducted are in Pennsylvania, unless otherwise noted. Hereinafter cited as COHC.

5. Interviews with Aldo R., California, 24 April 1974; Bill W., LaBelle, 27 August 1974; Steve C., Smithton, 2 August 1974; Anthony S., Allison, 1 May 1974, COHC.

6. Brophy, *A Miner's Life*, pp. 188-89. For information concerning the strike of 1922, the authors have a Xerox copy of a fascinating ledger (with "Strike Dope" printed on its cover) kept by a company official of a Westmoreland County mine during the conflict. This little book contains lists of miners evicted from company houses, names of men attending organizational meetings (collected by company spies), and numerous pamphlets urging miners to strike which were thrown from cars by union organizers. Hereinafter cited as "Strike Dope." See also Heber Blankenhorn, *The Strike for Union* (New York, 1924).

7. Muriel Earley Sheppard, *Cloud By Day: A Story of Coal and Coke and People* (Chapel Hill, N.C., 1947), p. 110; Anne Hard, "The Patch," *The Nation*, November 25, 1925, pp. 592-93.

8. Interviews with John W., Vestaburg, 10 December 1974; Helen A., West Brownsville, 21 April 1974; Mike U., California, 22 August 1974 , COHC; William Charles Oler, "Arnold City and the Coal Industry Crisis of the 1920s: A Social History of a Blighted Western Pennsylvania Coal Patch" (M.A. thesis, California State College, 1970), pp. 17-18.

9. Laurin Gilfillin, *I Went to Pit College* (New York, 1934), p. 107; interviews with George B., California, 1 May 1976; Rona B., Brownsville, 6 May 1974; George K., LaBelle, 13 August 1974; John B., New Eagle, 5 May 1975; Bob G., Charleroi, 14 August 1974, COHC.

10. Interviews with Sam D., Smithton, 20 April 1974; Mrs. George A., Charleroi, 1 December 1974; Margaret U., Larimer, 30 July 1974, COHC; Sheppard, *Cloud By Day*, pp. 7-8, 109-10.

11. Interviews with Walter C., California, 8 February 1976; Frank W., Irwin, 10 August 1974; Kenny D., Coal Center, 18 December 1974, COHC; Lorena A. Hickok,

Harrisburg, Pennsylvania, to Harry Hopkins, Washington, D.C., August 12, 1933, Box 67, Harry L. Hopkins Papers, Franklin D. Roosevelt Library, Hyde Park, New York. Hereinafter cited as FDRL.

12. Interviews with George T., Glen Campbell, 7 December 1974; John S., Vestaburg, 6 May 1976; Albert P., Victory Hill, 9 May 1977; Joe L., Connellsville, 12 May, 1977, COHC.

13. O. R. Check, Superintendent of Police, Ellsworth, Pa., to T. R. Johns, General Manager of Coal Mines, Bethlehem Steel Corporation, *Report of Police Operations for the Year 1927*, January 1, 1928; Check, Ellsworth, to Johns, Ellsworth, *Report*, 1928, January 1, 1928; January 23, 1929. The above are reports concerning the police activities of the Bethlehem Steel Corporation mines at Ellsworth, Cokeburg, Marianna, Slickville, and Heilwood, in western Pennsylvania. They are summaries of an entire year's operation, often include monthly reports, and describe almost every activity that went on in the Bethlehem patches. The reports cover the years of 1925-1930 and 1932-1935, and make fascinating reading for students of labor and recent American history. Xerox copy in California State College Library, California, Pennsylvania. Hereinafter cited as *Bethlehem Police Report*.

14. J. P. Shalloo, *Private Police—With Special Reference to Pennsylvania* (Philadelphia, 1933), pp. 61-64.

15. *Bethlehem Police Report,* 1932.

16. Ibid., 1926, 1930.

17. Ibid., 1927; interviews with Mike J., Clarksville, 5 May 1974; Stan M., Uniontown, 8 August 1974; Harry H., Mather, 5 May 1974; Mike M., New Salem, 4 April 1974; Steve P., Daisytown, 19 August 1974, COHC.

18. Shalloo, *Private Police*, pp. 64-65, 89-90. Shalloo reported that one county sheriff may have made as much as $30,000 in one month as his share of his deputies' salaries. Further, according to the recollections of old miners in the California Oral History Collection, apparently there were so many different groups of police in the coal fields that the individual forces have become almost indistinguishable through the years. Nevertheless, a miner usually could identify a policeman, irrespective of his title or uniform: he always seemed to fill out his clothes better than a coal digger.

19. Carol Lee Delbarre, "The Relationship Between Bituminous Coal Mines and Town Development Along the Monongahela River" (research project, California State College, 1973), pp. 2-3; Anna Rochester, *Labor and Coal* (New York, 1931), pp. 94-97; interviews with Ross M., Irwin, 22 July 1974; Harold H., Bobtown, 8 May 1976; John K., Crescent Heights, 18 May 1976, COHC.

20. Interviews with Russell U., Finleyville, 13 August 1974; Paul F., Uniontown, 25 August 1974; Joseph Y., California, 4 April 1975; Joe S., Belle Vernon, 18 April 1975, COHC.

21. Interviews with Walter W., Uniontown, 9 April 1974; Harold I., Bobtown, 8 May 1976; Frank M., Denbo, 14 May 1975, COHC.

22. Interviews with William W., Smithton, 2 August 1974; Bob M., Charleroi, 14 August 1974; B. E. T., Masontown, 30 April 1974; John F., Mather, 2 May 1974; George C., LaBelle, 8 August 1974; Henry Francis, Uniontown, Pennsylvania, to Harry L. Hopkins, Washington, D.C., 10 November 1934, Harry Hopkins Papers, FDRL.

23. Interviews with Frank C., Irwin, 10 August 1974; Bill H., LaBelle, 24 August 1974; Joe Z., Connellsville, 12 May 1977; Harold P., California, 5 May 1974, COHC.

24. *Bethlehem Police Report*, 1927, 1928, 1929.

25. The train of mine cars which transported the miners through the tunnels of the sections where they worked was called the "man trip."

26. Lists compiled from Jones and Laughlin Steel Corporation Papers, Jones and Laughlin California Office, California, Pennsylvania.

27. Interviews with Joe K., Denbo, 10 December 1975; Bruno J., Latrobe, 10 July 1974; John K., Uniontown, 4 August 1974; Earl L., Uniontown, 5 August 1974; Nick C., Blainesburg, 15 May 1977, COHC.

28. Interviews with Margaret N., Larimer, 30 July 1974; Lou L., Pittsburgh, 7 March 1974; Frank W., Irwin, 10 August 1974; Steve D., Uniontown, 5 August 1974; Attilio W., New Eagle, 13 May 1975; Pete Z., California, 21 August 1974, COHC. See also "Strike Dope"; also *Bethlehem Police Report*, 1933, 1934, 1935.

29. Interviews with Fred Y., Uniontown, 18 August 1974; Francis C., Herbert, 7 December 1974; John G., New Eagle, 3 May 1975; Mike F., California, 21 August 1974; Harold B., Bobtown, 8 May 1976, COHC.

30. Interviews with Frank S., Marianna, 11 December 1974; Valentine P., Buffington, 1 May 1974; Charles B., California, 18 May 1976; Joe U., Stockdale, 13 May 1977, COHC.

31. A large number of young men involved in various oral-history projects at California State College are sons of coal miners. Until the present economic troubles, none intended to become miners themselves. However, perhaps a score or more of this group are now working in the mines. As for the large families, one veteran miner gave a young interviewer this account: "Follow the coal mines back through the years. You'll find that when there's a strike it seems like the first grade had to build extra rooms on it [sic] six years after the strike to take care of the children." Interviews with Edwin J., West Brownsville, 21 April 1974, COHC.

32. Interviews with Stephen W., Jefferson, 1 February 1976; Mike S., Van Meter, 12 August 1975; Stan B., Greensburg, 11 December 1974, COHC; *Cloud By Day*, 41.

33. Interviews with Joe B., Pittsburgh, 7 March 1974; B. E. M., Masontown, 30 April 1974; Valentine P., Buffington, 1 May 1974; Anthony A., Allison, 1 May 1974, COHC; see also "Strike Dope."

34. Gilfillin, *Pit College*, pp. 7-8, 14; interview with Mrs. George M., Charleroi, 1 December 1974, COHC.

35. Interviews with LeRoy N., Herminie, 29 April 1977; Robert O., Marianna, 8 December 1974; H. A., California, 16 December 1974; John C., Monongahela, 20 August 1974; Joe G., Belle Vernon, 12 April 1975; Lincoln H., Washington, 3 May 1975, COHC.

36. Rochester, *Labor and Coal*, pp. 143-50.

37. Ibid.; Sheppard, *Cloud By Day*, p. 12.

38. Almost every veteran miner interviewed as part of California State College's oral history program has vivid recollections of mining tragedies which claimed the lives of friends. See also Dennis F. Brestensky, Evelyn A. Havanec, and Albert N. Skomra, *Patch/Work Voices: The Culture and Lore of a Mining People* (University Park, Pa., 1977).

39. Interview with Mason C., Washington, 10 December 1974, COHC.

40. Interviews with John W., Monongahela, 7 August 1974; Kenny B., Coal Center, 10 December 1974; John H., Connellsville, 12 May 1977, COHC.

41. Interviews with Harry K., Smithton, 9 December 1974; Robert L., Marianna, 8 December 1976; Paul W., Waynesburg, 11 December 1975; Rona T., New Eagle, 8 June 1977, COHC.

42. See Records of the United Presbyterian Church, Daisytown, Pennsylvania; interviews with Alexander T., Daisytown, 18 July 1976; Nick H. Blainesburg, 15 May, 1975, COHC, Sheppard, *Cloud By Day*, p. 5.

43. McAlister Coleman, *Men and Coal* (New York, 1943), pp. 124-25.

44. Bernstein, *The Lean Years*, pp. 128-32.

45. Shalloo, *Private Police*, pp. 105, 108.

46. *Bethlehem Police Report*, 1928; interviews with Albert W., Victory Hill, 9 May 1977; Sam T., Smithton, 18 April 1974; Francis S., Irwin, 10 July 1974, COHC.

47. *Bethlehem Police Report*, 1928; interviews with George H., California, 10 May 1976; Mike D., New Salem, 25 May 1974; Bruno T., Latrobe, 10 July 1975; Sam F., Uniontown, 5 June 1974, COHC.

48. *Bethlehem Police Report*, 1928; interview with Ray F., California, 27 April 1974, COHC.

49. Quotation from Bernstein, *The Lean Years*, pp. 130-31.

50. See *Conditions in the Coal Fields of Pennsylvania, West Virginia, and Ohio, Hearings*, Senate Committee on Interstate Commerce, Seventieth Congress, 1st session, 1928, 1:345-64, 1321; 2:3160-61.

51. Interview with Mike S., Fredericktown, 8 July 1974, COHC.

[2]
"But a Hungry Man Is Dangerous": The Marching Jobless in Philadelphia, 1930-1931

Pennsylvania coal miners were not alone in enduring a long depression. In Philadelphia, far from the semirural coal patches of southwestern Pennsylvania, mill workers in the "sick" textile industry also experienced years of hardship. Unlike the miners, textile workers lived in working-class neighborhoods, not in "coal baronies", and both places in their own ways were isolated. Moreover, as the long depression worsened, textile workers, like miners, increasingly employed strikes and other forms of protest to spotlight their economic misery. Violent activity of the early depression profoundly affected the life of the city.

In the early 1930s Philadelphia's textile and metal manufacturing district was wracked by the worst depression in the nation's history. There its severity had implications which extended far beyond the locked mill gates and darkened factories lining Allegheny and Richmond Avenues. As the ranks of Philadelphia's army of unemployed swelled and the misery of the jobless worsened, many upper- and middle-class city dwellers remembered the revolutionary turmoil of 1919 and feared not only for the survival of the capitalist economy but also for their own safety. In this fragmented metropolis, which Sam Bass Warner in his study of Philadelphia described as segregated by class, race, and ethnicity, different social groups seldom exchanged information about one another, and upper and middle-class families nurtured nagging fears about the intentions of the city's large, clustered working class.

The social climate of Philadelphia in the early 1930s and the contemporary debate over appropriate relief measures for depression-induced human suffering will be better understood if we examine the Kensington-Richmond working-class response to the Great Depression and contrast that response with middle-class Red-scare fantasies.

On the evening of November 7, 1930, the United States Department of Commerce interrupted scheduled radio programming with the terse query, "How is your city organization planning to organize to relieve unemployment?" Alexander Whillidin, a clearance engineer for the Pennsylvania Railroad, had just furloughed several men, and the message jolted him. Immediately he typed a reply and forwarded it to the mayor of Philadelphia and to the mayors of several nearby cities. Whillidin insisted that reasonable relief for the unemployed was imperative, but stressed that the wisest strategy would be "to urge the jobless to shun our large cities and towns, go into the country and work raking gardens, building fences or any other work which they are capable to do, and expect no more for some little time than perhaps their board and tobacco money. This may seem drastic, but a hungry man is dangerous."[1]

Like many Philadelphia engineers, technicians, professionals, executives, and managers of small and large business, Whilliden feared that the depression nurtured the evil of radicalism. Surrounded by the wreckage of the city's economy and tormented by gnawing personal insecurity, businessmen such as Whilliden lashed out at the radicals, or "Reds" for criticizing a system that had only yesterday afforded status and security — at least to successful Americans.

In addition, Whilliden reflected the fears and sentiments of Philadelphia's socially mobile second-, third-, and fourth-generation Irish- and German-Americans who, during the 1920s, had moved into the new row homes checkering the once sparsely settled northern fringe of the city. Areas such as Olney, which abutted suburban Montgomery County, burgeoned with row upon row of comfortable red-brick and white-frame homes. Almost 75 percent of the families in the forty-second ward were native-born, while over 44 percent of the foreign-born came from England, Ireland, or Germany; less than 5 percent emigrated from Poland, Czechoslovakia, or Austria-Hungary. Twenty-four percent of the employable males worked as small businessmen or professionals. Only 14.5 percent toiled in metal works, knitting mills, or other factories.

Approximately 11 percent worked in the building trades (a reflection of a current home-building spree). Clearly, the area bore the distinct markings of people who had found their niche in urban society. The forty-second ward affirmed the city's reputation as a "City of Homes," and the area's large professional and business community swelled the ranks of the Chamber of Commerce. These Olneyites eagerly supported campaigns for low taxes and expressed foreboding at the trumpetings of radicalism which they supposed accompanied the city's skid into the depression.

The rhetoric of these middle-class people and their upper-class neighbors in nearby Oak Lane and Chestnut Hill never gave even a sketchy description of the "Red" menace. The Reds were usually an amorphous "they." Only their lair was fixed with any certainty: in some Philadelphians' fantasies, the red flag of revolution fluttered brashly over the city's large Kensington-Richmond mill district; the amorphous "they" were the dour jobless and almost-jobless who slouched and shuffled at the chained entrances to closed mills. In reality, the people of Kensington-Richmond were unswervingly patriotic, as suggested by an inquiry into the contrast between their working-class way of life and the inferno conjured up in middle- and upper-class nightmares.

The Philadelphia mill district comprised a cluster of aging neighborhoods nestled in the shadows of Victorian factory architecture. The red-brick monotony of the district's two-story row houses, the pall of coal smoke, the oppressive presence of the mill was Dickensian — a scene from *Dombey and Son.* As early as 1830 Kensington enjoyed a reputation as a textile center. Mill operatives from Yorkshire and other British textile centers flocked to Kensington mills, drawn by good wages and the knowledge that their weaving and spinning skills were still highly valued. Indeed, Kensington's later attraction for skilled and semiskilled labor from Germany, France, and Poland persisted into the late nineteenth and early twentieth centuries. By 1930, over 70 percent of the residents of the four principle wards of the mill district were primarily native-born Americans of northern European extraction.[2]

Misunderstanding among different social groups in the city was not uncommon. As early as 1840, a common ethnic and working-class heritage forged strong ties of group loyalty which in turn produced a distinctly native American violence. Kensington bully boys fought pitched battles against neighboring Irish plug-uglies and, on at least one occasion in 1844, dislodged the "agents of the Pope"[3] with cannon fire. Like the Irish, the factory system steadily displaced the artisan, shifted the locus of work from the home to the mill, and threatened to disrupt the system of values and the social bond which held the community together. The artisan class assailed the factory threat with the same vengeance they wrought on the Irish. In 1843, state militiamen were called to quell Kensington strikers who rampaged through the district, invading homes and smashing the looms of weavers who refused to strike against the increasing regimentation of the factory system.[4]

Through the nineteenth and into the twentieth centuries the residents of Kensington-Richmond perpetuated the cohesiveness which inspired the nativist uprisings of the Jackson era. Despite an influx of Poles, Germans, and Italians, milltown conveyed to the world an image of tough native Americanism, boosted by pride in the community's Anglo-Saxon heritage. Also, milltowners continued to wear their reputation for toughness and boisterousness as a badge of Americanism. Hundreds of milltown youths joined the army in World War I, and to the Kensington-Richmond doughboys who marched from the textile mills and metal foundries to Chateau-Thierry and the Argonne, the spirit of the Philadelphia mill district seemed indomitable.[5]

Despite this sturdy spirit, the mill district declined in the 1920s. Throughout that decade Kensington-Richmond experienced a predepression slump initiated by several factors, including the vagaries of style. The trend to exposed hardwood floors hurt the city's carpet industry, and the short-skirt fad harmed the cotton fabric and sock industries. Automation was another serious problem, since Kensington-Richmond's aging millworks housed antiquated machinery which could not compete with the automated factories outside the city. The number of weavers employed in Philadelphia's upholstery mills declined 45 percent. Automation likewise undermined the security of Kensington's skilled tool and dye makers and other metal workers. By 1930 even the full-fashioned hosiery workers, who had prospered during the 1920s by catering to the flapper's penchant for short skirts and sheer seamless stockings, felt that sting of expendability as the price of full-fashioned hosiery plummeted together with wages and the number of jobs.[6]

The consequences of automation and style change on Philadelphia's industrial base prompted the University of Pennsylvania to undertake an extensive study of the city's manufacturing economy. The study concluded that automation had placed the city's skilled workers and their "quality products" at such a disadvantage that for Philadelphia industry to compete effectively in the face of ever-widening "labor-cost differentials" extraordinary labor tactics would be necessary.[7]

Throughout the 1920s, labor struggled to survive against paternalism, the open shop, and other anti-union blandishments of the "American system." Nowhere did labor find the battle to survive more difficult than in Pennsylvania, the stronghold of "old guard" management. And its Philadelphia bastion was armed with a full arsenal of injunctions, blacklists, and yellow-dog contracts.

Unfortunately for many workers, Pennsylvania's Federation of Labor (PFL) was hobbled in the 1920s by a disjointed leadership of conservative craft unionists such as Matthew Woll and "old guard" socialists such as James Maurer. In 1924, Robert M. LaFollette's Progressive Party campaign had created an alliance between the Socialist party and the Pennsylvania Federation of Labor. Socialists such as Maurer, who later headed the PFL, and Adolph Hirschberg, Philadelphia's Central Labor Union chief, touted the moderate Debsian socialism of Morris Hillquit, who regarded economic change as evolutionary and hoped to politicize the American Federation of Labor (AFL) with conservative Socialist ideals.[8] By 1930,however, both Socialist and non-Socialist union leadership suffered from lethargy, and this condition begged the appearance of A. J. Muste, a stalwart anxious to restore militancy to the labor movement. Muste, a former clergyman identified since the early 1920s with the Brookwood Labor College and its organ, *Labor Age,* preached a Trotskyite brand of socialism. Through Brookwood and other labor colleges (one located in Philadelphia), Muste attempted to sway the AFL toward what he called "progressive" unionism. Disillusioned with laissez-faire capitalism and the AFL's allegiance to capitalist dogma, Muste used Brookwood and *Labor Age* to bombard the labor movement with "facts" about the increased mechanization of previously unaffected craft industries. Muste stressed the necessity of bringing into industrial unions the unorganized workers of these newly mechanized industries.[9]

Matthew Woll, chairman of the Workers' Education Bureau of the AFL, closed Brookwood in 1928, contending that the college promulgated Communist ideas. In the wake of Woll's action, Muste formed the Conference of Progressive Labor Action (CPLA), whose leadership included prominent Philadelphia labor leaders such as Emil Rieve of the American Federation of Full Fashioned Hosiery Workers. By the 1930s, Philadelphia had become a stronghold of the CPLA, which spiced the city's labor rhetoric with acerbic attacks leveled at both the AFL and capitalism. Not a competing union, but rather a dissident element within the AFL, the CPLA expressed keen interest in the plight of Philadelphia's textile unions. Muste warned Philadelphia's flagging hosiery union

> to abjure . . . [the present AFL leadership] which thinks, feels, talks and acts like business men, and to go on confidently and militantly to attack non-union strongholds which are exploiting the workers and ruining the industry.

That was strong language in the "black pit of unionism."[10]

The shocking economic cataclysm of the early 1930s restored the spirit of activism in organized labor and kindled interest in

Musteite progressivism. By 1930, Philadelphia staggered under unprecedented unemployment, especially in its less fortunate neighborhoods. A fourth of the heads of households on a typical Kensington block were jobless; another fourth worked only part time. The black neighborhoods of south Philadelphia, where as much as 33 percent of the work force was unemployed, suffered even greater distress.

As one mill after another closed, poverty fell like a pall over the old mill district. To survive, jobless workers exhausted savings, insurance monies, and building and loan funds. However, such stopgaps carried most families no more than six weeks. Foreclosures increased between 1928 and 1933, more than 91,500 Philadelphia homes fell under the sheriff's hammer — many of them in Kensington-Richmond. When the last lines of defense collapsed, jobless mill workers swallowed their pride and turned reluctantly to charity.[11]

Since the 1870s Philadelphia had had a tradition of mobilizing voluntary charitable agencies against the massive poverty caused by economic depression. In late 1930, city socialites led by Horatio Gates Lloyd organized a well-oiled and, at first, well-heeled relief machine to supplant the potpourri of soup kitchens, missions, and ward organizations which had operated in the first months after the great crash. Lloyd formed the Committee on Unemployment Relief (CUR) according to the recognized tenets of contemporary charity and, through nine acclaimed citywide agencies, systematically disbursed the almost $5 million raised in the first United Campaign.

Despite efficient accounting for every relief dollar, the CUR failed to assuage the worst hardships of the Depression. Even poignant appeals to the "heart of Philadelphia," which included banners unfurled across Broad Street and emblazoned with a pair of outstretched hands and the slogan "THEY NEED YOUR HELP," could tap neither the wealthy's sense of noblesse oblige nor the middle-class's respectability. Month after month of business failures, plant closings, and slashed wages trimmed the incomes of the entire middle class and reduced its capacity for charity. By March 1932, Philadelphia's resources of voluntarism had been exhausted, and the CUR ceased operation.[12]

In federal hearings before the LaFollette Committee (December1931), Philadelphia social workers bemoaned the impotence of private relief and urged federal intervention. Karl DeSchweinitz supported his arguments with vivid descriptions of jobless families breakfasting on cocoa and bread and butter and dining on the discarded fruits and vegetables culled from the waterfront. Jacob Billikopf of Philadelphia closed his Senate testimony with the stinging words of the prophet Isaiah: "When a man is hungry he is likely to fret himself and in cursing his king and his God his heart is likely to be filled with revolt and rebellion."[13]

But Philadelphia's so-called Lloyd Committee, parading the kudos lavished on it by the Hoover administration,[14] ignored the carping of the city's labor press. "Let 'Em Starve, Say Wealthy," inveighed the *Labor Record*, going on to charge that "the city's so-called leaders scream that the lazy multitudes must look to private charity, and . . . give (us) little of that charity as they can."[15]

To the Communist party (CP), the sight of the jobless lined up before relief headquarters heralded revolution. In 1928, the CP had disbanded its Trade Union Education League, whose tactic of "boring from within" the American labor movement was deemed futile, brandishing, instead, the Trade Union Unity League (TUUL), whose mission was to supplant the AFL's "fake" unions with "legitimate" ones. However, as the economic crisis worsened in 1929, the party resurrected an earlier strategy of organizing the unemployed. While both the AFL and the Socialist party viewed the jobless as an unorganizable mass, TUUL agents approached unemployed millworkers in Kensington-Richmond in early 1930 and urged them to form neighborhood unemployed councils. Ideally, these councils would act as "transmission belts," moving the working class toward the impending revolution. Several unemployed councils sprang up in the mill district and, armed with slogans such as "Fight, Don't Starve," battled for adequate relief, unemployment insurance, clean bedding in the municipal flophouse, no evictions, and free gas and electricity.[16]

Given the enormity of the depression in Kensington-

Richmond and the inadequacy of relief, the district was presumably ripe for this militant appeal. However, the Communists in Philadelphia never mobilized great hordes to man the barricades, although the several hundred disciples who did brave the marches were unstintingly dedicated. The first "red assault" on City Hall in mid-February 1930 was countered by approximately 100 police, including a mounted contingent. Following shouts of "We want work" and "Down with politicians," someone bellowed, "Rush them" and the crowd surged against the police blocking the entrance to City Hall. In a fifteen-minute melee, seventeen marchers were arrested and a dozen were hospitalized.[17]

A week later, the councils regrouped before City Hall, this time demanding no evictions, a public-works program, and emergency relief amounting to $18 per worker. This second meeting attracted a crowd twice the size of the first; it was nevertheless peaceful. The next day, the *Philadelphia Inquirer* ridiculed the "horde" who stood shaking their fists while mannerly policemen "killed those Reds with kindness."[18]

At the demonstration on February 13, the police seized a quantity of TUUL handbills that announced an International Unemployment Day on Thursday, March 6. On that day – "Red Thursday" – violence erupted throughout the country, in Boston, Washington, D. C., and New York City. As a spectacular show of force, however, Red Thursday was a failure and nowhere did it fail so badly as it did in Philadelphia. Only about 150 demonstrators congregated before City Hall, where Communist speakers harangued three little knots of people. Once again, their themes were evictions, vagrancy laws, and the five-day week. Again the *Philadelphia Inquirer* commended the "brotherly care" and solicitude lavished by the police upon the "would-be overtossers of governments" and disparaged the gathering as a "three ring circus."[19]

Despite the failure of Red Thursday to generate a mass protest movement, it did stir a flurry of interest in the unemployed councils. By July 1930, there were seven chapters in Philadelphia. After 1930, however, the fervor waned. Periodically, as in January 1931, and on May Day 1932, the councils massed a respectable crowd at City Hall to protest the city's miserly dole. In 1932 Police Superintendent Kern Dodge hurled his motorcycle-mounted "Red Squad" into the marchers and littered the street and sidewalks with scores of injured. Seventy were hospitalized.[20]

Nevertheless, not even the spilling of Communist blood could renew interest in the CP. That, according to Muste, was precisely the problem. He scolded the CP for attempting to transform the jobless into a revolutionary cadre while ignoring the real task of building the strength of labor. The unemployed councils "are not unions," observed Muste, "but Communist sewing circles." A Trotskyite Socialist such as Muste did not view the depression as the seedtime for Socialist world domination, but rather as an opportunity for the emergence of a workers' party. In addition to the creation of a labor party, Muste's CPLA called for a planned economy, the socialization of the railroads, mines, and major utilities, and a five-day week. The CPLA insisted that the workers must have the right to control the introduction of labor-saving machinery. (Textile workers and machinists already attributed the vagaries of the economy to the reckless introduction of time-saving machines.) In fact, this very sensitivity to the American working-class psychology attracted rank and file support for the CPLA.[21]

Most Philadelphia milltowners were extremely pragmatic and balked at philosophical arguments of any kind, much less Marxism. Kensington-Richmond machinists, carpet weavers, and hosiery workers turned away from the strident Communist rhetoric and clung steadfastly to traditional labor tactics and objectives. In the midst of Red Thursday, the district fixed its attention on a two-month-old strike at the Aberle Hosiery mill, not on the mass protest at City Hall. Violence had erupted at the mill on March 5, at which time sixty-five strikers had been arrested, primarily for trying to keep strikebreakers out of the plant. And the next day, while the Communist party grouped at City Hall for Red Thursday, hundreds of seething hosiery workers in Kensington milled outside the Aberle plant.

That evening a carload of strikebreakers left the Aberle plant gate, followed seconds later by a carload of striking unionists. After a short distance the first car stopped, the union car right behind it. When the strikers jumped from their car, sudden gunfire felled three of them. One of the victims, Carl Mackley, lay mortally wounded. Within minutes of the shooting, thousands of angry Kensingtonians spilled into the streets in outrage over Mackley's death. Workers formed groups which roamed about Kensington, seeking revenge on any unwary strikebreaker. Alarmed, Mayor Harry Mackey rushed a special detail of 500 police into the area and put the city's entire force on riot duty.[22]

The Aberle strike had started in early January when the mill's management had again slashed workers' wages. But what rankled the workers even more than the reduced pay was Aberle's refusal to recognize the union. The company hired "new employees" and proclaimed to the union and to city officials that no strike existed. On Friday, the day after the death of Carl Mackley, Mayor Mackey declared the Aberle situation "intolerable" and insisted that the strike issues be arbitrated.

A distinguished arbitration board failed to resolve the main issues: union recognition and the right to arbitration. Accepting the grim realities of the industry's economic condition, the hosiery union consented to a reduction in wages in return for their demands for union recognition and collective bargaining. Furthermore, the union pledged to "turn its energies into the struggle to make the industry better." However, Aberle's old-guard management refused to budge.[23]

A. J. Muste believed that the Aberle strike prepared Philadelphia labor for political action, especially now that the union was convinced that the city's political machinery operated on behalf of the mill owners and against labor. Judges granted every injunction requested by the mills and granted mill "scabs" the right to carry guns. Indignant strikers made Mackley's funeral the largest protest meeting ever held in Philadelphia. Days later, the Northeast Progressive League was formed in Kensington-Richmond. Its first order of business was to plan the overthrow of Philadelphia's number-one textile magnate, Joseph Grundy.[24]

By early 1932, the CPLA – in league with the textile workers, the hosiery union, and the Central Labor Union (CLU) – was holding regular street meetings in the mill district, calling for the revival of militancy, and urging the jobless to organize into leagues. Over a thousand unemployed mill workers formed the Northeast Unemployed Citizens League in June 1932. The Northeast Unemployed Citizens League campaigned for unemployment insurance and old-age pensions, and opened a commissary where food collected from local merchants was distributed by League workers from an old truck donated by sympathizers. Like the unemployed councils, the unemployed leagues created active "eviction committees" to conduct peaceful, yet threatening demonstrations at the homes of the evicted.[25]

Significantly, by September 1932, the CLU had joined with the American Federation of Full Fashioned Hosiery Workers, the Carpet Workers' union, and the PFL to support the Unemployed Citizens Leagues (UCL). The CLU's endorsement of the UCLs reflected Philadelphia labor's leftward tilt. Emil Rieve marked the new departure in his 1932 Labor Day message, published in the *Philadelphia Labor Record,* challenging labor "to embark on a year of militant and purposeful activity to fight for unemployment insurance, and old age pensions . . ., and against injunctions." "We must assume," Rieve said, "that it is still possible to bring about in America a planned economy where real security will be gained for all who work, and where economic justice instead of a scramble for profits is made the basis for our whole social system." Rieve also called for a moratorium on "taking the depression on the chin in the meek and spineless manner so highly praised by the politicians . . .; a moratorium . . . that is, . . . on capitalism."[26]

To those untutored in Kensington-Richmond folkways, Rieve's words —cast against the backdrop of strikes, grim eviction demonstrations, and clashes with the police at City Hall — portended violent radicalism, if not revolution. Despite the strategy of the *Philadelphia Public Ledger* to portray radical activity as whimsy or the antics of a few pipsqueak "r-r-revolutionaries," many middle- and upper-middle-class Philadelphians regarded the mill district with trepidation. Kensington's traditional reputation for hooliganism, rowdyism, and mob violence, as well as evidence that Communists and Socialists were drumming the mill neighborhoods for recruits, convinced many "proper Philadelphians" that Kensington-Richmond, a drab district more European than American, festered with alien radicalism.[27]

Warnings of an impending revolutionary holocaust, *le deluge,* rang through the city in the early 1930s. In the mahogany-paneled sanctuary of Philadelphia's august Board of Trade (PBT), the city's business élite assigned the Communist threat top priority. A PBT member, Francis Ralston Welsh, reported to the board regularly on the dimensions of the "Red menace" and piped his intelligence directly into the Department of Public Safety. Welsh's most sensational discovery was reported four days after Red Thursday:

> The Communist party in Philadelphia is steadily growing, as is also the Communist menace. Membership in such Communist organizations as the International Labor Defense, the Trade Union Unity League, . . . etc., all purely Communist organizations, exceeds the total open membership of the Communist party. They have a number of members who do not call themselves Communists but style themselves Socialists or Libertarians . . . . such for instance, as James Maurer, ex-president of the Pennsylvania State Federation of Labor. . . .
>
> Something should certainly be done by businessmen here to fight against Communism. The Communists are openly and avowedly boring into our schools, our colleges, among our school teachers, youth organizations, the Boy Scouts in a few instances, among our mill workers, etc. . . . The thing has been steadily getting worse for several years and will continue to get worse until people recognize the menace and take steps against it.[28]

Welsh echoed the anxieties of many Philadelphians and the city took steps to counter radicalism. The mayor created an official radical squad which guarded virtually every bridge and public building in the city on Red Thursday. Despite newspaper reports of its solicitude, the Red Squad was ordinarily brutal in routing demonstrators.[29]

The preoccupation with the "Red menace" extended beyond corporate boardrooms and police stations. In fact, it had been very much on the minds of the 150 social workers, philanthropists, and other civic-minded individuals who assembled in November 1930 for a special luncheon at the Ritz Carlton Hotel. (At this meeting the Committee on Unemployment

Relief, the so-called Lloyd Committee, had been organized.) But if the speeches given there are any indication of the temper of the gathering, the diners were as preoccupied with combatting revolution as they were with providing relief. One prominent corporation lawyer accented his address by invoking the headless specter of Marie Antoinette, but the most sombre presentation was delievered by Herbert Tily, chairman of the board of the Strawbridge and Clothier department store. Tily vividly recounted the events preceding the Russian Revolution and observed that, if the Romanovs had been less stingy with their bread, Czardom would flourish still. "Obviously," exhorted Tily, "any dollar given today to unemployment relief is insurance against the overthrow of our Civilization." And in an allusion to World War I, he perorated: "We are fighting to save lives, not to take them."[30]

This theme would be struck time and time again in 1930,1931, and 1932 in pamphlets and speeches, in churches and corporate councils. Organized relief allayed "not only the direct results of unemployment, but its harmful by-products: a questioning of social and political forms, bitterness and discontent." According to the wealthy Lessing J. Rosenwald, the United Campaign for relief funds "was more than philanthropy, it touched the fundamental instinct of self-preservation, of making secure those things which we have grown to regard as basic in the life of this nation."[31] And when upper-class Philadelphia failed to dig deeply enough into its pockets, the middle-class Mayor Mackey unhesitatingly sounded the tocsin: if Philadelphia's wealthy could not find the dollars for relief, "the militia will be needed." Moreover, threatened Mackey, it would be absolutely impossible for the police force "to control the conditions which would be created."[32] In November 1931, with the city bankrupt, the public unable to support further relief, and winter approaching, Meyer Casman, an officer in the Pennsylvania National Guard, wrote his good friend J. Hampton Moore, the mayor-elect of Philadelphia, to advise him that the Guard was being drilled to "meet the possible mob rule that might take place during the hard times expected this winter." Casman urged Moore to have the city police trained similarly. When

Moore took office in January 1932 he complied, and proceeded to outlaw all future demonstrations in City Hall Plaza. Moore's Public Safety director forbade Socialists to frequent mill sites and, when questioned about this policy, explained: "Well, you know how it is — you start talking Socialism and go from that to a lot of things."[33]

The evidence shows that while Socialists and Communists actively courted the city's working class, upper-class businessmen, middle-class technicians, and other still upwardly-mobile Philadelphians reacted to the outburst of radical activity with a fear nurtured in part by the fragmentation of their metropolis. Philadelphia in1930 was segregated by income, race, and ethnicity. The broad boulevards built to facilitate the increasing volume of automobile traffic, as well as the subways and trolley systems, demarked the city with great physical boundaries and hastened the movement of the more mobile urban population toward the urban fringes and into the growing suburban communities. Communications about the values and intentions of different classes and races barely trickled across these boundaries. Social segregation served to confirm the "otherness," the "they"' of people living in mill districts such as Kensington-Richmond. In a period of economic and social insecurity such as the Great Depression, "their" labor agitation and "their" protests about unemployment and relief assumed a frightening character. Middle- and upper-middle-class phobias surged to the surface. In 1930 as in 1919, the fear and distrust were embodied in the "Red menace."[34]

But public meetings and labor demonstrations against wage cuts, stretch-outs, evictions, and inadequate relief were well within the tradition of American protest. This fact was illustrated in August1932. With all monies for relief exhausted, an angry crowd gathered in the Elks Hotel to denounce the inaction of both the city and the state. Unlike the unemployed council's gatherings at City Hall in 1930 and 1931 and the eviction demonstrations and union strikes of 1930, this meeting was convened by middle-class social workers to articulate the seriousness of the city's predicament. One desperate speaker threatened to take things into his own hands, insisting that he would "have hundreds if not thousands who will follow . . . If we want money we will hold up a bank, if we want food or clothing we will take it." Minutes later, a group of blue-shirted Communists urged the audience to join them in storming City Hall, but only a handful followed.[35]

Most of those who remained in the hotel wondered why the city was not already ablaze with revolution. Jacob Billikopf suggested that "the poor were too weakened . . . (to revolt), poverty had so deteriorated their morale that not even Stalin could incite them." Actually, the radicalism which gurgled in the recesses of the Kensington-Richmond mill district served in effect to underline basically conservative working-class demands for work, relief, and fair labor practices. Although Emil Rieve occasionally colored his speeches with Trotskyite verses on socializing industry and declared "moratoriums" on capitalism, it was the CPLA's militant commitment to working-class conservatism that made the conference program acceptable to Philadelphia mill workers. Their spleen was vented on capitalists such as Grundy and Aberle, not capitalism. Mill workers in Kensington-Richmond were in fact flag-waving patriots faithful to the mottoes emblazoned on the masthead of the labor weekly, *Progressive Labor World*: "Support American Manufacturers, for American Manufacturers Support the American Workingman," and "If Charity Begins at Home, It Is Equally True that We Should Buy Home Made Goods."[36]

The political temper of Kensington-Richmond was tested in November 1932. The CLU supported the Socialist candidates, Norman Thomas and James Maurer, and popular backing for the ticket was eagerly sought and expected in the district. "The twins are at it again," blasted the *Labor Record*, mocking the similarities between the Republican and Democratic platforms. But when the votes of Kensington-Richmond's seven wards were tallied, the Thomas-Maurer slate had won fewer than 1,200 votes, less than 2 percent of the total vote cast.[37] Truly, if "a hungry man" was dangerous, he was dangerous as a striker or defender of evicted neighbors, not as an overthrower of government. But that fact was not comprehended by urban society in the early 1930s. Much of the New Deal's initial drift to the left occurred in response to radicalism that was more figment than fact.

NOTES

1. Alexander Whilldin, November 8, 1930, to Department of Commerce, President's Organization on Unemployment Relief Papers, Record Group 173, National Archives, Washington, D.C., hereinafter cited as POUR.

2. U. S. Bureau of the Census, Fifteenth Census of the U.S., 1930, data taken from "Work Sheets" for Census Tracts 18, 19, 25, 31 and 42; Rowland T. Berthoff, *British Immigrants in Industrial America, 1870-1950* (Cambridge, Mass., 1953), pp. 39-43; Gladys Palmer, *Philadelphia Workers in a Changing Economy* (Philadelphia, 1956), pp. 53-55; Caroline Golab, "The Immigrant and the City; Poles, Italians, and Jews in Philadelphia, 1870-1920," in Allen F. Davis and Mark H. Haller, eds., *The Peoples of Philadelphia: A History of Ethnic Groups and Lower-Class Life, 1790-1940* (Philadelphia, 1973), pp. 203-26.

3. Sam Bass Warner, *The Private City: Philadelphia in Three Periods of Its Growth* (Philadelphia, 1968), pp. 142-53.

4. Peter Binzen, *Whitetown, U.S.A.* (New York, 1970), p. 89; Warner, *Private City*, p. 142; and Berthoff, *British Immigrants*, p. 37.

5. Binzen, *Whitetown*, pp. 81-87.

6. Gladys Palmer and Constance Williams, *Reemployment of Philadelphia Hosiery Workers After Shutdowns in 1933-34* (Philadelphia, 1939), pp. 1-13; Palmer, *Philadelphia Workers*, p. 36; Helen Hermann, *Ten Years of Work Experience of Philadelphia Machinists*, WPA National Research Project in Cooperation with the University of Pennsylvania, Report No. P-5 (Philadelphia, 1938), p. 2.

7. Gladys Palmer, *Union Tactics and Economic Change* (Philadelphia, 1932), pp. 129-33.

8. David J. Pivar, "The Hosiery Workers and the Philadelphia Third Party Impulse, 1929-1935," *Labor History* 5, no. 4 (Winter 1964), pp. 19-20; Bernard Karsh and Phillips Garman, "The Impact of the Political Left," in Milton Derber and Edwin Young, eds., *Labor and the New Deal* (Madison, 1961), pp. 79-115.

9. James O. Morris, *Conflict Within the AFL: A Study of Craft versus Industrial Unionism, 1901-1938* (Ithaca, N.Y., 1958), pp. 103-10; Philip Taft, *The A.F. of L. from the Death of Gompers to the Merger* (New York, 1959), p. 34.

10. A. J. Muste, "The Dilemma of a Militant Union," *Labor Age*, September 1930, p. 4; Louis Francis Budenz, "Following the Fight," *Labor Age*, May 1930, p. 19.

11. "Police Survey of Unemployment in Philadelphia," U. S. Bureau of Labor

Statistics, *Monthly Labor Review* (1930), p. 31; "Social and Economic Character of Unemployment in Philadelphia," U.S. Bureau of Labor Statistics, Bulletin, No. 555 (1930), pp. 7, 22, 23, 44.

12. On the Philadelphia Committee on Unemployment Relief, popularly alluded to as the Lloyd Committee, see John F. Bauman, "The City, The Depression, and Relief: The Philadelphia Experience, 1929-1939" (Ph.d. diss., Rutgers University, 1969), pp. 70-114.

13. Testimony of Karl de Scweinitz and Jacob Billikopf in *Federal Cooperation in Unemployment Relief*, Hearings, Senate Committee on Manufactures, Seventy-second Congress, 1st session, 1932, pp., 24-25, 121.

14. The "kudos" of the Hoover administration refer to the encouragement activity of Hoover's President's Emergency Committee on Employment and its successor, the Organization on Unemployment Relief. See Albert Romansco, *The Poverty of Abundance: Hoover, the Nation, the Depression* (New York, 1965).

15. The Philadelphia *Labor Record*, 2 October 1931, p. 1.

16. Daniel J. Leab, "United We Eat; The Creation and Organization of the Unemployed Councils in 1930," *Labor History*, 8, no. 3 (Fall, 1967), pp. 300-315; William Z. Foster, *American Trade Unionism; Principles and Organization, Strategy and Tactics, Selected Writings* (New York, 1947), pp. 188-93; Karsh, "Impact of the American Left," pp. 81-90.

17. *Philadelphia Public Ledger*, 15 February 1930.

18. *Philadelphia Inquirer*, 22 February 1930.

19. *New York Times*, 6 March 1930; *Philadelphia Public Ledger*, 7 March 1930; *Philadelphia Inquirer*, 7 March 1930.

20. *New York Times*, 1 May 1932.

21. "Left Wing Deserts," *Labor Age*, June 1931, pp. 6-7; Budenz, "Following the Fight," *Labor Age*, May 1930, p. 19; James Maurer, "March of the Machine," *Labor Age*, June 1930, p. 5.

22. *Philadelphia Inquirer*, 8 March 1930; *New York Times*, 8 March 1930.

23. "Statement of Research Department of the American Federation of Full Fashioned Hosiery Workers," n.d. (ca. November 1930), in Morris L. Cooke Papers, Franklin D. Roosevelt Library, Hyde Park, N.Y.

24. Muste commented on the consequences of the Aberle strike in *Labor Age*, May 1930, p. 12.

25. A. J. Muste, "The C.P.L.A. Policy in Unions," *Labor Age*, June 1931, p. 8; Philadelphia *Labor Record*, 26 February 1932.

26. Emil Rieve, "Unemployment Insurance and Moratorium on Capitalism Is Program for New Year," *Labor Record*, 2 September 1932, p. 1.

27. *Philadelphia Public Ledger*, 6 March 1930.

28. Francis Ralston Welsh, Philadelphia, to Henry N. Willis, Philadelphia, March 14, 1930; Henry N. Willis, Philadelphia, to Lemuel B. Scholfield, Philadelphia, January 11, 1930, both in Minutes of the Philadelphia Board of Trade Papers, Historical Society of Pennsylvania, Philadelphia, Pennsylvania.

29. On Red Squad see *Philadelphia Inquirer*, 7 March 1930.

30. *Philadelphia Inquirer*, 8 November 1930; Jacob Billikopf described the Ritz Carlton meeting in "Unemployment: What We Have Learned," *Proceedings of the*

National Council of Social Workers (Chicago, 1934), p. 35.

31. Rosenwald quote in *Final Report of the United Campaign* (Philadelphia, 1930), pp. 8-12, found in The University of Pennsylvania School of Social Work Library.

32. *New York Times*, 16 February 1931.

33. Meyer Casman, Harrisburg, to J. Hampton Moore, Philadelphia, September 15, 1931, J. Hampton Moore Collection, Historical Society of Pennsylvania, Philadelphia, Pennsylvania.

34. Warner, *Private City*, pp. 161-76.

35. *Philadelphia Public Ledger*, 17 August 1932.

36. David A. Shannon, *The Socialist Party of America: A History* (Chicago, 1955), pp. 111-31; Leab, "United We Eat," pp. 300-15.

37. *Labor Record*, 7 October 1932, p. 3; Pivar, "Hosiery Workers," p. 26; Shannon, *Socialist Party*, pp. 220-24.

[3]
The Rural Dimension: Welfare and Relief in Snyder County*

By the spring of 1931 the force of the Great Depression which had struck Philadelphia so suddenly and dramatically in 1930 rippled slowly through the economic, social, and political institutions of Snyder County in central Pennsylvania. Perceptions of its coming were blurred because there were no bread lines, no apple vendors on street corners, no other highly visible signs that men and women were becoming desperate. The "friction of space," typical of rural areas, the long history of destitution in some townships, the agricultural depression which was a legacy of the 1920s, and the absence of any heavy industry all meant that the ill effects of the larger economic crisis would only gradually appear in the county.

As with most rural people, Snyder Countians were commited to traditional verities and local autonomy. Central to their core of belief was that hard work bequeathed both individual success and independence. And they shared a concomitant belief that, when such work could not be pursued, local resources and energies should be the ameliorative agencies. Both would sustain individual integrity through the autonomy which individual or local achievements created.

The dilemma which the Great Depression presented to Snyder Countians was that these beliefs were no longer completely tenable. To sustain individual integrity through work assumed the existence of employment opportunities or returns

*This chapter is the contribution of Professor Housley, Associate Professor of History, Susquehanna University.

from the marketing of farm goods sufficient to sustain the produce-worker and his family. During the early 1930s these conditions failed to exist through no visible fault of local people. Moreover, individuals in Snyder County found that their destiny was increasingly intertwined with that of "translocal" economic and political institutions; that is, national or regional economic and political institutions determined the lives of local people to a greater degree than did local institutions.[1]

As regional and national economic institutions ceased to function normally, unemployment and economic hardship spread throughout the county. Local, private, and public agencies acted to ease the suffering, but they lacked the resources, the expertise and, perhaps, the willingness to meet the emerging needs of local citizens. Unlike urban social welfare, whose roots were implanted in the scientific efficiency of twentieth-century Progressivism, rural philanthropy had escaped the obsession with expertise. Yet, despite professionalism, urban altruism collapsed under the enormous weight of mass poverty. Meanwhile, relief agencies in America's less taxed rural counties very gradually succumbed. In fact, well into the depression decade, rural philanthropy only grudgingly relinquished its case-load responsibilities to a bureaucratically structured translocal welfare system. Yet, surrender it did, as the depression and the New Deal hastened the pace of modernization and brought rural Snyder County into the mainstream of the mass society. However, as will be demonstrated, modernization did not always involve the shedding of deeply internalized values.

During the 1930s a transformation occurred in those institutions created to ameliorate poverty. It involved essentially identifying the sources of the larger economic crisis, which were "translocal," and developing solutions for the problems the larger crisis had created. Unemployment and the accompanying personal distress did not come to Snyder Countians because of the failure of indigenous institutions, but rather because the national network of economic institutions had broken down. Thus, a larger network of welfare and relief organizations was required to make ameliorative policies efficacious and, perhaps, just. Even so, local beliefs and involvement were not eliminated by transition from a local to a national focus. Their influence did lessen, but this diminution reflected the reality of diminished individual and local autonomy in modernized America. The result of the transition in welfare and relief procedures in Snyder County had become clear by 1938, when the Pennsylvania Department of Public Assistance (DPA) was created. An efficient, specialized bureaucratic system, the DPA sustained both the degree of local involvement and the commitment to local beliefs, appropriate, perhaps, in modern society.

During the 1920s, the population and economy of Snyder County began to shift from rural-farm to small town-and light-industrial. The population of the boroughs went from 20 percent to 29 percent of the total population in that decade. The industrial sector had become relatively important during the 1920s as employment in light industry doubled from 519 in 1919 to approximately 1000 in 1930. These industries were labor intensive, nonunionized firms, a majority were textile-related industries such as the Beavertown Shirt Company, Groce's Silk-Throwing mills and the Sonny Blouse Company. The emergence of these firms during the 1920s opened opportunities as farm acreage and income declined. But in the early 1930s these industries slumped. The value of invested capital fell 23 percent from 1930 to 1934, and employment figures plummeted from a high of 922 in 1931 to a low of 866 a year later; several firms went bankrupt. Reflecting the deflating price market, the value of goods produced fell by 66 percent in these years.

Although the county's financial intermediaries — largely commercial banks — remained stable, they were understandably reluctant to extend credit in this unstable industrial market.[2] There was little growth in local industrial production (only two firms appreciably expanded their productive capacity); therefore, few opportunities arose for displaced farm workers, migrants from other counties, or young people to find jobs. Unemployment grew from 292 in 1930 to 1,530 in the winter of 1932-1933. Much of this unemployment existed in the eastern boroughs and townships of the county, where most of the industrialization had occurred.[3]

Interestingly enough, farm life in Snyder County from 1930 to 1937 reversed the declines which had begun a decade earlier in the depression of 1920-1922. This revival was not correlated to income opportunities, but to a return to a modicum of self-sufficiency on local farms in the 1930s. The following table depicts the changing status of farm life in the County:[4]

	1920	*1930*	*1935*	*1940*
Farms	1,753	1,596	1,712	1,667
Tenancy (1%		25.6	21.7	27.3
Acres tilled		85,500	82,661 (1937)	81,079
Crop value		1,737,200	1,548,180 (1937)	1,294,080

The increase of farmer-owned farms (with a decrease in the late 1930s) and the decrease in both farm size and the value of crops, combined with the immigration of adult males especially from more industrialized Northumberland County suggests that area farmers viewed their farms more as a method of survival than as a means to increase their income. Farm prices in the early 1930s were falling rapidly and with this fall consumer demand contracted. The prices received for cereal crops in 1932 were half those received in 1931, and the cost of raising potatoes was greater than their market value. Most local dairy farmers were in the Dairymen's League cooperative, which in 1932 received the lowest milk prices any dairymen had seen since 1879.[5]

As unemployment increased and farm income declined, many Snyder Countians became desperate in the early 1930s. Perhaps this desperation caused the appreciable increase in violent crime in the county, especially against those local wealth-holders who did not trust banks. One of the most bizarre criminal acts in these years was an extortion effort made by a Beaver Springs man against a woman from Selinsgrove. Although the state police thwarted this attempt, the extortionist's letter reflected a mood all too common in these years. He wrote:[6]

> I only had work 36 days last year and i have a family of six to feed and no work and no money my family is nearly starving and scarcely nothing to wear, and no coal to keep us warm it is driving

> me mad to think of it I have bought on credit all i can buy and cannot loan no money so i am driven to this method to get money and i will get it or the one i am asking will pay dear for not giving it to me.

Both private and public agencies assumed responsibility for ameliorating the harsh economic conditions. In the eastern boroughs of the county the first "Community Relief Committees" were formed, and soon others followed, especially in the more populated communities. This disbursement of food and fuel, donated to the poor by their more fortunate neighbors, was, of course, private charity. Community leaders coordinated this effort, sponsored fund raising projects, and tried to find jobs for the unemployed. The Red Cross gave out free flour, the American Legion delivered Christmas baskets to the poor; and the local Chambers of Commerce developed plans by which area farms could be rejuvenated through the cultivation and marketing of specialized crops. While observers lauded this "neighbor to neighbor" charity, the ranks of the dispossessed grew into an army swamping the resources of private benevolence. Thus, pressure grew on public relief agencies to come to the aid of the needy.[7]

The individuals elected to administer poor relief in Snyder County were Republicans and shared Herbert Hoover's distaste for governmental intrusion into the lives of individuals. Although the residents of the county had always been Republican (and would continue to adhere to this partisan affiliation during the 1930s), the administration of poor relief was marked less by partisan ideology than by the personalism and localism of rural politics. The structure of poor-relief administration itself suited the pre-industrial, rural society in which it had been founded and nurtured. The administrators were locally elected officials, not professional social workers. Revenue came from a local tax on farm-produce sales and on the assessment of real and personal property. Relief recipients were traditionally those who could not work because of a personal deficiency — age, insanity, infirmity. Snyder County had been among the last in the state to move from a township and borough basis for poor relief to a county system. This had occurred in 1925. By 1931 the budget of the County Directors of the Poor had grown 300 percent in four years ($9,535 in 1927 to $27,278 in 1931), and the directors had to resort to borrowed funds to meet the increased volume of need created by local unemployment.

The sources of poverty in the county had shifted since 1925 from personal attributes which disqualified one for work, such as youth, blindness, or insanity, to the absence of employment opportunities caused by the national economic crisis. The administrative structure and concept of relief based upon the older understanding of the roots of poverty was becoming outdated.[8]

Perhaps for this reason, criticism of poor-relief administration mounted in 1931. Local taxpayers, in trouble themselves, claimed that the directors were extravagant and irresponsible in their use of public funds. As an example of this, they cited the fact that an area physician had received $1,200 to care for three or four patients in 1930. And taxpayers in the more isolated agricultural townships were angry because their poor tax had been increased by the directors, but the money raised was being spent to help the unemployed poor in the eastern, industrialized boroughs and townships.[9] One year later this grass roots criticism would become organized.

Late in 1931 the state legislature reacted to these criticisms and passed a law which returned poor relief in Snyder County to the old-fashioned borough and township basis. Governor Gifford Pinchot tacitly acknowledged local opinion in his addendum to the bill:

> I sign this bill with full knowledge that a Commission appointed in 1921 recommended County units for Poor Relief Administration, and with the conviction that, when well administered the county unit is superior to the township system.
>
> I am informed, however, not only that the people of Union, Snyder and Juniata Counties are substantially unanimous in the desire that this bill be passed, but that they are indignant over the extravagance which is alleged to have occurred under the County system.[10]

The transfer of relief responsibilities from the county directors to the locally elected township and borough Overseers of the Poor occurred in January of 1932. For the next two years they were crucial elements in the relief machinery despite deficiencies in their revenue base. The overseers collectively never raised or spent more money than did the County Directors of the Poor (the highest local poor tax after 1931 was $2,000 lower than the director's tax of 1931). However, the changing locus of tax responsibilities underscored the incongruity of locally financed poor relief in a nationwide depression. For, while poor taxes fell in some townships, and all the overseers were more completely under the control of the public, those townships and boroughs with a high degree of unemployment could not generate adequate funds to sustain the needy.

The confluence of a contracting tax base and a quickened demand for public relief boded ill for a system based upon the smallest political units in the state system. In January of 1932 the overseers found that their predecessors, the County Directors of the Poor, had spent all the revenue collected from the poor tax of 1931. The overseers thus began with no money in their accounts. They were initially dependent on monies borrowed by the county commissioners and on emergency funds given to them by the state through the First Talbot Act of 1931. This latter source amounted to $14,529 (more than half the total budget of the directors in 1931). It was specifically for "food, clothing, fuel and shelter for residents within their districts who are without means of support."[11]

When the Overseers of the Poor finally received funds generated by the regular local poor tax, two complicating factors had diminished the amount collected. The value of real and personal assessments fell by 11 percent from 1930 to 1934 ($13,400,000 to $12 million) and the millage rate was raised to assure sufficient funds. In Selinsgrove, a borough with one of the highest unemployment rates in the county, citizens were "shocked" by the higher millage rate.[12] This shock reverberated throughout the other boroughs. The tax problem was further complicated by exonerations granted individuals and companies by local governmental bodies. In Selinsgrove tax exonerations numbered 9 in 1932, 99 in 1933, and 126 in 1934. Several struggling industries were released from local tax obligations in return for their promise to hire local people. A similar development took place in Middleburg. Thus, fewer taxpayers were being asked to pay more money.[13]

The resultant dismay of Snyder County's taxpayers, coupled with the residue of suspicion against all poor-relief administration, a legacy of the problems with the County Directors of the Poor, led to organized resistance to all governmental expenditures. The county's representative to the General Assembly, Dr. Harvey Surface, a Republican, was instrumental in creating the Snyder County Taxpayers' Justice League. There were chapters of the league in every borough and township; but, although traces of their lobbying were apparent, the league was more a symbol of taxpayers' unrest than a successful pressure group.[14]

Both the taxpayers and the poor were not served well by the personalized methods of the Overseers of the Poor. The title "overseers" suggested that these officials were more beholden to the electorate than to the indigent to whom they ministered. And their administrative procedures reflected both the paternalism inherent in the term "overseers" and the vagaries which were perhaps inevitable in an unsupervised and unstructured administrative operation. The overseers generally forced local relief applicants to take a "pauper's oath" before a justice of the peace, although this was not a legal requirement. Then commodity relief (food, clothing, medical service, or fuel) was granted for two weeks, after which the overseers conducted an investigation to establish the legitimacy of the indigent's need. If relief was to be continued, the recipient was expected to work in payment for his assistance; the work generally was done on local or state roads. The overseers kept no records of their investigations; some claimed they knew all of the applicants. Their records of disbursments were kept on scraps of paper, bank stubs, and the like, and audits of their accounts were rarely adequate, despite the fact that this was the only public check of the overseers' activities.[15]

The uneven performance of thirty-eight local poor-relief administrators spread throughout Snyder County meant that the effectiveness of the system varied. In some townships and boroughs it operated smoothly and responsibly despite an inadequate financial base. In other areas the overseers were suspected of being corrupt. Some overseers were accused of having arrangements with local merchants whereby both enriched themselves at the expense of the poor. Because there were no statutory categories for relief expenditures, a variety of supposed needs were funded by the overseers — from funeral sermons to barber services and rubber gloves. And while it was apparent that some of the community's wards needed social rehabilitation rather than custodial or remedial care, such services were beyond the capacities of locally elected poor-relief administrators.

Snyder Countians were no doubt aware of the financial and human complexities of handling poor relief in depression times. Elected for a four-year term, the Overseers of the Poor received no salary and little for expenses. Very few citizens sought the office, and several people elected to the overseer's post refused to serve. Others tried to quit before their term was up but were frustrated by the county judge's inability to find a replacement. It was not a popular job and many who did serve disliked the system and their responsibilities.[16]

However, after the fall of 1932, local responsibilities for relief diminished as the state took a more active hand in the administration of relief. This occurred because social workers, largely representing the state's beleaguered cities, finally won their campaign to have the state assume responsibility for the unemployed. In August, the Woodward Act provided for the creation of the State Emergency Relief Board (SERB), which, in turn, created the Snyder County Emergency Relief Board (CERB). Selected sales taxes provided short-term and long-term funding.

The percentage of relief aid given in Pennsylvania by various governmental levels from 1933 to 1936 reflected this change:[17]

	Federal	*State*	*Local*
1933	54%	40%	6%
1934	69%	24%	7%
1935	75%	21%	4%
1936	6%	94%	.05%

State and federal relief monies and personnel assumed the burden of caring for the unemployed after 1932, and the local overseers returned to their traditional assistance to those whose indigence stemmed from personal deficiencies. By 1936 much of this responsibility had shifted to other agencies. However, although the township and borough overseers were not significant elements in the welfare system after 1933, the emerging state and federal relief system perpetuated the involvement of local beliefs, people, and resources.

State aid to Snyder County's dependent poor had come in 1928, when the county had joined the Mother's Assistance Fund (MAF). This was a quarter century after the MAF had been created in Pennsylvania. The delay was probably due to the county's reluctance or inability to meet the requirement of matching state funds. The MAF gave relief to indigent mothers with children under sixteen years of age whose fathers were either insane or dead. A board of trustees supervised and administered the fund.

The board was composed of local women selected because they had been interested in charitable work and because they belonged to the party in power in Pennsylvania (that is, a majority would be Democrats or Republicans depending on the party that held the gubernatorial office). They had to investigate applicants and determine the legitimacy and level of need.[18]

In the mid-1930s the responsibilities and administrative structure of the MAF changed. The inroads of federal and state money were behind these changes, for with the introduction of monies gathered from a translocal tax base came demands for a strict accountability of the money's use. For example, after the enactment of Social Security in 1935, federal funds now assisted the aged, dependent children, and the blind, and professional social workers supervised the use of this money. Therefore, in April 1936, the voluntary supervision and administration of aid to these three welfare categories ended. The state hired an executive secretary to supervise professional case workers, who investigated applicants and administered assistance. The blind, the aged, and dependent children received welfare, which, as a permanent entity, was to be distinguished from the transitory nature of unemployment relief. The shift to specialized welfare administration thus relieved local personnel on both the Mother's Assistance Fund Board and the Overseers of the Poor of direct responsibility for these categories of the poor. The former became an advisory body, while the Overseers of the Poor were left to aid only the physically and mentally infirm.[19]

As in the case of the blind, the aged, and dependent children, so with the unemployed, the depression caused a shift in the responsibility for relief from the local community to the state and the nation. In the fall of 1932, as has been noted earlier, the State Emergency Relief Board was created, which, in turn, appointed the Snyder County Emergency Relief Board (CERB). This later board was composed of prominent local citizens who, although sensitive to the plight of the unemployed, also had a partisan affiliation which was in keeping with that of the political party then dominant in the state.[20]

The evolution of unemployment administration by this local board was similar to that of the overseers and the MAF board. It moved from a relatively chaotic, inefficient, localized effort burdened with great responsibilities to a professionalized, efficient system gradually relieved of total responsibility for sustaining the unemployed. The original CERB began to operate in September of 1932 with no clear-cut procedures and no indigenous administrative structure. It began to make its own rules and to establish its own methods of dispensing relief aid, although SERB provided some guidelines.

Originally the local board had intended to work through existing public relief agencies and governmental units. And some of this interaction between public agencies was sustained throughout the life of SERB. The procedures for giving commodity relief and the rules governing its issuance quickly came from the state, but the method of administering aid only gradually came under state control. Food orders amounting to $5.00 per week to a total of $20.00 per month were issued to the unemployed by a representative of CERB. These food orders were a type of demand deposit submitted to a vendor who listed the goods obtained for it on the back of the order, signed it, and then used it as a claim against the state to acquire either wholesale goods or money. The unemployed also received fuel to heat their homes. Rules for relief recipients included restrictions on their use of automobiles (for work only) and the requirement that all relief cases work for a sponsoring agency.[21]

The administrative operation of CERB was in constant flux from September of 1932 to September of 1933. Relief orders were initially granted to voluntary "lieutenants" and to the Overseers of the Poor for dissemination to those in need. The county was divided into three sections and relief was apportioned to each, roughly according to their level of industrial unemployment. Thus, the eastern third received 51 percent, the central third 27 percent, and the western third 22 percent. After the first few months CERB had separated the infirm indigent from the unemployed poor and relegated the former to the overseers. The "visitors" in charge of each section measured applicants for need, dispensed relief, and found work for the unemployed, generally on local or state highways.[22] The growth of this assistance was steady:[23]

Month	*Families*	*Individuals*	*Food Funds*	*Coal Funds*
September (1933)	51	241	209.60	
October	349	1423	2982.76	
November	626	2648	5713.18	467.10
December	675	2834	9818.93	234.81
January	968	4077	8156.21	362.35
February	1167	4875	8799.90	536.81
March	1287	6329	13,644.18	668.14
Average	731	3204	7046.45	453.84

In April of 1933 an executive secretary for CERB was hired, and the members of the board resigned as direct administrators and were reconstituted as an advisory body. The first executive secretary was not a professional social worker but an unemployed public school teacher-administrator. The responsibilities of the infant CERB, of the "visitors" who volunteered to work for it, and its executive secretary steadily increased. Shoes were added to the list of commodity relief, and "thrift gardens" were encouraged. Over 500 Snyder County families became "thrift gardeners."[24]

For rural Snyder County the personalized and local administration of unemployment relief came to an end in the fall of 1933. The infusion of federal relief monies, supplied by the Federal Emergency Relief Act of May 1933, necessitated a more efficient and professionalized account of the money's use. This was accomplished through a consolidation of the relief systems of five area counties, including Snyder, into Area No. 1 of the State Emergency Relief Board. Headquarters for the area was not in the county, but in Sunbury, the Northumberland County seat. Accounting and administrative procedures were centralized and professional supervisors and case workers were hired to work in each county. The visitors tried to see relief recipients once a month to certify continued need. This was necessary because the types of assistance available gradually increased to include medical services, clothing, and shelter, and because local taxpayers were, again, vocal in their criticism of relief measures. These visitors also had to locate work opportunities for the unemployed with local public and private sponsoring agencies.[25]

Paradoxically, just as the state's unemployment-relief system became more efficient, its responsibilities diminished. The federal government slowly assumed much of the administration of, and resource allocation for, unemployment relief. While many Snyder Countians found the growth of federal involvement to be disturbing, those who needed the assistance were quick to take it. The Civilian Conservation Corps (CCC) was created in March 1933 to employ young people in a variety of tasks. Snyder County's quota for CCC enrollment was thirty-six; it was quickly filled, and a waiting list existed. A CCC camp was built in the western end of the county. It was a small encampment with a mess hall, bath house, blacksmith's shop, garage, headquarters building for officers, a building for civilian foresters, and six barracks. Two different contingents of men were sent to this camp. The first was composed of World War I veterans drawn largely from the Philadelphia and Pittsburgh areas; the second were blacks, largely from Baltimore. The main task of these men was to build a road over an adjoining mountain, but they also afforded vital assistance during the damaging flood of 1936. The local community seemed to accept the presence of the CCC well; local teachers and recreational personnel worked at the camp under the auspices of the WPA and the National Youth Administration.[26]

During the difficult winter of 1933-34, the federal government became directly involved in local relief through the Civil Works Administration (CWA). The CWA was a hastily assembled effort to employ the unemployed. It relied on the local unit of SERB to supply names of the unemployed and local sponsors to supply materials and projects. The person who coordinated these two and supplied funds for wages was a Democrat employed by the CWA. Over 500 Snyder Countians worked for the CWA, building roads, draining swamps, rebuilding schoolhouses, shoveling snow, painting the court house and doing a variety of other labor-intensive tasks. While this federal assisance was appreciated, local recipients complained about the low wages and pressured for rent and food supplements.[27] The CWA ended in April 1934 and a "Works Division" of SERB assumed the funding and finished the projects initiated by it.

With the establishment in 1935 of the Works Progress Administration (WPA), this pattern of federal relief supplanting state efforts became even clearer. The WPA was a federally structured program, organized hierarchically along state, regional, county, and finally project-foreman lines. Over a million dollars was spent by the WPA in Snyder County from 1936 to 1939. Most WPA work was on local roads, but WPA workers also made clothes for the needy, mapped Selinsgrove, presented dramas and musicals, and operated the local community center.[28]

As later chapters will describe in greater detail, the WPA structure in Pennsylvania was the most politicized in the country. Although all of the administrative personnel down to the project-foreman level had to be Democrats, there was only casual evidence that the WPA in Snyder County was influenced significantly by partisan pressure. There was even less evidence that the use of the WPA for patronage purposes reached to the unemployed relief workers themselves.[29]

Almost all of the New Deal's "alphabet agencies" operated at some time in Snyder County. The National Youth Administration (NYA) employed 115 youths at its height, using teenage "workers" to supervise playgrounds, maintain game-feeding stations, and, for a time, operate the cafeteria at the local high school. Funds and plans supplied by the Public Works Administration contributed to the construction of a new post office and high school in Selinsgrove.[30]

By 1938 the federal and state systems of unemployment relief were wedded. The Social Security Act of 1935 contained a taxing provision which encouraged each state to establish its own unemployment-insurance system. Pennsylvania developed its system as an aspect of a general reorganization and consolidation of the various relief and welfare agencies in the state. A state Department of Public Assistance (DPA) was created. In turn, it created county Boards of Public Assistance, which were advisory bodies for state welfare supervisors and case workers working in the county. These professional employees were merely those who had previously worked for the now defunct Mother's Assistance Fund. They helped the aged, blind, and dependent children. The DPA established guidelines as to standards of eligibility and created a uniform system for records, reports, auditing and accounting forms, payroll forms, and purchasing requisitions. Local Boards of Public Assistance heard complaints and submitted policy recommendations to the state. The state also operated local employment boards as well as the unemployment-insurance system.[31]

The only welfare not under state control after 1938 was that operated by the County Institutional Districts. These districts were administered by the county commissioners. They raised funds from a local poor tax and used the money to provide custodial care and rehabilitation in institutions for county residents who needed such care. The Institutional Districts replaced the increasingly moribund township and borough Overseers of the Poor.

The standardized and professional public welfare system operating after 1937 was in marked contrast to that which had existed in Snyder County in 1931. The pressure of events had forced the welfare and relief systems to assume a modernized cast. But this process of modernization in the relief and welfare system created an atmosphere of disquiet among Snyder Countians. The criticism and pressure which had greeted the Directors of the Poor in 1931 and which distressed the Overseers of the Poor in 1932 continued as state and federal agencies transformed the nature of poor-relief administration in the county.

Unemployment relief and systematized welfare seemed to contravene the inherited values and the apparent needs of county residents. By 1934 relief and welfare were highly visible aspects of the county's social life. The CERB had become the biggest employer in the county. More local residents were on relief (23 percent) than was true in surrounding counties (from 19 percent in Union County to 8 percent in Perry County), although the average relief grant given was half that of other counties. Traces of corruption were evident; investigators discovered that, from 1933 to 1935, 5 percent of every relief dollar went to persons already employed.[32] Furthermore, it was charged that the federal relief system, especially the WPA, was being used to build support for the Democratic Party (these charges are discussed at some length in Chapter 10).

The suspicion and skepticism that these allegations generated in the county were probably convenient and surface explanations for a more profound sense of anxiety. The welfare and relief system developed in the county to resolve problems engendered by the depression proved anomalous and contradictory for county residents. There were two basic reasons for this. Relief contradicted certain traditional American values which were deeply rooted in the folk wisdom of this rural-farm area. Chief among these values was the virture of independent labor. The themes which dominated criticism of the relief and welfare system expressed this well. These themes included relief workers who would not take available jobs for fear they would lose their relief checks; workers who were not diligent; workers who came to get relief orders in their cars; relief orders which took income from area merchants. The thrust of this criticism was summarized by a local columnist:

"Older generations of Snyder County people, accustomed to earning a living by hard, honest toil, reared in an agricultural county where life is work, are most bitter about widespread distribution of relief."[33] This attitude was probably heightened by a long heritage of untended poverty in the county.

A second underlying source for the unease which relief caused in the county stemmed from the anomaly of a relief system oriented to a urban-industrial society which operated in a rural setting. On local farms, no matter how poor the farmers were, hands were seldom idle, food and the other necessities of life appeared to be at hand, a modicum of income was always to be had, and a residue of real and chattel property seemed to belie the supposed destitution of those desirous of relief. In this setting, citizens who did not need help were deeply suspicious of those who claimed to need it. This suspicion increased during planting and harvest seasons, when local relief recipients were reluctant to take seasonal jobs at a pay level which was lower than their relief checks.

Furthermore, those area farmers requiring relief monies had a difficult time obtaining, them, as the following letter to the director of SERB Area No. 1 indicates:[34]

> As I did not get a reply to my letter to you, so I called at the Middleburg office today and they told me that the reason I did not get relief was that I had 120 chickens and 75 turkeys, and that my wife got an inheritance. I do have the chickens and buy every bit they eat, but whoever said that about the turkeys must have counted them twice, and the tax collector owns them, as all the procedes [sic] must go to him by agreement and my wife did not get enough money to pay one of our banknotes. I am paying interest on $1,000, have a feed bill now of $70 and about $75 in small bills besides my fire and life insurance and back about $150 in tax.
>
> I had got 23 bushels of wheat but till it was recleaned for seed it was all. We get one quart of milk a day, and no butter. Can you figure out how to make ends meet?

The distress of farmers was supposed to be relieved through a variety of federal agricultural programs. But these programs were not designed, and certainly not locally administered, to give assistance to the many nearly self-sufficient farmers in Snyder County. Perhaps for this reason, and because of their already impoverished condition, local farmers were slow to take advantage of the opportunities presented by the federal government in 1933 and 1935. By 1936 only 16 percent of Snyder County's wheat and corn-hog producers subscribed to the federal programs created to assist them. Nor were the various farm credit agencies utilized by local farmers.[35] Relief seemed to be their only recourse and the emerging relief guidelines would tend to dislodge such farmers from their traditional way, rather than sustain them. Only the passage of time and personal readjustments solved the economic problems and ameliorated the hardships faced by this farming element of Snyder County.

It was perhaps ironic that the modernization of the relief and welfare system in Snyder County, rather than undermining local beliefs ultimately harnessed them to a more efficient and able system. The criteria established by the state Department of Public Assistance for relief recipients reinforced several basic American values. Those receiving assistance and refusing to work were effectively stricken from the relief roles. Automobiles could not be used by relief recipients other than to go to work. Women whose husbands refused to support them had to sue for nonsupport before relief could be granted. Those receiving unemployment insurance were easily located and stricken from relief roles. And, of course, this insurance had been partly paid for by the workers themselves through a tax on their previous salary. Relief recipients who refused to work because of illness had to have a physician's certification. These guidelines did not guarantee that there would be no evasion of personal responsibility, and they were perhaps demeaning for the person receiving relief. But at least from the public's perspective the system reinforced the traditional belief that dependency must be proved, and that, where possible, independent labor had to be sustained.[36]

Furthermore, a degree of local involvement and influence was continued by this modernized system. In 1938, the files, cabinets, and records concerning local relief were moved from Sunbury to Middleburg, the county seat. The professional supervisor hired to administer the program in the county was advised and influenced by the Snyder County Board of Public

Assistance, which consisted of prominent citizens. Finally, indoor or institutionalized welfare was funded and administered by local officials through the Snyder County Institutional District.[37]

The changes in the relief and welfare system which occurred in the1930s could not, of course, continue the degree of local autonomy which had existed prior to 1930. Such local control was made impossible, not by the administrative developments of the 1930s, but by the breadth and depth of the modernization process as it had worked into the county's economy and society over the course of a century. The Great Depression merely exposed the ineradicable presence of these translocal forces. The modernization of local relief and welfare was an extension, then, of this broader and perhaps irresistible process.

NOTES

1. A "translocal force" is an aspect of the economy, society, politics, and the like which is regional or national in scope and affects the local community in a significant, perhaps, determinant way. For a discussion of these forces in a Minnesota town see Don Martindale and R. Glenn Hanson, *Small Town and the Nation: The Conflict of Local and Translocal Forces* (Westport, Conn., 1969).

2. Statistics concerning the Snyder County economy in the 1930s can be found in the sixth through the tenth *Industrial Directory of the Commonwealth of Pennsylvania* (Harrisburg, Pa.: Pennsylvania Department of Internal Affairs, 1928-1941).

3. *Middleburg Post*, 26 June 1930, 5 February 1931; *Selinsgrove Times*, 29 September 1932.

4. *Industrial Directory of Pennsylvania*, sixth through tenth.

5. *Selinsgrove Times*, 13 March 1930, 31 March 1932, 22 January, 31 August, 1933, 31 January 1935.

6. Ibid., 30 March 1931.

7. Ibid., 9, 30 January, 6 February, 25 December 1931, 24 January, 17 April 1932; *Middleburg Post*, 24 December 1931.

8. *Minutes of the Snyder County Directors of The Poor*, January 11, 1926, to December 31, 1931.

9. Francis Hall, "Snyder County Poor Relief," Snyder County Folder, *Reports on County Poor Relief*, Department of Public Welfare, Folder No. 3, R6-23, Pennsylvania State Archives, Harrisburg, Pennsylvania.

10. *Laws of the General Assembly of the Commonwealth of Pennsylvania Passed at the Sessions of 1931* (Harrisburg, Pa., 1931), 181-82.

11. David K. Bruner, "The Township and Borough System of Poor Relief in Pennsylvania" (Ph.d. diss. University of Pennsylvania, 1937), p. 115; "Origins and Development of Public Assistance in Pennsylvania," Department of Public Welfare (May 1958), RG-23, Pennsylvania State Archives.

12. *Industrial Directory of Pennsylvania*, seventh through ninth; *Selinsgrove Times*, 14 July 1932.

13. *Minutes of the Selinsgrove Town Council*, January 27, 1937; *Minutes of the Middleburg Town Council*, July 17, 1933, June 7, 1937.

14. *Selinsgrove Times*, 13 and 27 October 1932.

15. Hall, "Snyder County Poor Relief," Pennsylvania State Archives.

16. Ibid.

17. Randall S. Stout, "The Financing of Relief in Pennsylvania, 1930-1943," (Ph.D. diss., University of Pittsburgh, 1943), pp. 33-34.

18. *Snyder County Tribune*, 6 January 1938; *Selinsgrove Times*, 17 April 1931.

19. *Snyder County Tribune*, 9 April 1936, 23 December 1937.

20. "Origins and Development of Public Assistance in Pennsylvania," Pennsylvania State Archives.

21. *Selinsgrove Times*, 1, 15, and 29 September, 22 December 1932, 12 January 1933.

22. Hall, "Snyder County Poor Relief," Pennsylvania State Archives.

23. *Selinsgrove Times*, 27 April 1933.

24. Ibid., 15 March, 19 July 1934.

25. Ibid., 21 September 1933, 27 September 1934, 31 January 1935.

26. Ibid., 23 December 1933, 2 February 1934, 5 March 1934, 7 April 1934.

27. Ibid., 7, 11, and 23 December 1933, 11 January, 21 June 1934.

28. Donald S. Howard, *The WPA and Federal Relief Policy* (New York, 1943), pp. 124-25; Edward N. Jones, *Accomplishments of the Works Progress Administration in Pennsylvania*, 4 July 1935, 30 June 1936, (n.p., 1936), Table E.; *Snyder County Tribune*, 2 January, 21 May 1936.

29. Priscilla Ferguson Clement, "The Works Progress Administration in Pennsylvania," *Pennsylvania Magazine of History and Biography*, 95, no. 2 (April 1971), pp. 245-47; *Snyder County Tribune*, 14 April 1938.

30. *Snyder County Tribune*, 20 August 1936, 2 September 1937.

31. Stout, *Financing Relief*, pp. 33-34.

32. *Selinsgrove Times*, 17 and 24 January, 28 February 1935, 14 April 1938.

33. Ibid., 21 September 1933, 31 January 1935.

34. Ibid., 7 February 1935.

35. Murray R. Benedict, *Farm Policies of the United States, 1790-1950* (New York, 1953), pp. 147, 184-87; *Selinsgrove Times*, 27 July, 23 November 1933, 12 April 1934, 20 August 1936, 17 June 1937, 9 June 1938.

36. *Snyder County Tribune*, 13 January, 3 February, 24 March 1938.

37. "Origins and Development of Public Assistance," Pennsylvania State Archives.

[4]
The Great Depression in Allentown*

In contrast to Pennsylvania's two major metropolises, Pittsburgh and Philadelphia, and the state's many rural towns, during the first quarter of the twentieth century Allentown was a prosperous and still growing middle-sized city. Between 1900 and 1930 its population rose from 35,000 to 92,000, and a diversified economic base of commerce, cement, steel production, truck manufacture, garment and textiles provided the jobs which attracted and held this expanding population. The city lay nestled in the Lehigh Valley, which not only contained some of Pennsylvania's richest farm land, but also plentiful limestone deposits, which formed the basis for Allentown's portland-cement industry.

Like that of other American cities, Allentown's growth lacked central direction. Interest groups and organizations competed and cooperated to shape the town in their image. Trade, labor, religious, charity, fraternal, beneficial, ethnic, and, above all, patriotic associations abounded. Under the booster injunction of "Dwell Here and Prosper," a remarkably stable municipal government gave only a loose coordination to the growth process. However, the inter- and intra-party factional politics which made governing so difficult in Philadelphia and Pittsburgh did not exist in Allentown. From 1920 to 1932 and again from 1936 to 1940 Malcolm Gross, a Democrat, was the city's mayor. Before Gross, Fred Lewis, a Republican in the

*This chapter is the contribution of Professor Fricke, Associate Professor of History, Indiana University of Pennsylvania.

Theodore Roosevelt tradition, had been mayor from 1898 to 1906, and was later a congressman. In 1931 he captured the nomination of both parties and served again as mayor from 1932 to 1936.

The Great Depression ended the region's growth and prosperity. In its stead came economic stagnation, underemployment, and unemployment. From October 1929 to April 1933 factory employment in Allentown declined almost 50 percent, plummeting factory wages 74 percent. At almost the same time unemployment rose from 2.2 percent to 37.6 percent of the work force. The number of persons dependent on relief burgeoned, rising on a monthly average to as high as 16 percent of the city's population; through 1939 the percentage on relief never dipped below 10 percent. Yet, because of the city's favorable economic mix the depression affected Allentown less severely than it affected other parts of the state. Although under- and unemployment racked the durable-goods industries such as construction and truck manufacture, the bulk of the city's work force employed in commerce and light industry continued to work, albeit at longer hours and lower wages.[1]

While the city approached the economic crisis in the glow of prosperity and political stability, Allentown, like other Pennsylvania cities, operated under severe handicaps. One was the lack of municipal experience in helping the poor. Normally, the Lehigh County Poor Board aided the destitute. Other people in temporary distress received charity from organizations such as the Family Welfare Agency. The only contact between the city government and the poor came from small, annual contributions from the city treasury to organizations such as the Family Welfare Agency and the hospitals.

A second factor impairing the city's ability to meet the crisis was a decline in revenues. The precipitous fall of industrial inventories, wages, sales, and real estate values undermined the city's tax base. While this plight was not unique, it was compounded in cities such as Allentown which had experienced a building boom in the mid-1920s. Like Philadelphia and Pittsburgh, Allentown experienced a very high rate of sheriff sales and tax delinquencies among property owners.

Still the city fathers felt compelled to act, for it was clear to them that the depression was a national catastrophe. Community opinion held that here was an emergency comparable to the world war and dictated that neighbors should not suffer because of something over which they had no control. So, instead of cutting the city budget, it was maintained at the same level; deficits were made up by borrowing. Internal economies provided monies for the Family Welfare Agency and other philanthropies. More important, the city used its prestige to encourage charity and to stretch relief. It encouraged and coordinated clothing drives, transient care, gardening, food distribution, and a community cafeteria. Ultimately, however, the voluntary relief structure collapsed. More borrowing became difficult. Charitable contributions to the Community Chest fell from $225,572 in 1930 to $146,606 in 1933.

Locally and nationally, the collapse of what social workers referred to as the "thin red line" of social welfare cast the unemployed adrift, dependent in the last analysis on their own resources and ingenuity. The garden projects, "Hoovervilles," doubling-up arrangements, food cooperatives, and jobless organizations which the unemployed jerry-rigged in order to survive during the 1930s constitute an important but overlooked chapter in the history of the Great Depression.[2]

At first the jobless used the institutions at hand, their churches, clubs, beneficial, fraternal, and patriotic societies, transforming them into lobbies and organizations of self-help. However, in time there emerged specific organizations of the jobless, designed to overcome the travail caused by the inadequacies of the private and public relief system. These organizations were inspired by various motives: the golden rule, humanitarianism, socialist and communistic ideals, and, of course, self-interest. In addition to examining their efforts on behalf of improved standards of relief, this chapter will explore another impact of these jobless organizations. The veterans groups, unemployed councils and alliances enlisted the jobless in extracommunity groups whose purview usually extended far beyond the boundaries of Allentown. Therefore, like public relief, labor unionism, and Washington-based New Deal politics, the organized jobless helped shed the veil of isolation and impel the engine of modernization.

Not surprisingly, Allentown's churches were among the first to provide an important vehicle for local and immediate bootstrap operations. In late 1930 the city's churches girded to face the Great Depression's first winter. The Allentown ministers' league inaugurated a program in November to survey the relief needs of local congregations, share work, and set up depositories for food and clothing. The Christ Lutheran Church cared for forty families over the winter by supplying them food, clothing, and on occasion rent monies. Meanwhile, the Evangelical and Reformed churches of Allentown used their traditional white gift Christmas offering to aid their unemployed families.

Among Allentown's small black population the church played an especially crucial role. Although in 1930 blacks in Allentown registered less unemployment than the state's Negro population at large, by 1934 joblessness among Lehigh County blacks reached almost forty percent. This growing need led the minister of the Saint James African Methodist Episcopal Zion Church, the city's largest black church, to solicit food and clothing, establish an unemployment bureau, and operate a cafeteria. From September 1932 until April 1933 the Saint James Colored Cafeteria served almost 7,000 free meals.[3]

Like Allentown's churches, the city's beneficial, fraternal, and patriotic societies provided food, clothing, and fuel for their members and on occasion operated employment bureaus. However, the fraternal organizations in particular offered a special service to their jobless brothers. Many fraternal societies waived the dues of jobless members, a consideration of particular importance where sickness, death, and other insurance benefits were at stake. For example, the Moose International convention reinstated all lapsed members throughout the world; the Knights of the Mystic Chain made similar provisions for its members. Among the veterans' organizations, the American Legion arranged for its unemployed members to remain in good standing by signing up a quota of new members.[4]

However, the American Legion, like the Veterans of Foreign

Wars (VFW), campaigned most vigorously for special aid from the national government in the form of the veterans' bonus. After World War I these veterans' organizations won the passage of the World War Adjusted Compensation Act, which provided veterans with twenty-year endowment policies. Veterans could borrow up to 25 percent of the policy's value. Beginning in 1930 the VFW and the Legion agitated for immediate cash payment of the certificates. In 1931 Congress enacted legislation over President Hoover's veto which allowed veterans to borrow up to 50 percent on their policies. Although nearly 1,000 Allentown veterans applied for the loans, the aid was insufficient. When in December 1932 another bill went to Congress providing for full and immediate payment of the bonus, veterans nationwide organized the Bonus Expeditionary Army (BEA) to march on Washington and fight for a favorable decision on the measure.

On June 8, led by Albert G. Sellers, 400 Allentownians arrived in Washington, D.C., joining a force of around 20,000 fellow marchers. After a few days, half the Allentown contingent returned home; the rest linked themselves with other units from the Lehigh Valley and, under Sellers' command, chose "the choicest spot on the Anacostia flats," and laid out a company street complete with company headquarters and shelter. Until General Douglas MacArthur — at bayonet point — drove the marchers from the flats, the Lehigh Valley troops earned the reputation as the best-housed and best-fed contingent in the BEA.[5]

While Allentown's churches, fraternal and veterans' societies existed before the depression, the jobless in the 1930s created a bevy of new organizations designed to address the problems of the unemployed. One such group, for example, consisted of over a hundred young teachers who in October 1932 formed the Unemployed Teachers Association of Allentown. Members were recently graduated Allentownians with faint prospects of school employment. The unemployed teachers demanded that all those eligible for pensions retire immediately, and that the school board enforce a 1927 policy requiring all female teachers to be unmarried. While the association did not wish to retrench women without other means of support, it did insist that those secretly married resign, and that Allentown residents be given preference in new hiring. By1932 most of their requests had been granted.[6]

Sharing importance with the Unemployed Teachers Association were the various organizations of the unemployed which admitted all jobless. Four such bodies operated in Allentown during the 1930s: the Unemployed Council, the Unemployed League, the Citizen's Welfare League, and the Labor Welfare League.

In Allentown, as in Philadelphia, the Unemployed Council emerged under the leadership of the Communist Party, U.S.A.'s labor wing, the Trade Union Unity League. And Allentown joined Philadelphia, New York, and Jersey City in experiencing a rash of demonstrations, hunger marches, and mass picketing aimed especially at city halls, relief centers, and eviction sites.

In early February 1931 the Allentown Unemployed Council (AUC) staged a march on city hall. Nearly 200 jobless paraded and presented Mayor Malcolm Gross a list of eleven demands. Late February witnessed a second march. Thousands of Allentownians watched as a hundred or more bedraggled jobless wound their way to city hall, where their numbers swelled to over 500. Unfortunately for the marchers, the city fathers had left — "sick" or "out of town on business." Usually timed to be held in conjunction with mass demonstrations of unemployed councils throughout the country, the Allentown marches lacked spontaneity and consequently failed to generate any sizable local support.

Indeed, lack of followers plagued the AUC. Patriotic groups considered them suspect, and the American Federation of Labor (AFL) shunned them. Since the AUC was concerned ultimately with gaining new followers among the unemployed, the council accomplished little toward alleviating the heavy burden of relief. Thus, although until 1932 the AUC had no competition in organizing the unemployed, it failed to grow.

The first of the unemployed groups to establish real strength in Allentown was the Unemployed League. As in Philadelphia, its roots were in Abraham J. Muste's Conference for Progressive Labor Action (CPLA), which, while trying to work as an educational unit within the AFL, steered "the haunted line between the socialists and the communists."[8] By 1932 CPLA leaders were organizing the unemployed not only in Pittsburgh, Youngstown, and Philadelphia, but also in Allentown. After being elected president of the Allentown CPLA in June 1932, Larry Heibach formed the Unemployed Citizens Relief League of Allentown and vicinity, which was shortly renamed the Lehigh County Unemployed League (LCUL).[9]

The LCUL grew rapidly. By November 1932 branches were counted in eight of the city's nineteen wards and several surrounding towns, and the progress of the LCUL became worthy of emulation. State and national CPLA propaganda lauded the Allentown unit's success, and sought to encourage lagging efforts in Pittsburgh and elsewhere. Eventually, Allentown became the headquarters of the 50,000-member Pennsylvania Unemployed Leagues (PUL), and, in fact, most of the major officers of the PUL came from the city.[10]

The rise of the Unemployed Leagues and the condition of the American labor movement finally prompted Muste to end his nonpartisan stand. At the end of 1933 he announced the abandonment of the CPLA and the formation of the American Workers party. In the summer of 1934 the Musteites moved further to the left by merging with Trotskyites under the banner of the Workers party. Now firmly radicalized, they led the National Unemployed Leagues to merge with the socialist-dominated Workers' Alliance of America. With a membership of 600,000, the Workers' Alliance was perhaps the most formidable organization of the unemployed in American history. By involving the jobless in organizations of national scope with a centralized administration, and by focusing the energies of the unemployed on national issues of hunger and jobs, groups such as the National Unemployed Leagues and the Workers' Alliance helped weld the disparate jobless of Allentown, Philadelphia, Pittsburgh, and New York into a respectable countervailing force, while at the same time forging a national consciousness of the problem of mass joblessness.[11]

The venturing of the CPLA into the politics of the left led the LCUL in its turn to emphasize politics over self-help. The result was greatly to weaken the LCUL by encouraging the growth of a rival group, the Citizens' Welfare League. Suspicious of socialism and staunchly anticommunist, the Citizens' Welfare League recruited at the expense of the LCUL. By the spring of 1935, the Citizens' Welfare League had become part of the statewide Pennsylvania Security League, and counted 1,200 members within its ranks in Allentown, plus another 1,300 in the county. Two years later the LCUL was moribund.[12]

The creation of the Works Progress Administration (WPA) in 1935 signaled not only a rising federal commitment to work relief, but also a national resolution to end what Harry Hopkins, work relief administrator, believed was the psychological miasma of joblessness. However, the creation of the WPA challenged the wary jobless organizations to police the adequacy of work relief and guard the unemployed against the exploitation of their labor.

Between 1935 and 1936 work-relief rolls in Lehigh County swelled from 5,111 persons (18.3 percent) to 14,022 (55.3 percent). In order to organize this growing force, the Pennsylvania Security League (PSL) formed the Keystone Workers' Association. Starting in 1935 with seventy-five members, by February 1936 all local PSL organizations were consolidated into one unit: the Lehigh Division, PSL. Work reliefers dominated the new organization, especially after Horace Geary, formerly president of the Keystone Workers' Association, became the head of the new organization. The local grew just as the Unemployed League deteriorated. In 1937 Geary became president of the PSL and pressed that body's strong anticommunist stand. In 1938 and 1939 the Lehigh Division broadened its program to include educational work and remained viable to the end of the decade.[13]

In the midst of the shuffle which created the Lehigh Division, PSL, in 1936 one group withdrew and formed the Labor Welfare League (LWL). Simon Levene, the initiator and lifelong president of the LWL, pursued a policy based largely on self-help. The Welfare League grew continually, branching into neighboring Hokendauqua, Quakertown, Fullertown, and Summit Hill. Although Levene talked of a statewide organization, the LWL never extended its geographic bounds.

Most of the WPA people in the LWL were the women of the sewing centers and project workers whom the league viewed as victims of a "boycott against renting homes to WPA workers." The LWL also involved itself in local politics, supporting candidiates favorable to more adequate relief benefits. Of the four unemployed organizations in Allentown during the Great Depression, this was the most durable; it was still active as late as 1959.[14]

Self-help constituted a basic policy of each of Allentown's four unemployed organizations. For example, all four instituted a barter system. The Lehigh County Unemployed League set the local model. In each city ward the LCUL acquired a vacant store as a meeting room and headquarters, and from there it served soup lunches, operated an employment bureau, and ran a bartering center. Through bartering the jobless traded not only goods, but also services such as shoemaking, carpentry, and barbering. In one case the LCUL announced itself ready to aid all farmers at harvest time in exchange for food, and to cut down or remove trees for firewood.

The exchange of labor for firewood was among the most successful bartering activities in the city. The twelfth-ward branch of the Unemployed League took trees out of the Lehigh Parkway project in 1932, and in 1938 the Labor Welfare League removed the trees from the city reservoir project. The LCUL gathered such a large supply of wood in 1932 that it donated 2,000 cords to the Lehigh County Emergency Relief Board of distribution to nonmembers on relief.[15]

However, bartering was only one of the devices used by the jobless associations to allay the need of the unemployed. The organizations also raised funds to assist jobless families. In time the leagues came to provide entertainment, hosting boxing matches, baseball games, ice cream festivals, block parties, card and bingo parties. Monies raised through these projects were used to buy fuel for the jobless, pay their rent and utilities, purchase medical services as well as to treat the children of unemployed families to picnics in the summer and Christmas parties in the winter.

It was not that the unemployed organizations refused charity. The LCUL ran its own bundle day in 1932 and collected over 400 garments. In 1937 the Labor Welfare League set up its own clothing center in Allentown's Americus Hotel. Much of the food served in the soup kitchens and at the summer picnics was solicited from grocers. Moreover, merchants also contributed the gifts, candy, and oranges for the children's Christmas parties.[16]

However, throughout the 1930s the relative importance of barter and charity to the unemployed declined. As Allentown's municipal government became more adept at handling large-scale relief, the city assumed some of the barter activities. For instance, the community cafeteria replaced the soup kitchens, "bundle day" replaced individual clothing appeals, and city "thrift gardens" replaced the cooperative gardening ventures of the unemployed organizations. More importantly, relief improved as state and federal relief funds became available. Public-welfare agencies such as the State Emergency Relief Board, the Civil Works Administration, and the Works Progress Administration convinced the unemployed that at least the bare essentials of living would be provided. Thus, the criticalness of self-help activities steadily diminished.

Although their self-help function declined, Allentown's unemployed organizations remained vital. Since the amount of help offered by the state was always inadequate, the need for barter operations continued. Under the Lehigh County Emergency Relief Board (LCERB), assistance initially took the form of food orders, ignoring all other needs of daily living. While eventually the LCERB provided clothing and utilities relief, critics deemed the level of provision inadequate, noting that the relief board had not expanded the relief budget but had in fact used the same amount of money to cover more things. Although the state declared an annual income of $3,500 to be necessary for a four person family to provide the necessities for an American standard of living, in 1934 the LCERB was granting each family only $803 a year. As it was,40 percent of the children of families on relief were found to be underfed in 1934. The situation was not greatly improved when Pennsylvania went from commodity to cash allowances in October 1936.[17]

The unemployed organizations also survived because of the

chaos created by the erratic funding of welfare. Relief crises arose with each fluctuation in government policy such as the cessation of state relief monies in 1931 - 1932, the dismantling of the Civil Works Administration in 1934, and the replacement of the State Emergency Relief Board in 1937. Other crises were produced by the frequent delays in state and federal relief appropriations. Each delay meant hardship for the relief client. Therefore, the unemployed organizations thrived because they interposed themselves between the client and the government, and helped mitigate the hardships stemming from the administration of relief.

In their role as mediators, the unemployed fought hard to improve the adequacy of relief. Often their efforts took the form of demonstrations. Both the Allentown Unemployed Council and the LCUL employed this tactic. In January 1933, twenty members of the LCUL complained to the County Relief Board that the agency's supply of coal to the jobless was too little and of poor quality. A month later the Unemployed League led 2,000 jobless to city hall protesting the state's adoption of the commissary system, which called for food to be distributed from government warehouses. Demonstrations such as this continued throughout the 1930s and on occasion even children were sent to picket relief headquarters.[18]

However, like self-help, mass protest in the city declined, especially after the State Emergency Relief Board moved its headquarters from Allentown to Bethlehem. But the most important reason for the decline of mass protest was the institutionalization of the complaint process. In the spring of 1934 the Relief Board stopped adjudicating complaints which could be handled by its staff in conjunction witht the LCUL. It also added another rule, that no more than three persons could present a complaint. After the LCERB offices were moved to Bethlehem the LCUL maintained its link to the Relief Board. In fact, during the spring of 1935 the Central Grievance Committee of the LCUL processed twenty to forty-five cases a week, including the complaints of a merchant who refused to accept clothing vouchers, a man unable to get blankets for over forty days, and a widow and her two small children living in the Lehigh Valley Railroad station after being refused relief because she believed in hexing.[19]

The number of complaints rose throughout Pennsylvania in 1935, touching off fourteen legislative investigations. In Lehigh County the investigators heard 150 complaints from the city of Allentown alone. This hearing helped convince the legislature to scrap the poor boards as well as the State Emergency Relief Board. And it was during the ensuing political battle between Democrats and Republicans that all welfare payments ceased, and 250 Allentownians joined thousands of angry relief clients in a massive protest in Harrisburg.

This so-called siege of Harrisburg, replete with catcalls and the occupation of the Senate gallery, produced not only emergency relief funds, but also impelled the legislature to produce a new state welfare system whereby County Boards of Assistance replaced the old poor boards. The new boards of assistance were only responsible for direct relief. A major reason for the limitation of the County Boards of Assistance in providing relief was the New Deal's decision in 1935 to create the WPA, which would provide work relief for the able-bodied unemployed.[20]

Throughout the state and nation the WPA was favorably received. In Allentown it was generally held that work was preferable to the dole. Most Americans felt that it was immoral to collect direct relief. Also, many were concerned about the type of work performed by the unemployed. Value-creating endeavors were preferred. The early projects of the Lehigh County Citizens Co-ordinating Committee for Welfare and Unemployment Relief and the Lehigh County Emergency Relief Board suffered in this regard. The projects frequently consisted of clearing weeds from roadsides, snow removal, cleaning streams, and manning charitable offices, transient shelters, and the cafeteria. Yet, Allentown's CWA, SERB, and the WPA projects were highly regarded. There had been time for planning. The city could boast a new airport, homes connected to sewers, paved streets, an assured water supply from a pump house, two reserviors, and, especially, an enlarged park system.

The city's park project was magnificent. In 1925 Allentown had only thirty acres of parks. In 1929 the city acquired a small two acre rose garden and, to protect its water supply, 625 acres along the Little Lehigh River. By 1938 there were 866 acres of park in the town. Each site was developed before the decade's end—the Little Lehigh Parkway, modeled after Philadelphia's Fairmont Park, as well as other swimming and recreation areas. In addition, plans were underway for a new stadium and a golf course.

However, the *quid pro quo* mentality which demanded work for assistance threatened the unemployed. In fact, as the depression continued and the sense of crisis eased, the sentiment of "no work— no relief" came precariously close to condoning forced labor. Consequently, the problems and conditions of work relief came to dominate the energies of the unemployed organizations. Forced to concern themselves with wages and hours, hiring and firing, these organizations began to think and act as labor unions.

In Allentown, as elsewhere in America, work-relief programs suffered an ideological crisis of identity — were they work, or were they relief? The early public-works programs were financed by extra food orders and regarded by the authorities as relief. This position was vigorously countered by the Unemployed Council, which charged that even the vacant-lot farming program was forced labor. Although the Unemployed League accepted the idea of work relief, they demanded that workers be paid union rates in cash, and not with food orders.[21]

Thus, both the Allentown Council and the Unemployed League had serious reservations about these local works programs. However, in the fall of 1933, they both welcomed the Civil Works Administration program. Under the CWA men were hired by their ability, not their need, and paid the prevailing union wages. When these rates were reduced in March 1934, a short, two-hour strike followed in Allentown. The call for a mass strike sponsored by the LCUL was forestalled when the CWA agreed to restore the cuts. The lingering fear of a wage reduction caused the Unemployed League to ally with the Central Trades and Labor Council of Allentown and the group began to organize the CWA projects. Then, in the spring of 1934, the CWA was terminated.[22]

The return of work relief to the SERB again changed the

emphasis from work to relief. Once more workers were drawn from the relief rolls, and although the SERB paid prevailing union wage rates, the relief agency calculated a worker's hours so as to produce an income equivalent to its relief budget. In January 1935, 200 Lehigh County project workers launched the Project Workers Section of the LCUL. The section sought to install grievance units at every project and to stage mass meetings every two weeks.[23]

The creation of the Works Progress Administration only exacerbated the underlying tensions between work and relief. WPA workers were to be hired off the relief rolls. However, because the WPA advertised the projects as "employment," the unions and the LCUL joined the newly formed Keystone Workers Association (KWA) in demanding that the WPA honor both the union wage scale and the prevailing wage. Yet, Allentown's unemployed organizations were unimpressed when the WPA announced its "security wage" formula. Days after the WPA published its security wage, the LCUL advertised its contempt by sending Mother Kimmel (an active seventy-year-old veteran protester) and ten others to picket the White House in Washington.

This dispute over the security wage stopped all Allentown's projects and burgeoned into the nation's second major WPA strike. The grievances which led to the strike prompted a catchy ballad:

Roosevelt and Hopkins
With bellies full of good,
Figured that the unemployed
Could go hung-a-ry and nude.

"Fifty-five a month," they said,
"For labor is good pay,
And we'll chisel down all union rates
On the WPA."

STRIKE! STRIKE! the cry went round
And workers downed their tools
We'll fight for living wages,
Too long we have been fools.[24]

While Mayor Fred Lewis agreed that the rates were too low,

most Allentownians decried the strike as ingratitude against the national bounty, especially after violence occurred. The strike began and proceeded peacefully. Following "three hours of persuasive oration," nearly all of the 206 WPA workers were "on vacation" throughout Lehigh County. The WPA closed down the projects, and when they reopened days later violence erupted. Strikers charged the police with brutal and insulting conduct, especially after the police arrested Mother Kimmel. Three relief workers who returned to their jobs were beaten by pickets, and the house windows of other returning workers were showered with stones and bottles. The strike ended on September 27, when the WPA agreed to an increase in wages and a decrease in hours.

Out of the strike emerged the Joint Labor Council of Lehigh County, composed of delegates from the Unemployed League, the Keystone Workers Association, and the Labor Council. Temporarily, the Joint Council became the official representative of all county project workers. This time the workers' grievances were quite basic. First, the workers were not getting their checks in time; delays of eleven to twenty-six days were not uncommon. In fact, the situation led the workers to dub the WPA as the "Wandering Paycheck Administration." The second problem was a ruling by Pennsylvania relief officials that clients must take a WPA position if it was offered. In retaliation, the Joint Labor Council urged fifty men who were getting less than their relief budget to quit. Since the Commonwealth clearly recognized the functional role of the WPA in alleviating the burden of the jobless, the state capitulated and worked out a system of supplementary budgets which satisfied Harrisburg's desire to be thrifty while relieving the jobless of being coerced to work for less than the relief wage.[25]

From 1936 to 1940 Allentown's unemployed organizations worked to soften the effects of the new public-assistance program and the unemployment-compensation law, neither of which made provisions for the newly jobless or partially unemployed to receive supplementary assistance. It was the persistent agitation of the unemployed organizations which helped convince Pennsylvania to change the relief rules to permit the County Boards to give aid to those waiting for unemployment compensation.[26]

Rent assistance was another serious problem. WPA wages were usually insufficient to cover the cost of shelter; therefore, relief workers became the most frequently evicted people in the city. Moreover, not only could a person be evicted, but his family could be broken up on the grounds that he failed to provide for his children. The unemployed organizations picketed evictions, proposed the purchase and conversion of the old Allentown post office as a temporary residence for the evicted, and supported efforts to build low-income housing in the city. At last, in February 1938, the Lehigh County Board of Assistance was empowered to pay rents for those threatened with eviction. However, if a person refused WPA work, the Board of Assistance denied him rent aid.[27]

All failures notwithstanding, the work of the churches, clubs, and societies in the early depression years and of the unemployed organizations in the later years did much to mitigate the often harsh terms of the official relief programs and helped strengthen the morale of the jobless. Therefore, all of the jobless organizations continued to function as long as they effectively voiced the grievances of the mass jobless and furnished the opportunity for needed self-help. It was only with the outbreak of World War II and the end of massive unemployment that the Lehigh Division, Pennsylvania Security League, and other jobless organizations disbanded. Only the Labor Welfare League survived into the postwar era, reflecting a continuing concern for evictions and a still critical housing shortage.

However, these bodies had an importance transcending their explicit functions of self-help and organized pressure. To a large degree the Allentown Unemployed Council, the Lehigh County Unemployed League, the Keystone Workers' Association, and other groups of the unemployed represented the bureaucratization of mass protest and the articulation of the frustrations of the jobless through centralized and structured units. As such, these organizations acted to broaden the forces of protest beyond the boundaries of Allentown, New York, or

Philadelphia, and into the national arena. Therefore, for the jobless participants and those who followed their tergiversations, the organizations helped define the problem of unemployment in a modern industrial society. Nor were their tactics of protest overlooked. The same tactics of sit-in, stand-in, and mass march characterized the civil-rights and antiwar movements of the 1960s and 1970s.

But violence and civil disorder were never the hallmark of the jobless demonstrations. Nationally, some violence accompanied certain early demonstrations of the Unemployed Councils, but most of the jobless emphasized peaceful protest. Certainly civil disorder played only a negligible role in the initiation and expansion of public relief in Allentown. In fact, the expansion of public-relief programs began prior to the appearance of any major demonstrations in Allentown. Then demonstrations hastened the formalization of grievance procedures to ameliorate the problems of inadequate relief.

However, in the end, one of the greatest impacts of these unemployed organizations was on the jobless themselves. Sociologists studying the effect of the Great Depression on the unemployed worried about those outside, not those within the ranks of the jobless organizations. For to the extent that the unemployed joined with their fellow jobless in self-help and protest organizations many of the unemployed preserved their initiative and self-respect. They retained their ability to determine their destiny; therefore they escaped the mire of dependency. Those who slipped beyond the pale into the pool of what social workers called the "permanently unemployed" became part of Michael Harrington's "Other America." Accordingly, it was one of the chief contributions of these jobless organizations to keep the jobless psychologically employable. In doing so, they helped define joblessness as a national problem begging federal solutions—and not simply the problem of Allentown.

NOTES

1. For most purposes Allentown was not a statistical unit for either the state or the federal government. The employment and relief figures are extrapolated from data collected for Lehigh County, of which Allentown was the seat. The Federal

Reserve Bank of Philadelphia's "Allentown Area"—Lehigh, Northampton and Carbon counties—provides the figures on factory employment and wages. For a complete explanation of how these figures were determined see Ernest B. Fricke, "The Impact of the Depression on Allentown, Pennsylvania: 1930-1940" (Ph.D., diss., New York University, 1974).

2. *Allentown Morning Call*, 18 November 1930, 9 January 1931, 16 and 23 December 1935; see also Albert U. Romasco, *The Poverty of Abundance: Hoover, The Nation, The Depression* (New York, 1965), and Clarke A. Chambers, *Seedtime of Reform: American Social Service and Social Action, 1918-1933* (Minneapolis, 1963).

3. *Allentown Morning Call*, 15 June 1935, 23 March 1938. The economic characterization is for the state as a whole. See Pennsylvania Department of Welfare, *Negro Survey of Pennsylvania* (Harrisburg, Department of Welfare, [19271]), p. 11.

4. *Allentown Morning Call*, 14 September 1930-10 December 1933, passim.

5. Ibid., 3 March 1931, 6 and 8 June 1932; Roger Daniels, *The Bonus March: An Episode of the Depression* (Westport, Conn., 1973), pp. 43, 52.

6. *Allentown Morning Call*, 17 March 1931, 15 October 1932.

7. Ibid., 11 and 26 February 1931, 31 August 1930; Irving Howe and Lewis Coser, *The American Communist Party: A Critical History, 1919-1957* (Boston, 1957), pp. 192-94.

8. Donald Meyer, *The Protestant Search for Political Realism, 1919-1941* (Berkley and Los Angeles, 1960), pp. 95, 183.

9. A. J. Muste, "Labor's Left-Wing Vanguard," *The World Tomorrow* 15, (September 28, 1932): 306; Clark Kerr, "Productive Enterprises of the Unemployed, 1931-1938" (Ph.D. diss., University of California, 1939), 1: 18; *Allentown Morning Call*, 15 June 1932, 23 May 1932. Heimbach had recently graduated from Muste's Brookwood Labor College.

10. *Allentown Morning Call*, 16 June 1932, 29 November 1932; 3 and 5 February 1933, 16 April 1933. The LCUL eventually developed its own Workers Scouts of America. (Lehigh County Unemployed League, "Voice of the Workers," 3, No. 2, October 21, 1935, p. 4 (mimeographed), hereinafter referred to as "Voice of the Workers"; Pittsburgh Unemployed Citizens League, "The Unemployed in Action: A Challenge to the Unemployed of Pittsburgh," Bulletin, no. 3, undated, but earliest October 1932, pp. 9-10 (mimeographed); Roy Rosenzweig, "Radicals and the Jobless: The Musteites and the Unemployed Leagues, 1932-1936," *Labor History* 16, no. 4 (Winter 1975), p. 60; *Allentown Morning Call*, 29 January 1934.

11. A. J. Muste, "The A.P.L.A. States its Case," *The World Tomorrow* 16, (October 12, 1933); pp. 569-70; James Cannon, *The History of American Trotskyism: From Its Origins (1928) to the Founding of the Socialist Workers Party (1938)*, 2nd ed., New York, 1972), p. 115.

12. Workers' Alliance of America, *Proceedings of the First National Convention . . . Washington, D.C., March 2-3-4, 1935* (Milwaukee, n.d.), p. 1.

13. Table 16, "Average number of persons dependent on work relief, by county: yearly averages, 1933-1940; Monthly Average, December, 1940" in Pennsylvania, Department of Public Assistance, "Pennsylvania Public Assistance Statistics, Summary, 1932-1940," p. xxviii (mimeographed.); *Allentown Morning Call*, 2 and 19 April 1935.

14. *Allentown Morning Call*, 14 August 1936, 28 January 1938, 22 March 1938, 22 September 1936.

15. Ibid., 20 August 1932, 14 September 1932, 12 August 1938. The AUC did not act so vigorously in this area as in the other three. It aimed to increase the amount of relief by pressuring the government. Its failure to do more than a minimal amount of self-help was one of the major reasons it did not overcome its other handicaps.

16. For instances of fund raising, see ibid., 15 July 1932, 23 February 1936, 22 September 1936; on fuel, ibid., 20 September 1937; rent, ibid., 30 March 1937; medicine, ibid., 25 January 1938; picnics, ibid., 26 May 1935; Christmas, ibid., 22 December 1936; *Voice of the Workers* 2, no. 1, January 12, 1935, p. 5.

17. Interview with an investigater reported in *Voice of the Worker*, 1, no. 22 December 17, 1934, p. 4; *Philadelphia Record*, 13 December 1934, noted in Pennsylvania State Emergency Relief Board, "The Unemployment Relief Digest," 2, no. 1 January 3, 1935, p. 35 (mimeographed); "The Preliminary Report of the Pennsylvania Planning Board," December, 1934, noted in ibid., 2, no. 2, January 17, 1935, pp. 18-20; Pennsylvania Department of Public Assistance, *Current Living Costs as Related to Standards of Public Assistance in Pennsylvania; December 1938* (Harrisburg, [Pa.]: Department of Public Assistance, n.d.), pp. 1-2 and 6-7; *Current Living Costs as Related to Standards of Public Assistance in Pennsylvania; December 1939* ([Harrisburg, Pa.]: Department of Public Assistance, n.d.), p. 11, and *Current Living Costs as Related to Standards of Public Assistance in Pennsylvania; December 1941* ([Harrisburg, Pa.]: Department of Public Assistance, n.d.), p. 4.

18. *Allentown Morning Call*, 14 January, 8 February, 9 April, 17 May 1933.

19. Ibid., 19 April 1933, 13 January 1935, "Voice of the Workers", 2, no. 3 February 9, 1935, p. 8; 2, no. 5 March 9, 1935, pp. 3 and 5; *Allentown Morning Call*, 25 May 1935.

20. Pennsylvania General Assembly, Joint State Government Commission, "Report on Relief," 1941, pp. 50-51; *Allentown Morning Call*, 15 June 1935; *Allentown Chronicle and News and Item*, 3 October 1939. In practice, food stamps lowered the amount of food received and more obviously marked a person as on relief.

21. *Allentown Morning Call*, 22 February, 5 April, 1, 20, and 28 June 1933.

22. Ibid., 3, 13, 15, 24 March 1934. This nascent organization disappeared in the period it took to form the SERB: Works Division.

23. "Voice of the Workers", 2, no. 2, January 26, 1935, p. 6.

24. Anonymous, "Ballad of the WPA Strike" in ibid., 3, no. 1 October 12, 1935, pp. 2-3; Allentown Morning Call, 12 September 1935; Workers Alliance of America, *Proceedings of the Second National Convention*, p. 10.

25. *Allentown Morning Call*, 13, 20, and 26 September 1935; *Voice of the Workers* 3, no. 1, October 12, 1935, p. 3; ibid., no. 6 November 18, 1935, p. 1.

26. *Allentown Morning Call*, 29 January 1938; Pennsylvania General Assembly, Joint State Government Commission, *Unemployment Compensation—Proposals for Increased Benefits and Benefits for Partial Unemployment: A Report of the Committee on Unemployment Compensation Benefits for Partial Unemployment of the Joint State Government Commission* (Harrisburg, Pa.): Joint State Government Commission, April 10, 1945), p. 13. Unemployment compensation was passed in 1936 and

amended in 1937, 1939, and 1940 to bring it into conformity with the federal Social Security Act.

27. *Allentown Morning Call*, 16 February 1938, 7 December 1936, 23 May 1937, 1 April, 2 October 1938.

[5]
1934: The Critical Election in Indiana County*

In Pittsburgh and in Philadelphia, as well as in many smaller cities like Allentown, the political gestation of the early 1930s involving relief and self-help organizations helped pave the way in 1934 for a new political alignment in Pennsylvania. This realignment is well illustrated in the case of Indiana County.

Feisty Francesco Biamonte, editor of the Italian-American weekly *The Patriot*, disrupted the midwinter doldrums of 1926 in Indiana County, Pennsylvania, with a searing front-page assault on the county's Democratic party. "Indiana County Democrats, disheartened by years of incompetent leadership, are beginning to wonder whether the party will ever have any better prospects in this 'bailiwick,' " he changed. "Shall the Democratic voters in Indiana County always be subject to the shame of a leadership which seems possessed of neither intelligence nor conscience?"[1] This attack symbolized the nadir of the Democratic party and the two-party structure in Indiana County. The party's leadership seemed unable to produce a winning ticket for any office. Additionally, the party's registration accounted for only ten percent of the county's electorate. Indiana County in the 1920s was truly a one-party county and the Republican hegemony seemed impregnable. Within ten years from Biamonte's blast, however, the county enjoyed a competitive and viable two-party system. The Republican party still enrolled a substantial majority of the voters and continued to dominate the county's political bureaucracy. But the Democratic party had enjoyed such a revitalization that its membership touted the hopes of carrying the county for

*This chapter is the contribution of Professor Smith, Professor of History, Indiana University of Pennsylvania.

Franklin D. Roosevelt in 1936.

The reconstitution of the Democratic party in Indiana County was part of a broader political revolution that characterized the New Deal era. The Democratic party overturned the Republican majority and emerged as the dominant party in the nation. The New Deal revolution in American politics, as most historians contend, gained its generative power from the laboring and ethnic pockets of urban America. A debate has arisen about the exact time or election that the political realignment occurred. Traditionally, scholars accepted Roosevelt's election in 1932 as the turning point, but the 1950s studies by Samuel Lubell and V. O. Key, Jr., concluded that 1928 was the "critical election." Key's "critical election theory" became the model to ascertain the precise timing of political realignment. Key suggested that the critical election occurred when there was an alteration in voter preferences, an abnormally high voter turnout, and a realignment of the voters that was evident in subsequent elections. Subsequently, a scholarly debate arose as various students laid claims to either 1924, 1928, or 1932 as the critical election. Allen J. Lichtman in a recent article suggested that the political shift occurred as early as 1916 and that "no election between 1916 and 1940 qualifies as a critical election."[2]

In this research historians have paid little attention to rural areas. They have made few attempts to determine if the New Deal revolution permeated rural America, too, or if it was simply an urban phenomenon. This chapter presents the results of such an inquiry. It focuses on a staunch Republican bailiwick in western Pennsylvania, Indiana County, and demonstrates that the New Deal revolution occurred there, too. The realigning or critical election, however, came in 1934, a much later date than in urban centers. Moreover, the reconstitution of the Democratic party came as a result not of shifting ethnic patterns, but because a reinvigorated labor union involved itself in politics. The county's Democratic party remained an ineffectual organization until the United Mine Workers of America (UMWA) allied with the Democrats in 1934. The UMWA provided the apparatus that mobilized the electorate and brought about the revival of a two-party system in Indiana County.

The reconstitution of the Democratic party in Indiana County was the last phase of a major transformation in the county's institutions. At the turn of the century Indiana County enjoyed a blissful somnambulence reminiscent of a Currier and Ives nineteenth-century farming community. Located fifty miles east of Pittsburgh away from any major transportation lines, Indiana County had escaped the impact of industrialization. Then in 1901–04, coal companies began to tap the bituminous coal deposits within the county. A boomlike atmosphere gripped the county as newspapers reported coal leases being sold, employment opportunities abounding, and profits enjoyed by all. Coal production in Indiana County rose by 50 percent from 1900 to 1905 and doubled again by 1910.[3] The demand for labor brought a corresponding increase in the county's population. From 1900 to 1910 the population increased from 42,556 to 66,210, an increase of 36 percent. The population explosion meant a qualitative change in the county because a substantial number of the immigrating laborers were Italians and Slavs. The process of industrialization quickly transformed this small county from its serene rural blissfulness to the hurly-burly climate of twentieth-century modernity.

While the county's economy and population measure these changes, the political system retained its preindustrial character. In the early twentieth century, the Republican party dominated Pennsylvania as well as Indiana County. The state and Indiana County were like Republican fiefdoms under the control of strong bosses and party machinery. Except for the 1910–14 campaigns, when the statewide Republican organization was disrupted by Progressive-conservative battles, the Republicans counted Indiana County a sure stronghold. In 1920 the county was among the top ten counties in the state with high Republican percentages. In 1926, when the county's favorite son, John S. Fisher, was elected governor, the county polled the highest Republican percentage in the commonwealth.[4]

As elsewhere in the state, the Indiana County Democratic organization was mired in a minority position. In the 1920 presidential election the Democrats polled only 16 percent of

Major Party Percentages of Total
Vote in Indiana County, 1900-1926

	Republican	*Democrat*	*Progressive*
1900 President	72.3	22.4	
1902 Governor	59.1	35.9	
1904 President	77.2	17.3	
1906 Governor	63.8	19.7	
1908 President	67.4	20.7	
1910 Governor	39.6	5.9	39.8
1912 President	20.2	18.7	39.0
1914 Governor	28.0	18.7	16.00
1916 President	57.6	28.3	
1918 Governor	69.9	16.1	
1920 President	71.8	16.1	
1922 Governor	52.0	41.1	
1924 President	69.7	11.3	
1926 Governor	86.7	8.8	

SOURCES: *Smull's Legislative Handbook*

the county vote; by 1926, the party enrolled only 11 percent of the registered voters.[5] Its farmer-immigrant coalition mirrored the similar contradictory divisions within the national organization.[6] The farm element of the Democratic party was the oldest component and exerted the preponderant force over the party. The principal Democratic organ, *The Indiana Democrat,* appealed to farmers with its regular grain and livestock price quotations, but seemed oblivioius to the problems of the miners and immigrants. In September 1922, when John A. McSparran, the Democratic gubernatorial candidate, toured the county, the Democrats boasted that "he has made a thorough study of the political game and knows just where to stick a pin in the Republicans where it hurts most."[7] Then the candidate, obviously advised by county leaders, epitomized the agrarian orientation of the party by visiting farming communities such as Cookport and Plumville and ignoring the mining towns. Still the party could rely upon the allegiance of some immigrant voters such as the Italian-Americans.[8]

Minority parties such as the Prohibition, Labor, and

Socialist parties vied in the 1920s with the Republicans and Democrats for voters. While the Prohibition party, especially in local elections, attracted a few voters from the Republicans, the Labor and Socialist tickets seriously weakened the Democrats. In 1924, for example, some miners and Italians supported the LaFollette-Labor slate when ordinarily they would have voted for the Democratic candidate.[9] The LaFollette ticket was popular enough to poll more votes than the Democrats in fourteen townships and boroughs. In the countywide totals the LaFollette ticket was only 121 votes behind the Democrats.[10]

The Republican monopoly and weak party competition contributed to a political malaise throughout the commonwealth of Pennsylvania. Voter indifference characterized the state as wells as Indiana County. In 1926 only two-thirds of the potential voters in the state were registered and only one-third voted that year in the gubernatorial election. While Indiana County was one of the counties with the highest number of potential voters registered, still only 32.5 percent of the county's registered voters went to the polls in 1926. Until 1928, voter turnout for the state and the county fluctuated between 20 percent and 45 percent.[11]

Though the party structure remained unchanged, the political issues of the mid-1920s reflected the altered character of Indiana County since industrialization. The ethnocultural antagonisms and the economic problems stemming from the recent industrialization increasingly found expression in politics. These antagonisms served as the seedbed of political change.

The prohibition issue, for example, was symptomatic of the ethnocultural divisions in early twentieth-century America. The "dry" crusade was part of the Progressive reform movement which frequently divided middle-class native Americans and the newly arrived ethnic laborers. The ethnocultural divisions were enhanced by the religious differences between "drys" and "wets." Evangelical Protestant denominations such as Presbyterians, Methodists, and Baptists were fervent prohibitionists while most Catholics either ignored or opposed the "dry" crusade.[12] In Indiana County, the dividing lines between the "drys" and the "wets" adhered closely to ethnocultural patterns. The Presbyterian and Methodist denominations were especially influential in the county and they echoed the prohibition refrains of their national leaders. The Italian community in Indiana County, on the other hand, formed the bulk of the "wet" component in the early 1920s. Biamonte's *Patriot*, the organ of the Italian community, frequently avowed its "wet" preferences in the early years of prohibition. The county's immigrant population also accused the Republican county administration and judges of unfairly raiding and punishing the Italian section of Indiana borough for bootleg liquor.[13]

A less evident but equally divisive issue in the county's politics was the Ku Klux Klan. Its revival in the 1920s also represented the ethnocultural divisions between middle-class WASP America and the newly arrived immigrant laborers. The Klan spread into Pennsylvania in the 1920s and organized in Indiana County in 1924.[14] While the miners' and immigrants' press attempted to counter the influence of the KKK, political observers estimated that the Klan could muster 5,500 votes for a candidate in a county election.[15]

A potentially explosive problem in Indiana County which both major parties wished to ignore was the battle over unionization between coal operators and miners. The 1920s were economically depressed times for the county's miners. The miners sought some remedy by striking and organizing with the United Mine Workers of America. But the miners met stubborn resistance from coal operators. The operators won court injunctions that prohibited striking and organizing near company properties. Judges sympathetic to the companies broadly interpreted injunctions that prohibited even miners' wives from activity against the company.[16] The Indiana County judge was among those judges who collaborated with coal companies to stifle union meetings and protests. According to one UMWA leader, as late as 1933 in "the heart of the R.& P. (Rochester & Pittsburgh) Coal and Iron Company Properties in Indiana County . . . a permanent injunction existed at all of their mines some dating as far back as in 1925 with Judge J. N. Langham still the sitting Judge and like a mighty Emperor of old."[17] The battle between the miners and coal companies intruded into politics, too. When the operators feared the miners might vote for a pro-labor candidate, the companies threatened layoffs and scheduled work on election days.[18]

During the 1920s Indiana County insured its reputation as one of the staunchest Republican areas in the state. Since the Civil War the county's population identified with the Republican party. The GOP represented the traditional American values of laissez-faire government, prohibition, Protestantism, and patriotism.

Epitomizing the traditional Republicanism of Indiana County was the party's gubernatorial candidate in 1926. Like many ambitious men, fifty-nine-year-old John S. Fisher by 1926 had enjoyed a varied career in public life. He began his career as an educator, turned to law and then to politics. He was elected to the state senate in 1899, where he served until voluntarily retiring in 1908. During his senate career he also served as a legal agent for coal companies and was instrumental in developing the coal industry in Indiana County. In 1908 he became a full-time entrepreneur as land speculator, banker, president of an electric as well as a brick company, and counsel for the New York Central Railroad. He returned to government in 1919 by accepting the position as Commissioner for Banking in Pennsylvania. Then in 1926 he vigorously sought the Republican nomination for governor. In a heated primary battle he won the nomination and then swept the state in the general election. Fisher won every county in the state and polled 86.7 percent of the vote in Indiana County. Fisher's election marked the end of an era in Pennsylvania's history, for he was the last governor to enjoy a one-party structure in the state and in Indiana County.[19]

From 1928 to 1932 the political system became more dynamic nationally and in Pennsylvania. For many areas in the United States this was a critical or realigning period as the origins of the New Deal coalition appeared.[20] For Indiana County the 1928-32 period was a time of preparation for change, encompassing, as it did, a transition from a one-party political hegemony to a healthier two-party structure.

Especially noticeable in this period was the awakened interest that voters took in the campaigns. Heretofore, voter turnout in the county ranged between 30 and 50 percent. But the 1928 presidential campaign elicited higher interest and 65.2 percent of the county's voters went to the polls.[21] Presidential elections traditionally stimulated a high voter turnout, but a higher voter participation became normal for the county and the state.

A second noticeable feature of the 1928-32 era in Indiana County was the disappearance of the Labor, Socialist, and Prohibition parties as influential vehicles. Some loyal members clung dearly to their banners but the minority-party vote and registration dropped from the 10 percent range to less than 1 percent. An analysis of the total vote at township level reveals that the Labor and Socialist advocates joined the Democratic party, while the Prohibition stalwarts fused with the Republicans.[22]

The disappearance of the minority parties did weaken the Republican party's majority position a bit. The GOP never again attained its 1926 high of 86.7 percent of the vote,but it still polled 75 percent of the votes in the 1928 and 1930 elections. While the Democratic strength nearly doubled as it gained from the minority parties, the Democratic clout remained ineffectual at the township level. The Democrats mustered strength to carry only one township in 1928.

It was the Great Depression which enabled Indiana Democrats to wreak revenge on the Republicans. The Democratic vote in Indiana County increased from fewer than 5,000 votes in 1928 to 8,606 in 1932, an astounding gain of 3,796 votes in four years. But the 1932 election was still not a critical or realigning election in Indiana County. The Democrats carried ten townships but only seven became identifiable Democratic areas. The remainder returned to their traditional Republican posture.[23] The 1932 vote in Indiana County represented some instability, but not realignment.

That the Democrats failed to concoct a permanent alignment in 1932 is evidenced by their disastrous loss in the 1933 county elections. The results indicated a return by voters to the old political order. The Republican candidates won decisively in every office. In the vote for the highest county office being contested, the register-recorder position, the Republican candidate polled 50.8 percent and won every township and borough except Blairsville. The Democrats polled only 16.3 percent and remained impotent at the township level. A Labor ticket, which polled 22 percent of the vote, portended a new voting bloc in the county. But in 1933, the Democratic and Labor candidates divided their strength and could not match the habitual Republicanism of Indiana County.[24]

The election of a Democratic administration in Washington and President Roosevelt's attempts to achieve economic recovery gave new life to local Democratic organizations everywhere. Democrats benefitted from FDR's positive reforms, his personal popularity, and the government patronage. The success of the national administration spurred local Democrats such as those in Indiana County to contend more energetically for local and state offices.

The revival of the Democratic party in Indiana County was apparent first in the 1934 gubernatorial campaign. For Indiana County that campaign and election best satisfies the definition of a critical election. The election was marked by (1) a sharp alteration in voter preferences; (2) an intense voter activity; and, (3) a permanent realignment of the electorate.[25] Though the Democrats failed to usurp the Republican hold on the county, a revitalized Democratic party helped to restore a two-party system to Indiana County.

Voter registration data for 1934 revealed a sudden shift of 10 percent of the voters to the Democratic party. These voters did not move over from minority parties, because that shift occurred between 1928 and 1932. The shift in 1934 came as disaffected Republicans abandoned the GOP for the Democrats. In addition, a large number of citizens registered for the first time and this registration benefitted the Democrats. By 1936 the Democratic voter registration accounted for 36.9 percent of the electorate and remained at that level for the next 20 years.[26]

Voter Registration in Indiana County, 1926-1940

Year	*Republican Percent*	*Democratic Percent*	*Third Party Percent*
1926	81.2	11.1	7.6
1926	83.1	12.3	4.6
1930	85.5	11.4	3.1
1932	85.3	12.3	2.4
1934	75.5	22.1	2.3
1936	61.8	36.9	2.7
1938	58.0	40.8	1.3
1940	62.0	36.8	1.2

A second indication that 1934 was the critical election can be derived from an examination of the voter turnout. More people regularly vote in presidential elections and, according to high turnouts in 1928 and 1932, one might surmise that these were critical elections. But the voter turnout declined in the 1930 gubernatorial election. In contrast, the 1934 gubernatorial election nearly equaled presidential levels and initiated a series of local, state, and national campaigns with high voter-participation.[27]

Voter Participation in Indiana County, 1926-1940

Year	*Percentage Voting*
1926	32.5
1928	65.2
1930	54.6
1932	63.9
1934	60.0
1936	84.6
1938	85.2
1940	80.2

In the 1934 election identifiable Democratic areas appeared in Indiana County. Certain townships and boroughs hereafter consistently polled heavy majorities for the Democratic ticket and indicated that a permanent realignment of voters had occurred. In all, eleven townships or boroughs became Democratic areas. Six were securely Democratic in every election from 1934 to 1940, but the mean vote of each ranged above 53.5 percent in this period.[28]

Democratic Districts Ranked by Mean Vote, 1934-1940

1. Center Township	68.9
2. Pine Township	63.1
3. Young Township	63.0
4. Jacksonville	62.5
5. Burrell Township	59.3
6. Conemaugh Township	56.2
7. East Wheatfield Township	55.4
8. Buffington Township	55.2
9. West Wheatfield Township	54.9
10. Clymer	53.7
11. Canoe Township	53.5

The mean percentage of the Democratic areas in 1934 was 58.9 percent, which was a considerable improvement over the 1932 mean of 49.2 percent. The 1934 mean compares favorable with the 58.7 percent mean of the Democratic districts in the 1934-40 period. This indicates a consistency of strength that began in 1934, not 1932. Moreover, the Democrats carried 18 areas in 1934 and only 10 in 1932.

A final indication that 1934 was the critical election was the strength of the party organization and identification in subsequent elections. Hereafter, the Democratic ticket consistently won in certain areas in county elections as well as state and local elections. In 1934, for example, the county commissioner election demonstrated that voters in county and local elections as well as in national elections possessed a strong sense of party identification. Voter turnout was an estimated 73.3 percent, which was extraordinarily high for a countywide election.[29] The Democratic poll was consistent with previous and subsequent elections and the Democrats carried their identifiable areas.

Democratic Percentage Vote in Democratic Districts, 1934-1940

District	*1934*	*1935*	*1936*	*1937*	*1938*	*1939*	*1940*
Center Twp.	71.7	67.5	73.6	61.5	67.9	68.5	72.0
Pine Twp.	62.1	56.7	66.2	58.6	65.4	65.8	67.1
Young Twp.	65.5	56.4	72.0	57.5	60.4	58.5	70.8
Jackonville	53.6	59.8	75.8	47.3	64.6	63.9	72.7
Burrell Twp.	54.8	56.4	65.7	59.9	60.5	58.7	59.7
Conemaugh Twp.	64.2	53.3	61.6	48.4	51.3	57.9	57.1
East Wheatfield	55.98	53.0	60.3	51.2	53.4	56.1	58.2
Buffington	45.3	61.3	53.1	53.6	52.8	60.1	59.9
West Wheatfield	55.9	54.4	55.2	53.4	50.5	60.8	54.3
Clymer	57.1	50.2	62.0	50.6	48.8	47.4	59.8
Canoe Twp.	61.9	50.3	58.1	52.3	47.8	50.3	54.4

Political observers in Indiana County recognized that 1934 was a significant year in the county's politics. After the campaign the *Indiana Evening Gazette,* a Republican daily newspaper, succinctly stated: "Democrats Planning Great Victory Parade— Coming Out of Obscure Position for First Time in 45 Years."[30]

The revival of the Democratic party was a major political phenomenon of the New Deal era. Its emergence marked the reestablishment of a viable two-party system in Pennsylvania. In some areas, such as Pittsburgh, the Democrats broke the Republican monopoly on local offices, but in Indiana County, as in Philadelphia, the Democrat party continued to operate as a minority party.[31] Nonetheless, a political realignment occurred in rural Indiana County as it had elsewhere. Explanations for this new political order have contended that the political restructuring during the New Deal was the result of urban, labor, and ethnic elements moving into the new Democratic constellation.[32] This interpretation is too mechanistic, perhaps, and fails to show the sequence and combination of events leading to the revival of the Democratic party in Indiana County.[33]

An obvious problem affecting local as well as national politics was the economic collapse of 1929–32. A survey of the economic data shows that the production of coal in Indiana County declined by 42 percent, which resulted in a 25-percent decline in mining employment. Mines which operated through the depressed years of the 1920s were closed by 1932. The unemployment in the mining industry undoubtedly affected retail sales, farming, and professional services. Unemployment data for 1932 showed that 5,959 Indiana countians were out of work, which amounted to 25.4 percent of the county's labor force. The hard-pressed and impoverished men and women soon channeled their frustrations into politics against the Republican administrations nationally and in Pennsylvania.[34]

To some degree the revival of the Democratic party in Indiana County came as a result of greater participation by ethnic groups in politics. As the following table shows, the Democratic areas, except for West Wheatfield, had sizable blocs of foreign-born in 1920 and 1930.

Democratic Areas and Estimated Percentage of Foreign Born[35]

	1920	*1930*
Center	18.8	9.6
Pine	16.8	11.0
Young	10.4	15.5
Jacksonville	unavailable	8.8
Burrell	14.8	9.2
Conemaugh	12.8	6.5
E. Wheatfield	14.7	7.7
Buffington	16.4	9.8
W. Wheatfield	5.2	1.6
Clymer	13.3	7.2
Canoe	11.9	6.7

Only one non-Democratic township, Rayne, had a sizable ethnic bloc, that being 14.4 percent in 1920 and 6.5 percent in 1930. This data suggest that the Democrats could depend on the support of the ethnic voters. It does not explain why they became more active in the 1930s. To understand that, one must also note that the Democratic areas were pockets of mining activity. This common demoninator made them seedbeds of unionizing activity in the 1930s. The revitalization of the UMWA and then its association with New Deal politicians best explains the reconstitution of the Democratic party in Indiana County.

During the 1920s the coal companies' tactics in obstructing negotiations and strike activity had greatly weakened the union. Membership in the UMWA declined as coal operators exercised the upper hand.[36] The battle between pro-union and anti-union elements affected the politics of the county as well as the daily lives of the miners. "The miner, who toils for his daily wage," lamented the *Patriot,* "must vote according to instruction or lose his job."[37] In the presidential campaign of 1932, for example, coal companies attempted to coerce miners to vote for Hoover:

> With instruction "to deliver" the vote for the Republican candidate, the boss has passed out the word that if Roosevelt is elected the plant or mine will shut down. . . . Another favorite method of high pressure campaigning is to gather a crew of foremen and inform these "key" men that some sizeable orders are on hand, but to be filled only on the condition that Hoover be elected.[38]

Spurred by encouragement from Roosevelt's election, UMWA President John L. Lewis in 1933 launched a new campaign for membership and sent Philip Murray into the western Pennsylvania coal fields. Murray toured the region soliciting miners to join the UMWA. He found an especially friendly reception in Indiana County. On May 14, 1933, an estimated 4,000 people braved inclement weather to attend a rally in Clymer, where Murray spoke, and after the meeting 700 new members joined the UMWA. Organizers followed with rallies and enlistments in other mining towns such as Ernest, Homer City, Iselin, and McIntyre.[39]

The following year, the reinvigorated UMWA in district 2 created a Labor Non-Partisan League. Headed by John Ghizzoni, UMWA organizer from Homer City, the Non-Partisan League became the political arm of the union in district 2.[40]

The union mobilized its membership in the gubernatorial campaign in 1934 behind the Democrat ticket because the candidate for lieutenant governor was Tom Kennedy of the UMWA. For the first time a working relationship between the Democratic party and the union was evident throughout Pennsylvania. That linkage was also apparent in Indiana County. That autumn the Non-Partisan League and the Democrats co-sponsored political rallies at union halls around the county. When state campaigners toured the county for the Democratic ticket, the Non-Partisan League sent delegates to the rallies.[41] At one political rally Bruce Sciotto, the Indiana County counsel for the UMWA, delivered a fiery tirade against the Republican gubernatorial candidate and the Republican administration in Indiana County. In urging miners who were Republicans to vote Democratic, Sciotto declared, "Party affiliations in the present campaign should and must be set aside." He continued by accusing the Republican gubernatorial candidate and the party of violating individual rights and human decency in their attacks on labor organizations. "Do they seek to cloud the memory of the union laborer who was clubbed, persecuted and otherwise abused by paid Coal Company Deputy Sheriffs," he asked, " . . . (or) the incarceration of mothers of children at unreasonable hours of the night because of their sympathy for union labor?" Sciotto claimed that the Republican administration in Indiana County was responsible for imposing injunctions to thwart union meetings and wage negotiations. Sciotto also directed his appeal to merchants who he said had been denied by coal companies the right to sell their wares in company towns.[42] Appeals such as Sciotto's and meticulous political organizing reaped rich harvests among the miners for the Democratic party in Indiana County. John Ghizzoni announced that in Indiana County 9,000 miners and 27 union organizations sanctioned the Democratic ticket.[43]

Republicans were alert to the alliance between the UMWA and the Democratic party in Indiana County. For the first time Republicans became more solicitous of the labor vote. "Whatever the advantages of joining a labor union may be," exclaimed the county's self-acclaimed most stalwart

Republican newspaper, "the Democratic party has been using its labor union policy as a smoke screen while it has been mischievously tunnelling under the industries by which our people live."[44] Other Republican newspapers cited arguments from the National Coal Association that New Deal hydroelectric power projects would cripple the coal industry.[45] The county GOP organization met the Democratic challenge with increased party rallies and meetings. One such meeting exemplified the increased Republican awareness of ethnicity as they advertised a GOP rally with a Polish speaker who would speak in the Polish language.[46]

The intense political activity by the UMWA aroused Democratic hopes in Indiana County. But reality does not always match expectations, as the Democrats learned in 1934. The state elected a Democratic governor, which brought considerable satisfaction, but Indiana County remained a Republican bastion. Nonetheless, the Republican margin of victory was a slim 1,219 votes, a marked contrast to its 4,121-vote margin in 1932. The Democrats polled 46.1 percent of the vote, which represented their highest poll in Indiana County in the twentieth century. To the Democrats, then, who had been accustomed to losing every campaign, the narrow defeat in 1934 was a moral victory. They had reduced the Republican margin in the county and certainly had assisted in the election of a Democratic governor. Therefore the Democratic organization felt a "victory parade" was in order for Indiana County. The Democrats paraded through downtown Indiana borough and ended with a rally at the county courthouse, where their newly elected congressman and UMWA officials addressed the party's rank and file. Perhaps one county wheelhorse captured the spirit of the rally most precisely when he exclaimed optimistically that "Indiana County has come into civilization 'after 40 years in the wilderness.'"[47]

That the UMWA activity on behalf of the Democratic ticket was a considerable asset for the party is undeniable. Though miners and ethnic groups may have voted Democratic before, the union served as the mobilizing agent for the party. It injected the county's labor problems into politics and identified the Democratic party as the pro-labor party. Additionally, the union staged rallies, circulated electioneering pamphlets, and "got out the vote" on election day. In 1934, the voter turnout for the gubernatorial election was 60 percent, which equaled previous presidential election turnouts.

Union involvement in the county's politics continued into the 1935 countywide campaign. The county UMWA organization endorsed candidates in the primaries and worked for the Democratic ticket in the general election. Using the sympathetic press as a vehicle, the labor Democrats urged miners to support the Democratic ticket. "Somehow it just seems natural," exclaimed Biamonte's *Patriot*, "for the man who makes his living with his hands to vote Democratic this year in Indiana County."[48]

An extraordinarily high turnout of 81.7 percent in 1935 indicated a high voter interest and active organizing by the parties. The Republican ticket won again, but the margin of victory in many races was slim. In the election of three county commissioners, for example, the leading Republican candidate exceeded the leading Democratic candidate's poll by only 700 votes.[49]

The 1936 campaign in Indiana County as in the nation was an acutely intense presidential race. Again county Democrats and labor leaders collaborated to swing the county to Roosevelt, staging a series of joint party-labor rallies at the county fairgrounds. One rally took on an especially festive note as John L. Lewis, president of the UMWA, visited Indiana County to speak on behalf of labor and the Roosevelt administration. Recognizing the closeness of the campaign in Indiana County, John Ghizzoni solicited Lewis's assistance in urging miners to vote for Roosevelt. The rally opened with a parade through Indiana borough and climaxed with Lewis's address. The press estimated that 20,000 people attended the rally.[50]

The Republican county leaders astutely met the Democratic challenge. On the one hand, they accused the Democrats of unceremoniously injecting politics into a Labor Day picnic; on the other hand, they imported Republican leaders to appeal to laborers. At one such rally also held at the county fairgrounds, Senator James J. Davis of Pennsylvania sought to assure the county's coal miners that he had a plan to stabilize the coal industry and that the Republican presidential candidate Alf Landon would support the Davis plan. The Republicans also invaded labor-Democrat strongholds such as Young, Buffington, and the Wheatfield townships to solicit votes.[51]

The active campaigning by all organizations resulted in a record turnout of 84.6 percent of the voters. Despite all their preparations, activity, and expectations, the labor-Democratic coalition failed to break the Republican grip on Indiana County. Republicanism was too deeply imbedded in the minds and hearts and habits of Indiana Countians. Still, a considerable political transformation had occurred in the county in ten years. The New Deal political revolution had extended to rural Pennsylvania and Indiana County. The county enjoyed a healthier political system with two competitive parties.

NOTES

1. *The Patriot* (Indiana, Pennsylvania), 16 January 1926. Hereinafter cited as *The Patriot*.

2. William E. Leuchtenburg, *Franklin D. Roosevelt and the New Deal* (New York, 1963), pp. 326-48; on critical elections, see V. O. Key, Jr., "A Theory of Critical Elections," *Journal of Politics* 17 (February 1955): 3-18; Samuel Lubell, *The Future of American Politics* (New York, 1956); Walter Dean Burnham, *Critical Elections and the Mainsprings of American Politics* (New York, 1970); David J. Alvarez and Edmond J. True, "Critical Elections and Partisan Realignment: An Urban Test Case," *Polity* 5 (Summer 1973): 563-76; John L. Shover, "Emergence of a Two-Party System in Republican Philadelphia," *Journal of American History* 60, no. 1 (March 1974), pp. 985-1002; Allan J. Lichtman, "Critical Election Theory and the Reality of American Presidential Politics, 1916-1940," *American Historical Review* 81, no. 2 (April 1976), pp. 317-51.

3. John J. Schanz, Jr., *Historical Statistics of Pennsylvania's Mineral Industries, 1759-1955*, Bulletin of Mineral Industries Experiment Station, 69 (1957), pp. 17-21.

4. Edgar Eugene Robinson, *The Presidential Vote, 1896-1932* (Palo Alto, Calif., 1934); Richard M. Scammon, ed., *America at the Polls: A Handbook of American Presidential Election Statistics, 1920-1964* (Pittsburgh, 1965); Harold F. Alderfer and Robert M. Sigmond, *Presidential Election by Pennsylvania Counties, 1902-1940* (State College, Pa., 1941); *Pensylvania State Manual, 1900-1930*, (Harrisburg).

5. Harold Alderfer and Fanette H. Luhrs, *Registration in Pennsylvania Elections, 1926-1946* (State College, Pa., 1948), p. 57.

6. David Burner, *The Politics of Provincialism: The Democratic Party in Transition, 1918-1932* (New York, 1968), pp. 1-26.

7. *The Indiana Democrat*, 27 September 1922.

8. *The Patriot*, 11 November 1922, claimed that a majority of Italians supported

the Democratic party. Unfortunately, a statistical analysis cannot verify this claim because the county was so deeply Republican that in areas where the foreign-born resided the borough and voting area still voted Republican.

9. *The Patriot*, 1 November 1924, printed names of union leaders, later identified with the Democratic party, endorsing the LaFollette ticket. In addition, some townships with a sizable foreign-born population revealed declines in Democratic percentages but large percentages for LaFollette, e.g.:

	Estimated Percent of Foreign-Born	Democrat *1922*	Percentage *1927*	LaFollette Percentage *1924*
Center	18.8	41.6	7.9	34.4
Conemaugh	12.8	60.9	25.2	13.5
Young	10.4	37.3	6.3	43.2

Estimated percentage of ethnic males is based on statistics of employed foreign-born garnered from 1920 census schedules, Bureau of Census, Pittsburg, Kansas.

10. Official Manuscript Election Returns, 1924, Indiana County Courthouse, Indiana, Pennsylvania.

11. Alderfer and Luhrs, *Registration in Pennsylvania Elections*, p. 55; *The Patriot*, 19 September 1925; *The Indiana Democrat*, 12 November 1930.

12. James H. Timberlake, *Prohibition and the Progressive Movement, 1900-1920* (Cambridge, 1963), pp. 29-32.

13. *The Patriot*, 22 December 1923; 25 July, 29 August, 12 September 1925, 4 February 1928; *The Indiana Progress*, 20 August, 30 September 1925; *The Indiana Democrat*, 2 September 1925.

14. Emerson H. Loucks, *The Ku Klux Klan in Pennsylvania* (Harrisburg, 1936); *The Indiana Progress*, 2 September 1925.

15. *The Patriot*, n.d. December 1923; 25 July 1925; The Indiana Democrat, 2 September 1925.

16. James P. Johnson, "Reorganizing the United Mine Workers of America in Pennsylvania During the New Deal," *Pennsylvania History*, 37, no. 2 (April 1970), pp. 117-32; Hyman Kuritz, "The Labor Injunction in Pennsylvania, 1891-1931," *Pennsylvania History* 29, no. 3 (July 1962), pp. 320-321.

17. John Ghizzoni, Indiana, Pa., to John L. Lewis, Washington, D.C., 12 June 1933, John T. Brophy Papers, The Catholic University of American, Washington, D.C.; also see *The Patriot*, 25 July, 29 August 1925.

18. *The Patriot*, 17 November 1928.

19. William A. Cornell, "The Political Career of John S. Fisher", (M.A. thesis, University of Pittsburgh, 1949); Harold F. Alderfer and Fannette H. Luhrs, *Gubernatorial Elections in Pennsylvania, 1922-1942* (State College, Pa., 1946), pp. 12-13, 23.

20. For Pennsylvania, see Shover, "Emergence of a Two-Party System in Republican Philadelphia," and Burnham, *Critical Elections*, pp.56-70.

21. Unless otherwise noted, the participation rates were computed from data in the *Pennsylvania State Manual*.

22. Official Manuscript, Election Returns, 1924-1930, Indiana County Courthouse.

23. *Pennsylvania State Manual*, 1933.

24. Official Manuscript, Election Returns, 1933, Indiana County Courthouse.

25. This follows the definition of a critical election established by V. O. Key, Jr., "A Theory of Critical Elections," pp. 3-18.

26. *Pennsylvania State Manual*, 1926-1940.

27. Ibid.

28. For suggestive methodology, see William H. Flanigan and Nancy H. Zingale, "The Measurement of Electoral Change," *Political Methodology* (Summer 1974): 49-82.

29. No registration data exist for 1935; therefore, the 1935 publication rate was computed by using the 1934 registration data.

30. 9 November 1934.

31. Shover, "The Emergence of a Two-Party System in Republican Philadelphia," p. 985.

32. Harold F. Gosnell and William G. Coleman, "Political Trends in Industrial America: Pennsylvania An Example." *Public Opinion Quarterly*, September 1940, pp. 473-86.

33. One historian has written: "To get at the 'why' of voter behavior we must probe more deeply and in greater detail than the discernment of party systems and the typologizing of elections according to voter alignment in aggregate terms." See Bernard Sternsher, "The Emergence of the New Deal Party System: A Problem in Historical Analysis of Voter Behavior," *Journal of Interdisciplinary History* 6 (Summer 1975): 147.

34. Schanz, *Historical Statistics of Pennsylvania's Mineral Industries*, pp. 17-21; Pennsylvania Department of Mines and Mineral Resources, *History of Bituminous Coal* (1964), p. 34; Pennsylvania Department of Mines and Mineral Industries, *Annual Reports*, 1927-28, p. 580; *Annual Report*, 1932, pp. 89-90, 112-13, 119-21; Pennsylvania Department of Labor, *Monthly Bulletin* 19, August 1932, p. 1.

35. The ethnic composition of these districts is suggestive, not definitive. It is an estimate based on the number of employed laborers at township and borough level compiled from the original census schedules for 1920 and 1930. The Census Bureau, Pittsburg, Kansas, compiled the data on special request.

36. Johnson, "Reorganizing the United Mine Workers," pp. 117-20.

37. 12 November 1925.

38. *The Patriot*, 5 November 1932.

39. Johnson, "Reorganizing the United Mine Workers," p. 121.

40. Interview with John Ghizzoni, Indiana, Pennsylvania, May 1977.

41. *The Indiana Democrat*, 17 October 1934; *The Patriot*, 20 October 1934; Edwin B. Bronner, "The New Deal Comes to Pennsylvania: The Gubernatorial Election of 1934," *Pennsylvania History* 27, no. 1 (January 1960), pp. 44-68, surveys the election on a statewide basis. A close analysis of Indiana County would modify his suggestion

that the labor vote played only a minor role in 1934.

42. *The Patriot*, 20 October 1934.

43. Ibid., 3 November 1934; Ghizzoni insists that many miners continued to vote Republican. Interview, 9 May 1977.

44. *The Indiana Weekly Messenger*, 30 August 1934.

45. *The Indiana Progress*, 10 October 1934; *The Indiana Weekly Messenger*, 1 November 1934.

46. *The Indiana Evening Gazette*, 27 October, 5 November 1934.

47. *The Indiana Democrat*, 11 and 12 November 1934.

48. *The Indiana Evening Gazette*, 16 September 1935; *The Patriot*, 2 November 1935.

49. Official Manuscript, Election Returns, 1935, Indiana County Courthouse.

50. Interview with Ghizzoni, 12 May 1977; *The Indiana Democrat*, 28 October 1936; *The Indiana Evening Gazette*, 24 October 1936.

51. *The Indiana Progress*, 9 and 23 September, 21 October 1936.

A stranded mining town in Pennsylvania, circa 1933. *Courtesy of the National Archives.*

Housing conditions in Depression Allentown. *Courtesy of the National Archives.*

An unemployed miner in Shenandoah, Pennsylvania, scrounging for coal. *Courtesy of the National Archives.*

A WPA citizenship class in Southwestern Pennsylvania. *Courtesy of the National Archives.*

A WPA sewer project in Connellsville, Pennsylvania. *Courtesy of the National Archives.*

The Richard Allen Homes: a housing project for black Philadelphians. *Courtesy of the Philadelphia Housing Authority.*

Senator Joseph F. Guffey and John L. Lewis during the debate of the Guffey-Snyder Act. *Courtesy of the Washington and Jefferson College Library.*

David L. Lawrence, Joseph F. Guffey, J. David Stern, and George H. Earle emerging from a political meeting at the White House. *Courtesy of the Washington and Jefferson College Library.*

[6] The New Deal and Pennsylvania Coal Miners

While the New Deal and the United Mine Workers of America (UMWA) failed to produce Democratic majorities in Indiana County, both effected great changes in the lives of coal miners throughout Pennsylvania. Acting often in concert —certainly not always—leaders of both the rejuvenated union and the resurgent Democratic party won union contracts for the UMWA while eliminating most of the competition for the miners' loyalty from competing unions and brotherhoods. Further, union and party leaders helped to destroy the old feudalism of the notorious coal patches and developed the militancy necessary to win union recognition in times that perhaps were not always right economically, but surely right politically. Finally, union and party leaders pushed federal legislation which proved beneficial to both operator and miner alike, and brought a new stability to the coal fields of the state.

The Great Depression spared neither operator nor miner in Pennsylvania. From 1929 to 1932, the output of bituminous coal dropped 42 percent, the average price per ton fell from \$1.78 to \$1.31, average hourly earnings plunged from 68 cents to 50 cents, average weekly hours fell from 38.4 to 27.2, and the yearly average of working days declined from 219 to 146. In 1932, 32 percent of the region's miners were paid less than \$2.50 per day, and only 16 percent of 1,900 mining operations reported net incomes after taxes. A year later, prices, wages, output, and profits had dropped to levels not touched since the turn of the century.[1]

The economic poverty in the coal fields reached a state perhaps unprecedented in American history. Labor leaders almost to a man testified that they had never seen conditions so bad. Governor Gifford Pinchot of Pennsylvania was so sickened by the "pitiable conditions" in the state's southwestern counties that he and his wife financed six milk stations for children. In 1933 Pinchot told President-elect Franklin D. Roosevelt that some miners were working over forty hours a week, yet they could not feed their families. Old miners by the score have recalled the suffering of their children. Their young virtually "took turns" at eating every other day, especially during the winter months. Meat, milk, and fruit were rarities; malnutrition, common. The incidence of tuberculosis rose significantly, and the "flux" (bleeding dysentery of the stomach and intestines) ravaged children. The day-to-day diet of many miners consisted of beans, or of "bulldog gravy" (flour, water, and a bit of grease), or of stale bread soaked in lard and water, called a "water sandwich" or a "miner's sandwich." The real toll will never be known; perhaps it has been revealed best by the miners' devotion to the union after it returned with the New Deal.[2]

The collapse of the coal industry also witnessed the disintegration of the United Mine Workers of America. After a series of defeats from 1925 to 1928, union president John L. Lewis advised local leaders to negotiate contracts as best they could. The resulting chaos led thousands of miners to believe that Lewis had deserted them, and many grabbed at whatever possibilities existed to organize anew. Such conditions attracted rival groups intent upon winning the allegiance of the hapless diggers. One group was the Communist-led National Miners' Union, which operated from 1929 to 1935 in southwestern Pennsylvania.

As the UMWA disintegrated in the Central Competitive Field (Ohio, Indiana, Illinois, and western Pennsylvania), Communists organized the Pennsylvania-Ohio Relief Committee to care for the down and out. At the same time, Moscow directed the Communist International to form competing unions designed to crush the affiliates of the American Federation of Labor (AFL), including the UMWA. In September 1928, leftist dissidents among the miners met in Pittsburgh to form the National Miners' Union (NMU).

Working with the Trade Union Unity League, the same Communist group which organized the Unemployed Councils in such locales as Philadelphia and Allentown, the NMU attempted to exploit, in the words of one leader, "the growing radicalization of the American working class." In southwestern Pennsylvania, the TUUL-NMU strove to array class against class, to conduct massive violations of labor injunctions, to appeal especially to Negroes, and to replace capitalism eventually.[3]

In the years before the New Deal, when the UMWA was in decline, the NMU was able to organize a handful of locals in southwestern Pennsylvania. Screaming "Mussolini" at operators, police, and UMWA officials, NMU leaders kept the few areas under their influence in constant turmoil with their revolutionary rhetoric. They set up "National Miners' Relief Stations," advertised for the Young Communist League, distributed the *Daily Worker,* and sent truckloads of singing children to Pittsburgh to beg for relief. In a few instances there were armed clashes between the UMWA and the NMU, and the latter group once dragged UMWA District 5 president Patrick Fagan from a platform and beat him.[4]

In June 1931, the NMU called a strike to substantiate its demands for union recognition, higher wages, and a checkweighman. As a result, within a seventy-five-mile area from Washington County to New Kensington, a number of violent skirmishes took place. Two miners were killed in a riot near Pittsburgh on June 8, and at Ellsworth hundreds of strikers erected highway barricades and battled the Coal and Iron Police. On June 13, the Pittsburgh Terminal Coal Company, which had rejected collective bargaining in 1927, suddenly announced a new wage agreement with the UMWA.

Furious NMU leaders watched helplessly as Governor Pinchot negotiated with the UMWA in the executive mansion. On June 16, the NMU marched through Harrisburg denouncing both Pinchot and the agreement. That same day, in response to the threats of the NMU, an injunction was issued that forbade the union from picketing the Consolidation Coal Company at Wildwood. Defiantly, 7,000 miners and their families protested before the Washington County Courthouse. On June 22, an armed clash between miners and police occurred at Wildwood. One miner was killed, a dozen were injured, forty-two miners were arrested, and the federal government instituted deportation proceedings against a score of aliens.[5]

Still the NMU fought on. A storekeeper was killed, and four miners were injured in a melee at Arnold City on June 23. Six days later, deputies armed with tear gas and clubs routed three truckloads of NMU pickets at Ellsworth. In July, NMU organizers attacked a UMWA meeting at Canonsburg and 100 people were injured. By the end of the bloody summer, over 2,000 miners and their supporters had been wounded, injured, or gassed by deputies, police, and the UMWA. The NMU had won nothing but bruises; indeed, even the Comintern denounced the union for its conduct of the strike.[6]

However, the NMU continued to meet and picket through the early days of the New Deal. The union was active in Bentleyville, Vestaburg, Marianna, and other areas in Washington County. Company spies reported NMU doings to their superiors, and the police continued to harass NMU pickets. Eventually the NMU withered away and most of its rank and file joined the UMWA.[7]

Out of the fiery rubble of the NMU arose a rejuvenated United Mine Workers of America, led by the irrepressible John L. Lewis. If, as one historian has written, organized labor "underwent a revolution" in the 1930s — tripling its membership, changing its attitudes toward government, and strengthening its position versus management — no union and no union leader commanded these changes more ably than did the UMWA and Lewis. Everywhere in the coal fields Lewis capitalized on the popularity of the Roosevelt administration and its apparently friendly attitude toward labor. He took full advantage of the economic plight of the coal operators, of the desire of the coal miners to organize, and of the new political arrangements that the Great Depression had wrought. In southwestern Pennsylvania, where the mood was electric and the hopes widespread, Lewis and the miners succeeded in unionizing the commercial mines. However, even though they won new contracts and better working conditions in the captive mines (those owned by the steel companies), they would not win union recognition there until 1941.[8]

Aware of the intense suffering of Pennsylvania coal miners, as well as that of millions of workers over the nation, the Roosevelt administration's rhetoric, promises, and action released among workingmen a new hope and a new militancy. The New Deal offered relief to the needy, and through its federal projects and agencies, promised jobs for the able-bodied. During the famous First Hundred Days (the Congressional session of 1933), Roosevelt pushed through Congress a variety of recovery and reform measures, one of which, the National Industrial Recovery Act (NIRA), carried major implications for the labor movement and for American workers. Under Section 7a of the NIRA, the federal government guaranteed the right of workers to organize into unions of their own choosing and to bargain collectively with their employers. Thus, the New Deal and the federal legislation it sponsored not only brought a new stability to the coal industry while providing for the revival of the UMWA, but also destroyed the old feudalism which had prevailed in Pennsylvania coal fields.[9]

Even before the passage of the NIRA, Lewis had decided to revive his strife-ridden, demoralized forces. Committing the union's entire treasury to the cause, Lewis sent over 100 organizers and field workers into the coal fields. "The President wants you to join the union," they claimed, not bothering to specify which president they meant. The Pennsylvania fields were alive with optimism and action as the miners became convinced that the New Deal offered them their best hope in over a decade. There was "really no need to campaign," one mine leader later recalled. "An organizer had only to see that he had a good supply of application blanks and a place to file them, and the rank and file did the rest." Thousands of miners joined up in every coal area of the country; by the end of June, Pennsylvania UMWA leader Philip Murray claimed that 128,000 miners in southwestern Pennsylvania alone had joined the union.[10]

The time set for the drive was April 1. On that date union leaders spoke at Blythedale to almost 2,000 miners eager to join the union. Defying repeated injunctions, thousands of miners listened to Murray and other organizers speak in dozens of coal towns during the following weeks. In retaliation, some companies pressured local officials to cancel meeting permits and to harass miners attending union meetings. Companies continued to secure injunctions against union activities, to send company spies to union meetings, to compile lists of those miners who had participated in strikes and had attended organizational conferences, and to remove strikers and organizers from company property.[11]

However, the companies failed to stay the determination of the men to organize. In June, two days after Congress had passed the NIRA, over 50,000 miners joined Murray to celebrate the union's new militancy at the first union meeting in years in Uniontown. Even miners in such traditional nonunion areas as Connellsville in Fayette County and Greensburg in Westmoreland County hastened to sign union cards. The years of frustration had finally produced a unity that drove the miners — trapped in their isolated company towns — to seek outside help in the form of the UMWA and the New Deal.[12]

At the same time, the long years of economic depression had convinced many of the commercial coal companies that a revitalized union, coupled with a new federal paternalism, might equalize wage rates in the North and South and bring a new stability to the industry. Consequently, when negotiations to draw up a coal code began in Washington, some company officials, desiring to gain as great an advantage as possible, no longer looked upon the UMWA as the adversary that they had virtually destroyed during the previous decade.

As the coal operators, UMWA leaders, and the National Recovery Administration gathered to draw up a code agreement, the captive mine owners, on the other hand, prepared to resist the recognition of the union. In fact, H. C. Frick, the coal supplier for U. S. Steel and the coal subsidiaries of Crucible Steel and Weirton Steel, sponsored plans for company unions. Although the Frick company inspired some loyalty in its men by paying higher wages than the prevailing wage and by offering pensions, fair rent, and relief programs for its unemployed, UMWA organizers were particularly anxious to crack this bastion of the nonunion captives.

Frick and the UMWA clashed on July 23 at the Frick mines at Maxwell, where sheriffs tossed tear-gas bombs at UMWA pickets, and again two days later at Grindstone, where pickets roughed up company deputies and erected barricades on the roads leading into the three Colonial mines. After these incidents, the strikes at the captive mines spread so rapidly that many miners were left underground when strikers walked out above. After a week, almost 15,000 miners were out, immobilizing four Frick and two Jones and Laughlin mines. In all, at least twenty mines in Fayette County were closed by the strike, which soon spread into adjoining counties to shut down another dozen mines.[13]

In the midst of the spreading mine war, Governor Pinchot and Sheriff Harry Hackney of Fayette County bickered over how to control the difficult situation. The governor proposed that Hackney, whose job depended upon how well he served the operators, turn his police authority over to the state. Hackney refused. Instead, he issued a proclamation forbidding picketing and ordered 100 more deputies to disperse all groups of more than three persons on public highways and public property. In retaliation, Pinchot ordered the state police and the National Guard into the area. Besides collecting over 1,200 assorted weapons from pickets who blocked entrance into the mines, the troops established martial law and posted machine guns at several locations in the county.[14]

Pinchot, who insisted publicly that the troops were to protect the miners' right to organize, assemble, and picket peacefully, as well as to protect mining property, attempted to mediate the dispute. Although UMWA officials agreed to accept the governor's offer, Thomas Moses, president of Frick, refused to meet with the union leaders.

As negotiations broke down, the strike spread. Miners at the Republic, Crucible, and Pittsburgh Steel mines in Greene County joined the walkout. Pickets armed with American flags, union banners, and placards piled out of cars and trucks and formed their lines, urging nonunion miners to join the strike. Armed with sticks and stones, they roamed the highways and stopped cars at barricades built of rail ties. At Frick's Colonial No. 3 mine, near Grindstone in Fayette County, deputies fired a volley of shots from a speeding car. Louis Podorsky, a thirty-eight-year-old veteran of World War I who was picketing, was hit. He died later that same day in the Brownsville Hospital.[15]

More violence occurred at Frick's Star Junction mine, where six strikers were shot by deputies. These skirmishes forced Pinchot to threaten to send in more troops. Finally, UMWA leaders agreed to give advance notice when they planned to picket or parade. But because of the new militancy of the miners they could not guarantee that all their local organizers would be able to carry out the agreement.

Because the strike threatened to undermine the New Deal's recovery plans, John L. Lewis, Governor Pinchot, and Pennsylvania Democratic party leader Joseph Guffey appealed to Washington for help. Roosevelt responded by asking NRA administrator Hugh Johnson to investigate the dispute and to speed up the negotiations between operators and mine leaders for the coal code, which would cover the entire coal industry.[16]

On August 4, the federal government negotiated a temporary truce. By its terms, subscribed to by the commercial mines, by the captives, and by Lewis and Johnson, the commercial mines would not discriminate against miners because of their union affiliation or their participation in the strikes. Also, the truce guaranteed a checkweighman. Most importantly, the President appointed a board to settle all disputes until the coal code was written.

Significantly, when H. C. Frick president Thomas Moses tendered his agreement to Johnson, he omitted any mention of the UMWA. Johnson accepted this omission as necessary in getting Moses to sign. Lewis signed the agreement and agreed to call off the strike, if the conditions were carried out. Johnson then journeyed to Hyde Park to get the approval of President Roosevelt, who declared, "Never in our country has a strike of such threatened proportions been settled so quickly and so generously."[17]

But it was far from over. Suspicious of the truce and remembering that in 1922 Lewis had sent them back into the pits before they had achieved their goal, Fayette County miners refused their leader's order. Only after President Roosevelt had sent his personal representative to talk with them in Uniontown did they agree to return to work.

The hearings on the coal code began again on August 9. When further delays and postponements were announced a few days later, Pinchot warned of trouble if the proceedings did not move along. Roosevelt then moved up the code hearings and urged prompt action, insisting that he would write a suitable code if the operators could not draft one. Even in the face of a threatened strike by 60,000 miners in southwestern Pennsylvania, the hearings stalled again in early September.[18]

Meanwhile, at an open-air rally in Uniontown, Pinchot urged over 15,000 rain-soaked miners to be patient and to trust the president. The next day he penned a "Dear Franklin" note to Roosevelt, describing the precarious situation in Pennsylvania: "The feeling is still intense," he wrote, and "if the code fails to give recognition" to the miners "they will go out in a body." If that happens, he went on, "their leaders will be entirely powerless to get them back." In such circumstances, Pinchot insisted he would not be able to get the men to return, and "it will be extremely doubtful whether even you could get them to return to work without recognition."[19]

Still the negotiations went slowly, and miners began to walk out again. On September 14, over a dozen miners and one deputy were shot in fighting near the Frick mines at Footedale, Edenborn, and Gates. Within three days, over 30,000 pickets surrounded almost every captive mine in western Pennsylvania.[20]

In dreary conference rooms in the Commerce Building and in the Shoreham Hotel in Washington, meanwhile, commercial coal operators and union officials began to draw up a bituminous-coal code as provided for in the NIRA. When the negotiations dragged, miners conducted short-lived strikes — often against the wishes of UMWA leaders. Lewis, who wanted a coal code and a new contract more than he wanted a strike, pleaded with his leaders in the commercial fields to urge the miners to be patient. With President Roosevelt pushing them, the negotiators met in virtually continuous session seven days a week. Finally, on September 18, Roosevelt signed the commercial coal code, which was to become effective as of October 2. "As Lincoln freed the Negro of the South," a group of Cambria county miners enthusiastically wired the president, "you have delivered the miners out of the wilderness."[21]

The code provided for important changes in the coal fields. It abolished child labor, outlawed scrip wages, and eliminated the enforced patronage of the company stores. Through the code, the coal industry granted the forty-hour week and, by agreeing to minimum wages, was able to set minimum prices for its coal with the cooperation of the federal government.

Perhaps even more important than the code was the Appalachian Agreement, which was signed on September 21. This agreement not only included the features of the coal code, but also established a new geographical arrangement for collective bargaining in the bituminous industry. By shifting coverage from the Central Competitive Field to a new North-South Field, the agreement meant that for the first time in its history the UMWA could bargain at the same time with both Northern and Southern operators. Affecting 340,000 miners (the largest group ever included under one wage contract), the agreement provided for the election of checkweighmen, pit committees, the checkoff for union dues, and the machinery for settling coal disputes.[22]

Tired but happy union leaders, "dazed with joy," praised the agreement as "a fitting culmination to their union drive." The *United Mine Workers' Journal* labeled the code and the Appalachian Agreement as "the greatest victory ever won by organized labor." One reporter wrote that the operators now agreed "to all the things that deputy sheriffs (used to) shoot people for demanding." One union leader later wrote that "unashamed tears" filled the eyes of UMWA leaders as the "United Mine Workers of America lived again!"[23]

However, the steel companies which owned Pennsylvania's captive mines did not sign the code and refused to deal with the union. In September, steel executives proposed a captive-mines code that offered their miners the wages, hours, and general working conditions of the commercial-mines agreement. But their proposal did not include the checkoff of dues or union recognition. When President Roosevelt insisted that "working conditions" included the checkoff, the captives resisted and refused to negotiate with UMWA leaders. H. C. Frick officials then put into operation the wages, hours and other conditions of the Appalachian Agreement, excepting, of course, the checkoff and union recognition.

The steel industry and the nation's most powerful union were now locked in a conflict which gravely threatened the president's recovery program. By early October, 75,000 miners—commercial and captive—were again absent from the pits, and Governor Pinchot complained that three-fourths of the state's coal production had stopped. Moreover, looting and violence were rampant throughout many Pennsylvania coal fields as the impasse continued. Within days, local leaders—in defiance of UMWA officials—had led over 100,000 miners out on strike.[24]

Typical of the local leaders who encouraged the men to stay out was Martin Ryan, a forty-four-year-old Irish immigrant from Fayette County. Ryan, who had resisted an earlier UMWA call to return to work before the commercial agreement was signed, now rallied recalcitrant captive miners at Frick's Colonial No. 3 mine to his side. Called a "communist" or a "Red" by mine officials and union leaders, Ryan led a march on U. S. Steel's Clairton works to ask steel workers to join the miners' cause. However, he abandoned this tactic when Governor Pinchot asked the miners to confine their picketing to their own areas. Still, the captive miners roamed the coal fields, even after UMWA leaders Philip Murray and William Feeney urged them again and again to return to work.[25]

Besides insurgents such as Ryan, the UMWA was confronted with company unions, especially in the Frick mines. At Frick, the Workmen's Brotherhood—in some areas supported by the Ku Klux Klan—and the Miners' Independent Brotherhood supported the company's labor policy. The brotherhoods presented lists of "good men" to Frick officials. These miners were not only hired first, but also were given the best places to work. On the other hand, miners loyal to the UMWA had to work in the worst areas, often dubbed the "UMW (A) section" or the "Feeney Section"—the latter in honor of the union's district president. Nevertheless, the insurgent miners continued to hold out through October. "We are not going back to work until (Frick) recognizes the union," insisted miners at Footedale. At Pricedale, miners passed a resolution to remain on strike until the entire district was organized.[26]

Throughout Fayette and Greene counties, union leaders were unable to control the captive miners. At Rowe's Run, pickets and deputies waged a gun battle between company houses. Near Isabella, pickets almost destroyed a coal train coming from West Virginia. When a UMWA district president tried to address a meeting at Searight's, Martin Ryan's insurgents shouted him into silence. Governor Pinchot's entreaties of late October failed to halt the walkout, and even rumors that the New Deal might hold back relief from striking miners did not produce peace.

Finally, however, President Roosevelt brought the strike to

an end. By the time Martin Ryan and a few of his followers met with the President in early November, Roosevelt had worked out an agreement. After having consulted with the fourteen largest captive operators on October 30, the president ordered the National Labor Board (NLB) to hold an election in November to determine bargaining representation. The agreement provided that the striking miners not be discriminated against; that the checkoff be collected; and that wages, hours, and working conditions be those of the Appalachian Agreement. The UMWA apparently won because the agreement was signed with their leaders; this also constituted a victory over their own insurgents, if not one as yet over the steel companies and the brotherhoods.[27]

The miners went back to work on November 6. Later that month, elections were held at the U. S. Steel mines of Frick and at captive mines owned by Inland, Wheeling, Crucible, Republic, Weirton, Allegheny, and the Jones and Laughlin steel companies. UMWA representatives won in twenty cases, lost in nine, and one contest ended in a tie. In the victorious twenty, the men voted to be represented by UMWA officials—Lewis, Murray, and Thomas Kennedy—but not by the union itself.

Since none of the steel companies entered into contracts with the bargaining representatives in the ten-day period as required in Roosevelt's agreement, outstanding issues such as the cheokoff and the question of the legal parties to the agreements were referred to the National Labor Board. Faced with the studied unwillingness of the steel companies to recognize the union, the NLB capitulated, and the union failed to win recognition in the captive mines.[28] In January 1934, the NLB ruled that, while the steel companies had to sign agreements with the individuals elected as the miners' representatives, they did not have to sign with the UMWA itself. The board refused to consider whether this arrangement constituted "legal recognition." However, the NLB did rule that the companies had to honor the checkoff, which was to be paid to the miners' elected representatives.

All parties accepted the decision of the NLB. Lewis, Murray, and Kennedy executed agreements in the captives where they had won election. The agreements did not mention the UMWA by name. Company unions and brotherhoods prevailed in the mines the UMWA did not win.[29]

H. C. Frick officials were still unhappy with the modest gain of the captive miners. At Colonial No. 4, Frick-controlled miners voted to abolish the checkweighman. UMWA miners who boycotted this election were replaced by loyalists of the Workmen's Brotherhood. Convicted of assaulting a company official, Martin Ryan was fined and then lost both his job as checkweighman and his position as local union president. Frick still fired miners for loading "dirty coal," still evicted union members, and still maintained its cadre of deputies who continued to bomb and gas those militants who refused to give up the cause of union recognition.[30]

Despite the union gains and the new contracts in the captive mines, many unemployed miners remained poor and isolated. In 1933 and 1934, New Deal social workers visited Pennsylvania to investigate living conditions. At Vestaburg, a Jones and Laughlin patch in Washington County, Henry Francis found children who were unable to attend school because they lacked shoes. Others had only one change of hand-me-down school clothes, and many had no underwear for the fall and winter. At Bobtown, a Jones and Laughlin patch in Greene County, the entire population of 400 families was idle. Although about fifty of the patch's young men were with the Civilian Conservation Corps—an early New Deal project—the rest of the patch worked their gardens and awaited the reopening of the mine. At Cokeburg, a Bethlehem Steel patch in Washington County, the mine had shut down in July 1934, and there was little likelihood that it would reopen soon.[31]

Despite Fayette County's rich deposits of coal, fewer than fifty of the county's 150 coal and coke plants were operating after eighteen months of the New Deal. Nearly 70 percent of the county's miners were unemployed. Thousands were without adequate shoes, clothing, and bedding, and in the fall of 1934 children were found living in coke ovens outside Uniontown. It was estimated that since 1928 the county had failed to collect 50 percent of its taxes. At Weirton Steel's Isabella patch, 300 families were on relief. "There's not a ray of hope about the place," one visitor commented, despite over 2,500 acres of underground coal. "We don't know if we'll ever work again," one mine official lamented. At the Frick mine in Maxwell, only fifteen men of a force of 550 were working in November 1934. At Republic Steel's mine in Republic, 900 miners had averaged four days per month in the previous four months. Even worse, the pits were closed at Allicia, Orient, Tower Hill, Herbert, Thompson, Palmer, and Buffington.[32]

Scores of other mines were shut down all over Pennsylvania. The unemployed miners and their families sought work elsewhere, tried to get on one or another of the New Deal projects, lived off relief or off others who were fortunate enough to have some sort of income. Relief was difficult to obtain when coal companies insisted that unemployed miners still had credit at the company store. Because the credit was counted as a "resource" by social workers, many miners were thus unable to qualify for relief. The coal companies and local businesses, which paid most of the county taxes, complained bitterly that relief only prolonged the strikes.[33]

By early 1935, however, the coal industry was on the upswing. At Youngstown Sheet and Tube's Nemacolin mine in Greene County, the men were promised work for at least two days a week through the winter. At Jones and Laughlin mines, a three-day week was becoming routine. Also, miners' payroll records were now recording payments for federal old-age programs, for checkweighmen, and for union dues, thus reflecting the impact of the New Deal and improved job security. Although some of the brotherhoods continued to rival the UMWA in the captive mines, the union was not so worried as it had been; local UMWA meetings scheduled for the previous December 1 were canceled because that was the first day of deer season.[34]

While the administration of the recovery measure brought

neither recovery to all Pennsylvania coal mines nor recognition of the union in the captive mines, it had brought a measure of stability to the chaotic coal industry. But the National Industrial Recovery Act was due to expire on June 16, 1935, and operators and the UMWA alike shared the uncertainty of what would replace it when the Supreme Court invalidated the measure on May 27. Earlier, the two groups had begun to consider new legislation because more and more operators were writing contracts below the code's minimum prices, and in the absence of strong federal regulation, Southern operators could reduce wages in their nonunion mines. Moreover, before the Supreme Court decision, a lower court had enjoined the National Recovery Administration from enforcing the wage-hour provisions on a number of Kentucky operators. Thus, fearful of a return to the price-cutting and wage-slashing times of the 1920s, the UMWA joined a group of Northern operators to draft a new coal measure. Both groups were also under the pressure of a new wage contract that was to replace the one expiring on April 1.[35]

John L. Lewis submitted the new measure to Pennsylvania Senator Joseph F. Guffey, who agreed to introduce it in the Senate. Although Guffey, a former coal operator who claimed to have been born in the shadow of a coal tipple, was in his first year in the Senate, he was hardly an ordinary freshman in Washington. Long active in Democratic politics, Guffey had remained faithful throughout the party's dismal years since World War I; in fact, he had led its resurgence under Roosevelt, a resurgence which had culminated in sweeping Democratic victories in the state's congressional and gubernatorial elections of 1934. Guffey believed fervently that the party's future in Pennsylvania and in the nation rested upon its appeal to labor, minority, and urban groups. Therefore, Lewis had little convincing to do.

Introduced in the House of Representatives by Pennsylvania Congressman John Buell Snyder, the Guffey-Snyder Act proposed a Bituminous Coal Labor Board. The board would set up a new code of fair competition, rule on the legality of certain labor practices, and create a National Coal Producers' Board, which would assign coal tonnage quotas and set minimum prices in the coal districts. The old Section 7a of the recovery act was included in the new measure, which would enable the UMWA to enter into wage contracts with operators who produced two-thirds of the nation's coal.

Southern coal operators, the steel industry, business lobbies, the railroads, and the utilities opposed the new coal bill. As usual, commercial coal operators split North and South, but the UMWA was united in its support. Moreover, the union agreed to extend the existing contract to June 16 in return for the administration's support of the Guffey bill.[36]

In the wake of the court's invalidation of the NIRA, and given the apprehension of a nationwide coal strike, Lewis and Guffey believed the new coal bill would pass. After intensive lobbying on their part, and after the UMWA had agreed to extend the new wage deadline for two more weeks, President Roosevelt came around, too. But as opposition to the measure remained, on June 29 Lewis dictated a telegram to be sent to 6,000 local union leaders calling for a strike in the absence of a new wage settlement. President Roosevelt urged Lewis to reconsider, and the latter agreed to delay the strike for still another month.

Congress, believing that the president was demanding too much in this session (the historic "Second Hundred Days" of 1935), worked slowly on the Guffey-Snyder bill. In July, Roosevelt made a special but unsuccessful plea for its early passage. Lewis again extended the wage-negotiations deadline, this time until September 16. He hoped that this extension might move the measure through the appropriate House committee; he also calculated that a threatened strike would have a greater effect in the fall than in the summer, when the demand for coal was not so great.[37]

In August, Congress finally passed the Guffey-Snyder Act. The measure allowed the National Bituminous Commission to compute average costs of production from which district coal boards would establish minimum prices for their districts.

Operators agreed to abide by fair-trade practices included in the act, namely, to recognize collective bargaining and to allow miners to assemble peaceably, to join any union they chose, and to select their own checkweighmen. The Bituminous Coal Labor Board was created to decide labor disputes not settled by the usual union-operator contracts.

Lewis, who called the measure a "bill of rights" and a "triumph of rational thought," had played his hand well by staging his strike threats carefully. Nevertheless, the wage negotiations were not yet settled. As the fifth deadline approached and no agreement was near, Lewis and the operators agreed to another weeks' extension. When it ran out, Lewis called the miners out on September 22. The walkout lasted only a few days; on September 27, the union won a 10-percent wage increase.[38]

This agreement and the Guffey-Snyder Act further stabilized the coal industry. Fewer mines closed, and labor disputes remained only sporadic. Further, among miners both the agreement and the legislation enhanced the stature of Roosevelt, the first political figure in their memory who had provided the link between them and the help they needed to bring some order to the nation's coal fields.

Then, in 1936 the Supreme Court invalidated the Guffey-Snyder Act, declaring its labor provisions void because they regulated production having only an indirect effect upon interstate commerce. Despite this setback, the UMWA, many Northern operators, and their supporters within the federal government remained committed to the further stabilization of the coal industry. Consequently, Senator Guffey, John L. Lewis, and others quickly wrote a new measure that excluded the labor provisions of the earlier act. Although the UMWA would not obtain direct labor protection in the new bill, wages were so tied to prices that the union willingly supported legislation designed to stabilize prices. Although the act failed to pass Congress in 1936, it became law in April 1937. The measure empowered the National Bituminous Coal Commission to fix minimum prices on all interstate coal transactions. Eventually, an intricate area-by-area schedule established thousands of different price arrangements over the nation.[39]

The coal industry never returned to the competitive wars of the1920s. Prices remained stabilized through the late 1930s, and, while much of this stability resulted from the operators' willingness to keep prices high, it was primarily the UMWA which kept them there. Because union contracts prevented operators from cutting wages at will, they could not judiciously cut prices either. One student of the coal industry has written that the "UMW(A) proved the single most effective force for stabilization within the industry. It won original passage of a price bill and then policed wages and thus maintained what few profits there were in soft coal." Ironically, the coal stabilization program, which was "intended to allow industrialists to work together . . ., depended for its success on the one group excluded from the actual working of the act" – the United Mine Workers of America.[40]

The greater stabilization that New Deal measures had brought to the coal fields affected Pennsylvania coal miners more than just economically. There was probably less job mobility during the 1930s than during the previous decade because there were so few jobs elsewhere. But there were also positive factors which eliminated barriers that had isolated these "colonies of forgotten men." The stability of the industry encouraged men to stay at their present jobs, and the continued use of machinery lifted the formerly unskilled miners into skilled categories. While most of the mine bosses continued to be English, Irish, and Scotch-Irish, there was a greater incentive for job improvement among all nationalities. The rapid growth of the UMWA not only increased morale and job security but also led the union to act as a sort of conduit between the miner and an outside agency committed to his betterment. Moreover, the revival of the Democratic party occurred concomitantly with the appearance of a bonanza of new state and federal patronage jobs; not surprisingly, coal field recruits for these jobs were both numerous and willing. All these factors seemed to encourage a more meaningful community life. This sense of unity emanated not from misery and deprivation as before, but from promise and hope — a belief in emancipation from the oppressive forces of earlier times.

While the gains in the coal fields were real enough for those commercial and captive miners who had jobs, the latter group had not yet won union recognition from the steel companies. Beginning in the fall of 1941, UMWA president John L. Lewis — now estranged from Roosevelt and the New Deal — started the drive for recognition in the captives, a drive which would succeed by the time the United States entered World War II.[41]

In 1939, commercial miners had signed a new contract that included the union shop. Two years later, they won a continuation of the union shop, as well as significant wage increases. The war in Europe had increased the demand for coal, and both commercial and captive miners were heading for greater job security and higher wages than most of them had ever known.

In the fall of 1941, Lewis asked the steel companies to accept the new Appalachian Agreement (commercial contract), including the union shop. Of the twelve largest steel companies, only Jones and Laughlin agreed. The other eleven, which employed over 50,000 miners — most of them in southwestern Pennsylvania — offered the wages and hours of the Appalachian Agreement, but refused the union shop.

On September 15 the captive miners struck, and the mines shut down.[42] By this time, German and Japanese conquests over the world were so extensive than many Americans felt threatened. The U. S. Navy was virtually at war in the Atlantic. Further, President Roosevelt portrayed the nation as an arsenal for the British, and insisted that any interruption of heavy industry threatened that role. The mine dispute went to the National Defense Mediation Board, which had been created to minimize labor disputes and to accelerate the production of war materials. On September 19, when the steel companies agreed to the wages and hours provisions of the Appalachian Agreement, and while further negotiations continued over the union-shop demand, Lewis agreed to send the miners back to work for thirty days.

Again, the board failed to find a solution, and after a few days' delay, Lewis struck the captives on October 27. By this time, the international situation was grave indeed: the German advance had forced the Soviet government to flee Moscow, the anti-U.S. militarist Tojo had assumed power in Japan, and U. S ships had been torpedoed in the Atlantic.

World affairs seemed bent upon intruding into the lives of Pennsylvania coal miners, both those who still worked in the state's coal pits, and those who had already entered military service. The coal supply for steel production was running low, and if the strike continued, the industry would have to bank its furnaces in two and a half weeks. Further, if coke furnaces were allowed to cool, it would take a few weeks to get them operable again. At the same time, Congress was threatening to pass anti-strike legislation.

Under pressure from many sides, Lewis sent his men back to work on October 30. He agreed that they would work until November 15 while the mediation board continued further discussions. Lewis expected that the war crisis would push the board toward accepting the union shop. If not, he still had his strike option.

To his surprise, the board rejected the union shop, and despite the president's threats to take drastic action against the determined labor boss and his men, Lewis took the miners out for a third time, on November 17. By then, the Germans were at Sevastopol in the Crimea, Tojo had begun his countdown for war with the U.S., and the Navy was carrying out its shoot-on-sight policy in the Atlantic. Britain's back was to the wall, and she desperately needed more war supplies.

Roosevelt had failed to coerce Lewis, and the latter had picked up support in his struggle with the steel companies and the president. Commercial miners by the thousands now joined their captive brothers on strike, and CIO officials—in many cases former UMWA leaders—now supported Lewis and his men. They refused "to scab," even for a commander-in-chief they revered.

Rather than urge an anti-strike measure that would alienate labor just when war appeared inevitable, Roosevelt decided to surrender. He selected a panel of three members to decide the dispute; the group included Lewis, the president of U. S. Steel, and a "public" member who Roosevelt knew would side with the union. Both sides agreed in advance to abide by the panel's decision, and Lewis sent his men back to the pits once again, on November 22.

Two weeks later the panel awarded the union shop in the captive mines. It was a historic moment and a great victory for Pennsylvania coal miners. But as one historian has written, "Hardly anyone noticed." The board issued the decision on December 7, 1941.[43]

The Japanese bombers that attacked Pearl Harbor ended an era not only for the nation and the world but also for Pennsylvania coal miners. The times had witnessed a slow but steady rise in their living standards, a rise engineered by a solicitous federal government. Coal miners now belonged to one of the nation's most powerful labor unions, a union which had not only had benefited them individually, but also had helped save an industry as well. Hard times would return when the war was over; but, for the moment, at least, a new sense of self-worth and greater economic security now characterized the lot of thousands of Pennsylvania coal diggers.

NOTES

1. Glen Lawhorn Parker, *The Coal Industry: A Study in Social Control* (Washington, 1940), pp. 63, 72-73; Morton S. Baritz, *The Union and the Coal Industry* (New Haven, 1955), p. 48. See also Homer L. Morris, *The Plight of the Bituminous Coal Miner* (Philadelphia, 1934).

2. Irving Bernstein, *The Lean Years: A History of the American Worker, 1920-1933* (Boston, 1960), p. 362; Van Bittner, Charleston, West Virginia, to Phil Murray, Washington, D.C., June 27, 1930, CIO Files, United Mine Workers Papers, Washington, D.C., hereinafter cited as UMWP; Gifford Pinchot, Harrisburg, Pennsylvania, to Franklin D. Roosevelt, Albany, New York, February 20, 1933, Official File (OF) 52, Franklin D. Roosevelt Library, Hyde Park, New York, hereinafter cited as FDRL.

3. Bernstein, *The Lean Years*, pp. 133-134; O. R. Check, Superintendent of Police, Ellsworth, Pa., to T. R. Johns, General Manager of Coal Miners, Bethlehem Steel Corporation, *Report of Police Operations for the Year 1928*, 23 January 1929. The later are reports concerning the police activities of the Bethlehem Steel Corpora-

tion mines at Ellsworth, Cokeburg, Marianna, Slickville, and Heilwood in western Pennsylvania, hereinafter cited as *Bethlehem Police Report.*

4. Laurin Gilfillin, *I Went to Pit College* (New York, 1934), pp. 216-17; *New York Times,* 9, 14, and 17 June 1931; interview with Bill R., Marianna, 8 December 1974. This interview is part of the California Oral History Collection, an ongoing project involving both faculty and students which numbers over 400 taped interviews to date. The locations where the interviews were conducted are in Pennsylvania, unless otherwise noted. Hereinafter cited as COHC.

5. *Bethlehem Police Report,* 1931; Frank Butler, "Pennsylvania's Bloody Mine War," *The Nation,* July 8, 1931, pp. 38-39.

6. *Bethlehem Police Report,* 1931; "The Struggle in Coal," *New Republic,* 5 August 1931, pp. 301-302; *New York Times,* 24 June, 20 July 1931; interview with John Y., Vestaburg, 10 December 1974, COHC.

7. Nevertheless, the NMU's idealism and militancy contributed to the resurgence of organized labor during the Great Depression. Ironically, the union aided the UMWA in securing new contracts with many coal operators because the latter—believing that the recognition of some coal union was inevitable—preferred to deal with the UMWA rather than the NMU. Perhaps, too, the racial harmony promoted by the NMU effected a renewed racial unity within the UMWA which aided its cause. Finally, when John L. Lewis formed the Committee for Industrial Organization (soon the Congress of Industrial Organizations), the largest drive for organization in American labor history, he called on former NMU-TUUL leaders to help organize the movement. See Lynda Nyden, "Black Miners in Western Pennsylvania, 1925-1931: The National Miners Union and the United Mine Workers of America," *Science and Society* 41, no. 1 (Spring 1977), pp. 69-101. Also interviews with Gene W., Canonsburg, 7 July 1976; Alex H., Avela, 11 October 1975, COHC.

8. James P. Johnson, "Reorganizing the United Mine Workers of America in Pennsylvania During the New Deal," *Pennsylvania History* 37, no. 2 (April 1970), p. 117.

9. For a discussion of the National Industrial Recovery Act see Irving Bernstein, *The New Deal Collective Bargaining Policy* (Berkeley, 1950).

10. John Brophy, *A Miner's Life* (Madison, 1964), p. 236; Phil Murray, Pittsburgh, Pa., to John Boylan, Washington, D.C., June 30, 1933, UMWP.

11. Johnson, "Reorganizing the UMWA," p. 121; *Bethlehem Police Reports,* 1933; interviews with Lawrence Z., California, 24 April 1974; Brian W., Latrobe, 10 July 1974; Anthony T., Allison, 1 May 1974, COHC.

12. Muriel Earley Sheppard, *Cloud by Day: A Story of Coal and Coke and People* (Chapel Hill, 1947), pp. 122-27; interviews with Steve S., Smithton, 20 May 1974; Mike W., Uniontown, 8 May 1976, COHC.

13. Sheppard, *Cloud by Day,* pp. 127-28.

14. Morris, *Plight of the Bituminous Miner,* pp. 74-78; Sheppard, *Cloud by Day,* pp. 128-130; *Time,* 7 August 1933.

15. Daniel Allen, "Mine War in Pennsylvania," *The Nation,* 16 August 1933, pp. 176-77.

16. Pinchot Memorandum, August 2, 1933, OF 175; Joseph Guffey, Pittsburgh, Pa., to President Roosevelt, Washington, D.C., August 2, 1933, FDRL.

17. *Newsweek*, 12 August 1933; *United Mine Workers' Journal*, 15 August 1933.

18. Joseph Guffey, Washington, D.C., to Marvin McIntyre, Poughkeepsie, New York, August 5, 1933, President's Personal File (PPF) 451; Hurd Memorandum OF 175, FDRL.

19. Gifford Pinchot, Harrisburg, Pa., to Franklin D. Roosevelt, Washington, D.C., September 5, 1933, Box 2554, Gifford Pinchot Papers, Manuscript Division, Library of Congress, Washington, D.C., hereinafter cited as Pinchot Papers.

20. Gifford Pinchot, Harrisburg, Pa., to the President, Washington, D.C., September 12, 1933; telegram from Duncan McCallum, Harrisburg, Pa., to the President, Washington, D.C., September 14, 1933; Myron Taylor Statement, September 15, 1933, OF 175, FDRL.

21. Telegram from Dan Moriarty, Chairman, Barnesboro, Pa., to Franklin D. Roosevelt, Washington D.C., September 18, 1933, OF 290, FDRL.

22. For a discussion of both the coal code and the Appalachian Agreement, see James P. Johnson, "Drafting the NRA Code of Fair Competition for the Bituminous Coal Industry," *Journal of American History*, 53, no. 3 (December 1966), pp. 521-41.

23. *United Mine Workers' Journal*, 1 October 1933; *New Yorker*, September 1933; David J. McDonald and Edward A. Lynch, *Coal and Unionism* (Silver Spring, Md., 1939), p. 200.

24. McAlister Coleman, *Men and Coal* (New York, 1943), pp. 151-52; Gifford Pinchot, Harrisburg, Pa., to the President, Washington, D.C., October 1, 1933, OF 175, FDRL.

25. *Time*, 25 September 1933; telegram from J. D. A. Moran, Pittsburgh, Pa., to Franklin D. Roosevelt, Washington, D.C., October 12, 1933, OF 175, FDRL.

26. FDR, Washington, D.C., to Myron C. Taylor, New York, New York, October £, 1933, OF 175; Edward T. Leech, Pittsburgh, Pa., to Joseph F. Guffey, Washington, D.C., October 4, 1933, OF 175; Gifford Pinchot, Harrisburg, Pa., to the President, Syracuse, N.Y., October 4, 1933, OF 175, FDRL; *The New Republic*, 4 October 1933, *Newsweek*, 7 October 1933; *United Mine Workers' Journal*, 1 October 1933; *Time*, 2 October 1933.

27. FDR, Washington, D.C., to Myron C. Taylor, New York, New York, October 16, 1933, OF 175; William J. Hynes, et. al., Uniontown, Pa., to Mister President, Washington, D.C., October 25, 1933, OF 175; Congressman J. Buell Snyder, Somerset, Pa., to Franklin D. Roosevelt, Washington, D.C., October 26, 1933, OF 175, FDRL; *The Literary Digest*, 28 October 1933; *Time*, 6 November, 13 November 1933; Gifford Pinchot, Harrisburg, Pa., to Franklin D. Roosevelt, Washington, D.C., November 1, 1933, Box 2554, Pinchot Papers.

28. *United Mine Workers' Journal*, 1 December 1933, *The New Republic*, 6 December 1933; *Time*, 4 December 1933.

29. Johnson, "Reorganizing the UMWA," pp. 129-32; *The New Republic*, 31 January 1934.

30. *New York Times*, 21, 22, 24, and 28 February 1934; *United Mine Workers' Journal*, 18 February 1934.

31. Henry Francis, Uniontown, Pa., to Harry L. Hopkins, Washington, D.C., November 10, 1934, Harry Hopkins Papers, FDRL; *Bethlehem Police Report*, 1934.

32. Lorena Hickok, Uniontown, Pa., to Harry L. Hopkins, Washington, D.C., August 12, 1933, Hopkins Papers; Henry Francis, Morgantown, West Virginia, November 18, 1934, Hopkins Papers, FDRL; *Bethlehem Police Report*, 1933, 1934.

33. W. H. MacDonald, Scotthaven, Pa., to Franklin D. Roosevelt, Hyde Park, New York, September 30, 1934, OF 175, FDRL; Also see *Stabilization of the Bituminous Coal Industry, Hearings*, Senate Committee on Interstate Commerce, Seventy-fourth Congress, 1st session, February 19-March 7, 1935; also *Bethlehem Police Report*, 1934.

34. Henry Francis, Uniontown, Pa., to Harry L. Hopkins, Washington, D.C., November 3, 1934, Hopkins Papers, FDRL; Jones and Laughlin Steel Corporation Papers, Jones and Laughlin California Office, California, Pennsylvania; Lorena Hickok, Uniontown, Pa., to Harry Hopkins, Washington, D.C., July 24, 1935, Hopkins Papers, FDRL; *Bethlehem Police Report*, 1934.

35. See *Stabilization of the Bituminous Coal Industry, Hearings*, House Committee on Ways and Means, Seventy-fourth Congress, 1st Session, June 17-28, 1935.

36. See James E. Burrows, "The Congressional Career of John Buell Snyder, 1933-1946" (M. A. thesis, California State College, 1968); Ray Sprigle, "Lord Guffey of Pennsylvania," *American Mercury*, November 1938, pp. 273-75.

37. Arthur M. Schlesinger, Jr., *The Age of Roosevelt*, Vol. 3, *The Politics of Upheaval* (Boston, 1960), pp. 334-36; S. D. Spero, "Trouble in Coal," *The New Republic*, 3 July 1935, pp. 17-18; FDR, Washington, D.C., to Congressman Samuel B. Hill, Washington, D.C., July 6, 1935, OF 175, FDRL.

38. *New York Times*, 16, 17, and 18 August, 13, 14, 15, and 16 September 1935; telegram from Edward F. McGrady, Washington, D.C., to Marvin McIntyre, Washington, D.C., September 20, 1935, OF 175, FDRL.

39. John L. Lewis, Washington, D.C., to Frederich A. Delano, New York, May 19, 1936, Frederich A. Delano Papers, FDRL; *Coal Age*, June 1936, pp. 260-61.

40. James P. Johnson, "A 'New Deal' for Soft Coal: The Attempted Revitalization of the Bituminous Coal Industry Under the New Deal" (Ph.d. diss., Columbia University, 1968), p. 267.

41. C. K. McFarland, *Roosevelt, Lewis, and the New Deal, 1933-1940* (Fort Worth, Tex., 1970), pp. 109-10; Irving Bernstein, *Turbulent Years: A History of the American Worker, 1933-1941 (Boston, 1971), p. 752.*

42. Accounts of the captive-mines settlement are in James A. Wechsler, *Labor Baron, A Portrait of John L. Lewis* (New York, 1944), pp. 154-68; Saul Alinsky, *John L. Lewis: An Unauthorized Biography* (New York, 1949), pp. 238-47; Walter Galenson, *The CIO Challenges to the AFL: A History of the American Labor Movement, 1935-1941* (Cambridge, 1960), pp. 225-33. This account follows closely Bernstein's *Turbulent Years*, pp. 752-67.

43. Bernstein, *Turbulent Years*, p. 767.

[7]
Paved Roads and Coal Politics: The New Deal and Relief in Southwestern Pennsylvania

Long before the captive miners finally won the union shop, the New Deal had made the federal government a powerful force in southwestern Pennsylvania. Spearheading the federal presence were the New Deal's relief programs. First under the Federal Emergency Relief Administration and finally through the Works Progress Administration, federal relief played a major role in reshaping social and political relationships in southwestern Pennsylvania.

Despite the severity of the depression, America's system of poor relief in 1930 had changed little from the early eighteenth century, when colonies such as Pennsylvania fashioned relief-giving after the model of the Elizabethan poor laws. Faithful to the model, Pennsylvania established county poor boards, which were authorized to dispense meager assistance to needy residents. In the nineteenth century, asylums for the poor, soup kitchens, missions, and charity organizations supplemented the thin fare of the poor boards. By giving relief sparingly and making it contingent on the supplicants' conformity to local values, local relief agencies functioned to reinforce provincial customs and help preserve the insularity and isolation of many small towns. This conjunction of sparse relief and social isolation characterized the company-dominated mining towns which sprang up in southwestern Pennsylvania in the late nineteenth and early twentieth centuries.

Between 1929 and 1932, severe unemployment overwhelmed the resources of Pennsylvania's local poor boards and voluntary welfare agencies. Both the state and the federal government had to assume increasing responsibility for unemployment relief. In May 1933 Congress set up the Federal Emergency Relief Administration (FERA), introducing a highly centralized federal relief system. Although political pressure from business convinced the New Deal to dismantle the FERA in 1935 and replace it with a more decentralized system comprising Social Security and the Works Progress Administration (WPA), the federal role in relief remained sizable throughout the 1930s. By establishing, at least temporarily, national standards for the granting of assistance to the jobless poor, federal relief freed unemployed miners and coke-oven and steel workers from dependence on company-dominated standards of local relief. Not surprisingly, the issue of federal relief—especially its potential for disrupting local convention—dominated the political battleground in the 1930s.[1]

The isolation of southwestern Pennsylvania's mine towns magnified the impact of federal relief. In their site selection and plans for company towns, in their choice of an immigrant work force, and in their policing of the miners' lives, the mining companies attempted to bar all outside influences, especially the relief-giving kind. While poverty haunted towns plagued by low wages, mine closings, and strikes, the company encouraged home-brewed forms of assistance. Whatever his background, whether Slavic, Italian, Hungarian, or German, almost every miner supplemented his wages by gardening and keeping chickens, pigs, or a cow. More importantly, until the 1930s, weak, maimed, discouraged, or disruptive miners were driven out of the towns—not to the poor boards. Therefore, despite the decline of the bituminous-coal industry in the 1920s, during which time companies tried to increase profits by cutting wages and tightening their Coal and Iron Police security, southwestern Pennsylvania managed to provide traditional care for the poor. The strike of 1927, however, left the mine fields of southwestern Pennsylvania a veritable wasteland of human suffering. Red Cross workers, the American Friends Service Committee, government observers, and others spoke about "stranded" mine town populations, and warned that without help the area was doomed.[2]

When the stock market crashed in September 1929, the weight of depression had already crushed the people of southwestern Pennsylvania. Just as in the textile and other beleaguered industries, mine operators fought the depression by cutting wages and closing mines; when the miners responded with strikes, the owners countered by reinforcing their garrison of private police, employing scabs, and evicting militant miners. Violent strikes in the late 1920s had permanently scarred the bituminous-coal fields, especially in places such as Washington and Fayette Counties. The region's economy rested on coal and coke production, and the bulk of the population lived in small company towns housing fewer than 500 people. A visitor to Fayette County in 1934 reported many mines closed. All 300 residents of the Isabella patch subsisted on relief. Only a violent demonstration prevented the operators of the closed Allicia mine from evicting the town's remaining fifty families. At the Maxwell, Briar Hill, Republic, Tar Hill, and Allison mines—all in Fayette County—many miners were jobless or worked only two or three days a week.[3]

Although Washington and Westmoreland counties had more diversified economies, coal dominated. The 1928 strike had ravaged Washington County coal towns such as Cokeburg. Every morning in the early 1930s Cokeburg miners traveled from town to town in rickety trucks searching—usually in vain—for a day's work in the mines. Therefore, those residents of Daisytown and Richeyville who worked in the Jones and Laughlin Vesta mines considered themselves fortunate. Throughout the 1930s the men worked three days a week; however, their biweekly wages, which averaged about $20.00, hardly provided a decent living. Gnawing poverty, not just reduced circumstances, eroded the lives of the people of southwestern Pennsylvania. Twenty-five percent of the male work force in Fayette, Westmoreland, and Washington counties was unemployed in 1934. Over 60 percent of the miners in Fayette and 54 percent of the miners in Washington counties were either jobless or worked only part time. Towns such as Dunbar and Everson in Fayette, Cokeburg in Washington, and

Livermore in Westmoreland had unemployment rates in 1934 of 40 percent or more.[4]

In the winter of 1932–1933, life in these gray villages presented a tragedy of deepening poverty. People patched and repatched clothing until tattered rags draped their bodies. Bedding deteriorated beyond use, forcing many to sleep on newspaper-covered box springs. Shoes were an especially serious problem. Eyewitnesses reported seeing men wearing gunny sacks tied around their feet or wearing shoes soled with tire rubber. Teachers feared the effect of poverty on their pupils. A teacher at a Brownsville Catholic school told Henry Francis, a roving reporter sent by Federal Emergency Relief Administrator Harry Hopkins to investigate the coal regions, that cold weather would create insurmountable hardships for the scantily dressed students. "Some have only canvas shoes, and if snow came they couldn't go to school." Many children were undernourished, she noted, and "we need a doctor too."[5]

The housing situation compounded the misery of the coal region. Despite state laws restraining the coal operators from wholesale evictions, mine owners had little difficulty finding a judge and a sheriff willing to turn the hapless miner and his family out of the patch. Evicted mine families often "doubled up" in one house. "Doubling up" seemed preferable to seeking makeshift shelter in caves, shanties, and coke ovens. Nevertheless, in 1934 at least sixty families in Fayette County lived in coke ovens, forty-four found refuge in "dilapidated shanties," and many others dwelled in caves.[6]

Jack Conroy called the victims of the depression the "disinherited." While the term easily applied to the mining poor of southwestern Pennsylvania, other commentators of the period preferred the term "stranded." One observer painted an especially dreary picture of the conditions in Fayette County. Not only were fewer than fifty out of the county's more than 150 coal and coke plants operating, but, wrote Henry Francis, "a large proportion of those shut down will never reopen; many of these operating have only a few years' coal ahead of them. Coal is 'going back' on the county; what was a rich empire is almost ready to be dumped by its rulers; it has been bled white both above and below ground. Populations have been left stranded not only without work, but without the prospects of ever being re-employed in coal mining. What are they to do? Are they to remain indefinitely on direct relief?"[7]

Unfortunately, relief (the "lifebelt" as Francis called it) was usually too inadequate to reach the stranded. Prior to 1932, poor boards and voluntary agencies dispensed local relief in the time-honored fashion. The Fayette County Director of the Poor parceled out scant portions of food, fuel, and clothing. Poor directors were political appointees and southwestern Pennsylvania miners believed the directors took their orders directly from the coal barons. Politics notwithstanding, in Fayette County a miserly one-and-one-half-mill tax financed poor relief, raising only a pittance. During the strike of 1928, outside organizations attempted to fill the gap. The United Mine Workers of America (UMWA) built tent cities for the evicted miners and operated soup kitchens. Between 1929 and 1932 the Federal Council of Churches aided the stricken mining populations with food and clothing, and the Red Cross distributed flour purchased by the state from funds made available for relief through the Reconstruction Finance Corporation. In a different vein, the American Friends Service Committee worked to rehabilitate "stranded" miners' families by supplying materials and technical help to construct a community of small subsistence homesteads in Greene County. This homestead and subsistence garden theme reverberated throughout the 1930s and received its quintessential expression in the New Deal's Resettlement Administration.[8]

In 1932 Republican Governor Gifford Pinchot appointed Eric Biddle head of the new State Emergency Relief Board (SERA). In contrast to the old poor boards (which existed until 1937,) the new relief system operated through professionally run county relief boards (CRB). In fact, the state required a social caseworker on each county relief board staff. Biddle ordered county boards to investigate fully all relief cases and carry extensive files on every client. At first, relief families received commodities through "commodity markets" and "food commissaries." When these food handouts proved unwieldy, SERA gave clients food order slips acceptable at local stores. At the same time, SERA distributed clothing directly to the poor and, through its "thrift garden" program to promote subsistence gardening, supplied clients with seed and fertilizer.

In September 1933, after one year of operation, SERA carried close to 329,000 clients statewide on its rolls, 11,000 in Fayette, 8,000 in Washington, and 10,000 in Westmoreland. Many were miners. Regardless of the reason for the workers' unemployment, Pinchot insisted that relief be granted solely on need. Therefore, strikers in Pennsylvania were eligible for relief. Cornelia Pinchot, the governor's wife, expressed this position in 1933 at the Miners' Day celebration in Uniontown. Praising the "New Deal, FDR, and Unionism," she told the miners and their families that "if we must decide between profits and human welfare, human welfare comes first."[9]

State relief funds depended, however, on legislative appropriations, which Pennsylvania's Republican legislature made grudgingly. For example, in early 1935, the state exhausted its relief monies. The legislature took weeks to replenish the fund. Meanwhile, from throughout the state, thousands of relief marchers converged on Harrisburg to protest the "heartlessness of state politicians." By the time Franklin D. Roosevelt took office in March 1933, social workers, civic, labor, and many business leaders joined in imploring the federal government to help the states feed and clothe the unemployed.

Washington heard the pleas. Through FERA, headed by Harry Hopkins, the New Deal undertook to fund and orchestrate unemployment relief in America. Social workers, striving since 1900 to supplant "philanthropy" with scientifically administered casework, viewed FERA ecstatically. Understandably, social workers dominated FERA ranks, and strove to develop a national welfare system.

As the pivot of the national relief system, FERA endeavored to establish uniform standards for client eligibility and relief adequacy. Since the states contributed to the relief fund, FERA enforced neither the type nor the amount of individual relief grants. In 1934, outside of Philadelphia and Pittsburgh, Pennsylvania relief boards refused to make cash grants, and continued to dole out relief commodities.[10] When in 1934

Harry Hopkins rushed Assistant Administrator Arch Mandel to Uniontown to investigate a charge that jobless families in Fayette County were "starving," Mandel found an "efficiently" operated CRB staffed by fifty-nine social workers giving clients "48 hour service." Typically the CRB refused to assist unemployed people who owned cars or homes, or "hid" savings in the bank.[11]

The strictly enforced eligibility rules infuriated the jobless. After deducting expenses for lamp tending, explosives, rent, house coal, the doctor, the checkweighman, and the company store, hundreds of miners carried home pay statements marked "no earnings." These poor miners unsuccessfully demanded relief. Unemployed miners on relief objected to youthful CRB "visitors" violating their privacy by "snooping" in pantries and cellars for "hidden resources." Moreover, visitors treated residency in the company patch as an "asset." Because of these difficult relief requirements, the jobless suspected CRB motives. United Mine Workers spokesmen accused the Fayette, Washington, and Westmoreland relief boards of "having the operators' point of view." Some operators, on the other hand, protested that the Washington County Relief Board conspired with the UMW to finance strikes.

Eighty percent of the complaints against relief concerned the failure of the board to provide necessary clothing. On a cold November day in 1934, Henry Francis, one of Hopkins's roving reporters, found the Fayette County Relief Board missing many sizes of men's work clothing, sweaters, hosiery, and men's work shoes. Conditions were worse in Washington County, where in November relief-board workers pigeonholed 7,000 unfilled orders for shoes. Ernest Cole, the director of relief in Fayette County, described the situation in 1934 as "ready to boil over" —so serious that "there is the basis for a conflagration."[12]

On different visits two of Hopkins's agents detected seething discontent in southwestern Pennsylvania, and activists such as Dr. George Teagarden fueled the discontent. A Greene County physician and professor of sociology at Waynesburg College, Teagarden headed the UMWA's General Relief Committee. According to Francis, the miners "idolized" the doctor.

Teagarden badgered the state relief organizations not only for making grossly inadequate grants, but also for corruption and the willful denial of relief to "persons who did not stand in" (i.e., union agitators).

Despite Teagarden's activities, Francis found the UMWA striving to improve its relations with the CRB. The Unemployed Councils (UC) leveled a different charge at the relief authorities. An offspring of the old Communist-backed National Miners' Union, the radical UCs staged relief demonstrations on the doorsteps of relief-board headquarters, and urged jobless miners to treat CRB visitors abusively. Others accompanied Teagarden and the Unemployed Councils in vilifying the handling of relief. On the eve of the 1934 gubernatorial election, Democratic politicians in Washington County harangued a large election-night crowd before the courthouse in Washington, Pennsylvania. "Go to the polls Tuesday," a politician shouted to the group, "and take the relief administration out of the hands of the crooks."[13]

Throughout the 1930s Americans heatedly debated the handling of relief. Early in SERA's history, Pennsylvania Democrats charged that Gifford Pinchot packed the agency with Republican patronage and used relief in an unsuccessful effort to win a seat in the Senate. The victory of Democrats George Earle and Thomas Kennedy in 1934 raised Democratic hopes that finally they would feast on SERA spoils. Governor Earle, however, crushed these expectations by appointing Robert Johnson, a Republican *Time* editor, to replace Biddle as the czar of Pennsylvania relief. Even more than Biddle, Johnson stressed efficiency and professionalism in relief-giving and held the line against courthouse politics. Needless to say, Johnson's probity failed to put an end to criticism of relief. Exasperated Democratic politicians grieved over what they considered the denial of rightfully won patronage. On the other side, Republican opponents of the Earle regime denounced relief chiseling. Meanwhile, social workers joined labor spokesmen in denouncing the terrible consequences of the dole, at the same time assailing its horrible inadequacy.[14]

But the ramifications of the relief issue extended beyond charges of labor demoralization and political patronage. The dimensions of poverty in southwestern Pennsylvania compelled the isolated peoples of the region to seek help in the federal offices of Washington, D. C. As a result, new configurations of social and political power formed, built around big labor and federal relief-giving. New Dealer Lorena Hickok found the impact a little disquieting. She told Hopkins that the soft-coal miners "seem to have no faith at all in anyone save the President. They carry his picture in their picket lines and their little parades . . . with the American flag and queer little bands made up of saxophones and accordians . . . The people on relief generally seem to have that same feeling about him. The state government they ignore. They look to the Federal government for aid and are inclined to hold the Federal government responsible when it is not forthcoming."[15]

While social workers cheered the FERA for its effort to establish standards of adequacy and vigorously crusaded for a permanent federal relief system, labor opposed FERA's emphasis on direct relief and campaigned for more job-producing public works. Although labor also lobbied for more sufficient unemployment relief, union leaders deplored the destructive consequences of the dole on the human spirit. Wholeheartedly agreeing that direct relief had a psychologically debilitating effect on the unemployed worker, Hopkins and Roosevelt stressed that jobs were needed both to pump cash into the national bloodstream and to restore human dignity.

Historically, in times of depression Americans followed their denunciation of the dole with the cry for public works. Throughout the nineteenth century, work houses and wood yards were traditional accoutrements of relief. Serious depressions in 1873 and 1893 produced modest public-works programs in many American cities. In 1932 and 1933 SERA, through its Local Works Division, employed hundreds of the jobless on road-building projects. In 1933 unemployed miners in southwestern Pennsylvania complained that SERA forced them to earn their relief flour and shoes by working on the "Pinchot roads."

Over the winter of 1933-1934, the New Deal launched America's first massive works-relief program. At that time Roosevelt created the Civil Works Administration (CWA), headed by Harry Hopkins, which established a nationwide works program designed to help the jobless through the expected harsh months ahead. The CWA aimed to put 3,000,000 people to work in a few weeks. Workers were not expected to demonstrate need, and to avoid conflict with labor unions, the CWA paid workers the "prevailing wage." Virtually overnight the CWA created jobs building roads, constructing paths, making mattresses, even researching the history of the safety pin. In southwestern Pennsylvania most CWA workers swung picks and wielded spades on road and street projects. For example, CWA workers in Fayette County laid sidewalks in towns such as Dunbar and paved the main street of Belle Vernon.

Social workers acclaimed the CWA, especially its speed in putting thousands to work and its freedom from the "means test," a freedom which liberated CWA workers from the opprobrium of being "on relief." On the other hand, the critics of the CWA rebuked the program for "boondoggling" — too many CWA workers were busied with "leaf-raking" jobs.[16]

Washington, however, remained steadfastly convinced of the superiority of work over direct relief. As a key part of its 1935 program to give Americans Social Security and end the depression, the New Deal created the Works Progress Administration (WPA). The WPA dramatized the commitment to "getting out of the direct relief business" by giving jobs to the employable jobless. Social Security assisted the old, the blind, the disabled, and dependent children, leaving to the states the nondescript poor outside these categories. The WPA promised to lighten state relief case loads by giving the employable member of a relief family a "relief" job. Like the CWA, the WPA emphasized salaries. State and federal agencies, counties, cities, boroughs, and towns paid the cost of materials, while the WPA covered the labor costs. Wherever possible "for humanity's sake, manpower replaced steampower."[17]

Harry Hopkins, the administrator of the WPA, transferred the bureaucratic efficiency of the FERA to the WPA. Although scientifically trained social workers dominated the FERA, military-trained engineers filled the administrative ranks of the WPA. In military fashion the latter organized the nation into regions and the states into districts, and placed an administrator over each state. Supervisors and project foremen directed the WPA's activities in the districts.

Like the CWA, local political subdivisions originated WPA projects. The gamut of approval stretched all the way from the district office, to Harrisburg, to Hopkins, to Roosevelt. Once a project was approved, the district supervisor selected the work force and ordered the necessary material and equipment. Because projects frequently required supervisory and technically skilled personnel rarely found on the relief rolls, the WPA allowed 10 percent of the employees to be "predesignated" from nonrelief sources. Events illustrate that "predesignation" left ample room for the play of politics.[18]

Hopkins vowed to keep work relief nonpolitical. However, the patronage potential of WPA overwhelmed the administrator's vigilance. From the outset politicians in southwestern Pennsylvania understood the political significance of the federal relief dollar; clearly, the prospect of work-relief jobs whetted the appetites of Pennsylvania's patronage-starved Democratic party. Although federal observers gave CWA head Eric Biddle high grades for integrity and efficiency, state Democrats continually charged him with packing the organization with Republican social workers. To the chagrin of local politicos, Robert Johnson, who replaced Biddle in 1934, also drew the applause of efficiency-conscious New Dealers.

Behind the Democrats' opposition to Biddle, Johnson, and the whole social-work orientation of SERA, loomed conflicting interpretations of both relief and public employment. For example, SERA's scientifically trained social workers condemned patronage in relief as a violation of efficiency. This conflict between political versus bureaucratic administration moved foresquare into the limelight when Edward N. Jones was appointed Pennsylvania's WPA administrator. A former newspaperman and political protégé of Democratic Senator Joseph Guffey, Jones had directed the publicity for the successful 1934 Guffey-Earle campaign. His main qualification for the post of WPA administrator in Pennsylvania was Guffey's endorsement; Jones fully vindicated Guffey's expectations by running Pennsylvania's WPA along political lines.

From the start Hopkins considered the WPA situation in Pennsylvania exasperating. Jones immediately experienced difficulties compelling Hopkins to dispatch a team of field representatives to Pennsylvania. Their report to Assistant Administrator Colonel Lawrence Westbrook accused Jones of refusing "approval to our personnel to visit any of the districts and . . . (making) it uncomfortable, if not impossible, to gain anything useful by conferences with his administrative staff . . . We have felt powerless to contribute to his administration as we have been able to do in each of our other states."[19]

The problem stemmed from Jones's refusal to cooperate with SERA in transferring the "employables" from the relief rolls to WPA. He scored SERA for "doing everything in its power to cripple President Roosevelt's work relief program." Jones frankly considered the WPA the domain of the state Democratic party. Lorena Hickok beheld with incredulity his replacing experienced SERA work-relief personnel with political types. "Let's be charitable," explained Hickok, "and say that he is employing—as he apparently is—able men . . . They are being selected entirely on a political basis . . . They've got to start in from the bottom and learn the whole problem."[20]

Charges of political activity sharpened in the presidential election year of 1936. In May, Pennsylvania's Republican press pilloried the WPA as "Wholesale Political Assistance," and insisted that a Democratic party chairman was the best person to see for a work-relief job. Throughout that summer, Republican State Senator Mason Owlett attempted to investigate the state WPA. Time and again Democrats such as Philadelphia party chairman John B. Kelly thwarted Owlett by publically scolding the senator for conducting a political investigation. Owlett's probe ceased when the U. S. attorney general declared the state's investigation of a federal agency unconstitutional. Immediately, Pennsylvania's Republican U. S. Senator James Davis championed Owlett's cause in Congress. In October, Davis presented a whole sheaf of complaints before the Senate's Lonergan Committee, which had been formed to investigate charges of political corruption. Most of

Davis's charges involved the WPA's right to "predesignate" 10 percent of its personnel. His stack of affidavits purported that predesignated personnel received the "political endorsement" of party henchmen and were then victimized by vicious Democratic macing. Party bosses allegedly coerced WPA foremen into contributing 3 to 5 percent of their salaries into Democratic slush funds, and forced workers to buy a WPA magazine published by Eddie Jones called *We The People*. A newspaperman for the *Washington* (Pennsylvania) *Observer* reported WPA supervisors lined up at a Democratic beer-drinking club contributing to the party war chest. Similar reports came from Fayette and Greene counties.

Despite an interminable Republican litany of WPA political wrongs, Louis Glavis, the investigator for the Lonergan Committee, labeled the charges unfounded. Glavis found no connection between the WPA and the people who accused it of macing or discrimination. Ironically for the Republicans who hoped to use an investigation to discredit the WPA, in January 1937 the Lonergan Committee indicted for politically intimidating their workers several southwestern Pennsylvania Republican strongholds, namely, the Jones and Laughlin and Carnegie-Pittsburgh Steel companies.[21]

Accusations of WPA involvement in state politics electrified the political climate in 1938, but now the heaviest charges were unleashed by Democrats against Democrats. In 1938 rival Democratic factions in Pennsylvania vied for control of the party, each claiming to be the state's "real" Democratic party. Governor Earle, allied with Pittsburgh's David Lawrence, headed a faction which ran Earle for the U. S. Senate and Charles A. Jones for governor. Led by Joseph Guffey, Eddie Jones, and United Mine Workers' boss John L. Lewis, a second faction slated Lieutenant Governor Tom Kennedy for governor and S. Davis Wilson for the Senate.

Although Edward N. Jones stepped down from his WPA post in 1937, J. Banks Hudson, his successor, had aligned himself with the Guffey-Lewis faction and kept the WPA embroiled in politics. The storm of complaints in 1938 against WPA misuse suggests that Guffey wielded the WPA weapon with a vengeance. A WPA worker in Fayette County pleaded with Hopkins to investigate the charge that John L. Lewis forced WPA workers to pay dues of thirty-five cents monthly to Lewis's Citizens Committee for Social Welfare, headed by Dr. George Teagarden. Moreover, complained the worker, "The only men who get consideration (for WPA jobs) are ones who supported Kennedy for Governor or are members of the UMW." At one point in the primary battle a panicky Dave Lawrence begged his old friend William Bullit to warn Hopkins that "the state organization was being beaten to a pulp by the WPA."[22]

In its investigation of WPA skulduggery in the 1938 Pennsylvania elections, the Sheppard Committee of the U. S. Senate heard testimony about WPA trucks used to transport voters to the polls, WPA workers forced to change their registration, workers fired for not supporting the Kennedy-Wilson ticket, and workers made to buy tickets to a Kennedy-Wilson picnic in Hershey, Pennsylvania. WPA laborers in Westmoreland County reportedly constructed a political map and placarded the county with Wilson-Kennedy posters. Although the Sheppard Committee dismissed the charges against the WPA in January 1939, an investigator informed WPA field representative F. H. Dryden that "the active macing of employees in the Pittsburgh area during this period (May 1938) is a known fact, and your representative has seen concrete evidence of many contributions for party funds and tickets obtained under duress and threats."[23]

The political volatility of the WPA in Westmoreland, Washington, and Fayette counties reflected the gestation of a region emerging from decades of social isolation. The WPA was instrumental in bringing about this change. Federal monies for projects and relief outranked coal as an important medium for political activity, and Guffey and Lewis used the WPA to construct a new political hegemony replacing the dominion of King Coal. Whereas for decades the coal barons and the Republican party used the hiring apparatus of the mines to control the people and politics of the coal fields, Guffey and Lewis based their suzerainty on local control of federal relief.[24]

In addition to its reordering of social and political power in southwestern Pennsylvania, the WPA had a significant physical impact on the area's urban and rural landscape. Not surprisingly, the WPA's building program in southwestern Pennsylvania confronted enormous economic obstacles. When Lorena Hickok visited the area in 1935, she found Lyell Buttermore, the WPA administrator for Fayette, Greene, and Washington counties, uncertain "where he was going to get ANY projects." In Fayette, Hickok explained, "the only body that has any borrowing capacity at all is the poor board! Towns like Uniontown can barely pay their police, firemen, and teachers." Buttermore figured out that, after he had paid his labor and administrative costs, he would have "just about enough for truck hire."[25]

For poor communities in Fayette, Washington, and Greene counties, the smallest material costs overtaxed the town resources. Yet these were the towns that desperately needed WPA projects. Not only did "red dog" roads connect town to town, but the cheap paving material covered the streets of most coal towns. Dirty streams laden with yellow mine seepage, refuse, and raw sewage snaked through many of the towns and mining villages of southwestern Pennsylvania. Stinking rivulets in summer and raging torrents in spring, these open sewers advertised the underdeveloped state of the region. Wretched school buildings, untreated drinking water, and unsidewalked streets compounded the impoverishment of coal field living conditions.

Although the WPA's requirement that sponsors pay for the cost of materials limited its program in the region to heavy-construction projects, the WPA greatly narrowed the extent of isolation in the region. Both Washington and Fayette counties joined the state in sponsoring large street and highway projects. For example, between 1935 and 1938 the WPA spent $2,500,000 to improve 193 miles of Fayette County roads and fifteen miles of streets. Many of these newly paved roads tied isolated mining patches to small cities such as Uniontown. In Washington County towns such as California, Burgettstown, and Canonsburg, the WPA built curbing, constructed sidewalks, and paved streets. In addition, relief workers constructured almost two miles of storm sewers in Fayette County and spent over $20,000 in Washington County replacing foul outhouses with modern sanitary facilities.[26]

The WPA also operated a host of other, less costly projects. WPA workers sealed abandoned mines, cleaned and rebound textbooks for the Donora High School, and copied and catelogued all the ordinances for the towns of California, Charleroi, Monongahela, and Washington. WPA workers raised a second story on the Charleroi Municipal Building and remodeled the California State College Science Building; WPA archeologists uncovered lead plates planted by French soldiers in southwestern Pennsylvania in the eighteenth century. One of the largest WPA projects employed only women. Throughout the region the WPA operated sewing rooms where women produced clothing and blankets to be distributed among the needy. Women relief workers conducted health surveys and delivered medical care to the poor. One project trained women for domestic-service jobs, and another employed women teachers to instruct first-generation Slavic and Italian immigrants in citizenship, English, and home economics.[27]

Whether WPA workers quarried stone for roads or walls, leveled a field in California for a baseball diamond, or painted murals in local post offices, they labored in the presence of the red, white, and blue sign of the WPA. Everybody in the region knew a friend or relative working on a WPA project, and all formed an opinion of the caliber and permanent benefit of the work. But regardless of differing opinions, none denied the project's impact. The WPA bound the region to the nation with roads, sewing rooms, administrative personnel, pay envelopes, and a common interest in continued federal appropriations. In a plea to the president not to cancel her sewing project, a seamstress employed on a WPA sewing project summed up the impact of the WPA most eloquently:

> I am supporting a home and an elder sister and I am past the age to get employment. Knowing what you did at Norvelt, I felt you would help the Democratic women in our trying crisis.[28]

NOTES

1. Leah H. Feder, *Unemployment Relief in Periods of Depression: A Study of Measures Adopted in Certain American Cities, 1857-1922* (New York, 1936), passim; Josephine Brown, *Public Relief, 1922-1939* (New York, 1940), passim; Robert H. Bremner, *From the Depths: The Discovery of Poverty in the United States* (New York, 1967), passim.

2. Henry Francis, Uniontown, Pa., to Harry L. Hopkins, Washington, D.C., November 10, 1934, Harry Hopkins Papers, Franklin D. Roosevelt Library, Hyde Park, New York, hereinafter cited as Hopkins Papers, FDRL; Muriel Earley Sheppard, *Cloud By Day: A Story of Coal and Coke and People* (Chapel Hill, N.C., 1947), pp. 2-5.

3. Sheppard, *Cloud By Day,* pp. 112-20.

4. Pennsylvania State Emergency Relief Board, Department of Research and Statistics, Bulletin 40-A, "Unemployment in Washington County," 15 April 1934, mimeo, in WPA Library, HD 5725, Record Group 69, Records of the Works Projects Administration. Hereinafter cited as WPA Records; SERA, Bulletin 36-A, "Unemployment in Fayette County," 15 April 1934, mimeo, WPA Library, HD 5725, WPA Records; SERA, Bulletin 39-A, "Unemployment in Westmoreland County," 15 April 1934, WPA Library, HD 5725, WPA Records.

5. Francis, Uniontown, to Hopkins, Washington, Hopkins Papers, FDRL, November 3, 1934. Francis to Hopkins, November 10, 1934.

6. Ibid.; Bruce McClure, Uniontown, Pa., to Homer Cummings, Washington, D.C. July 10, 1934, in Federal Emergency Relief Administration State Files 1933-36, Box 257, Pennsylvania General Minutes, WPA Records; D.P.F. Lowry, "Significant Facts Revealed by Real Property Inventory of Washington County," n.d., mimeo, in WPA Library, HD 268/WPA4, WPA Records.

7. Francis, Uniontown, to Hopkins, Washington, November 18, 1934, Hopkins Papers, FDRL.

8. *Uniontown Herald*, 11 April 1934.

9. *Pennsylvania Emergency Relief Handbook* (Harrisburg, 1933); W. R. Whitacre, "Preliminary Report of the Pennsylvania Thrift Garden Program," 26 July 1933, in Lorena Hickok Reports, October 28, 1933, Hopkins Papers, FDRL.

10. Gertrude Springer, "For Welfare and Security," *Survey* 70 (March 1934): 67-69; Frank J. Bruno, *Trends in Social Work, 1870-1956: A History Based on the Proceedings of the National Conference of Social Work* (New York, 1957).

11. Report of Arch Mandel to Aubrey Williams, March 11, 1934, on "C.W.A. and Relief, Fayette County, Pennsylvania (Uniontown)", in CWA, State Series, Pa., WPA Records.

12. Francis to Hopkins, November 18, 1934, Hopkins Papers, FDRL.

13. Ibid.; Francis to Hopkins, November 3, 1934, Hopkins Papers, FDRL.

14. Edwin Bronner, "The New Deal Comes to Pennsylvania: The Gubernatorial Election of 1934," *Pennsylvania History*, 27, no. 1 (January 1960), pp. 44-52; memorandum, Arch Mandel to Hopkins, April 10, 1935, Hopkins Papers, FDRL; telegram, Karl de Schweinitz, Philadelphia, to Hopkins, Washington, November 28, 1934, FERA State Files 1933-36, Box 257, Pa., Gen. Minutes, WPA Records.

15. Field Report on Pennsylvania, Lorena Hickok, Uniontown, Pa., to Hopkins, Washington, August 7-12, 1933, Box 67, HP.

16. J. C. Glassburn, Uniontown, Pa., to Hopkins, Washington, March 28, 1934, and Bruce Sterling, Uniontown, to Hopkins, April 5, 1934, in CWA, State Series, Pa., WPA Records.

17. "The Works Progress Administration in Fayette County: From The Beginning of the Program to June 30, 1938," WPA, Division of Information, Appraisal Report File, Pa., WPA Records.

18. Searle F. Charles, *Minister of Relief: Harry Hopkins and the Depression* (Syracuse, 1963).

19. George Babcock, Acting Field Representative, Harrisburg, Pa., to Colonel Lawrence Westbrook, Assistant Administrator, WPA, Washington, November 4, 1935, WPA, State Series, Pa., 610., WPA Records; "Excerpts from letters from Pennsylvania . . . sent to Miss Dewson by Mrs. [Emma Guffey] Miller, to Whom the Original Letters were Addressed," n.d., circa. 1934, CWA, State Series, Pa. Official, WPA Records.

20. Press Release, "Statement of Works Progress Administrator Edward N. Jones," 21 June 1936, WPA, State Series, Pa., 610, WPA Records; Field Report, Hickok to Hopkins, October 17, 1936, Box 68, HP; State Emergency Relief Administration Minutes, December 14, 1935, Record Group 23, Box 1, found in Pennsylvania Museum and Historical Commission, Harrisburg, Pennsylvania.

21. *Philadelphia Inquirer*, 7 and 30 May, 4 and 18 June 1936; *Pittsburgh Post-Gazette*, 11 May, 2 June 1936.

22. David Lawrence, Pittsburgh, Pa., to William C. Bullitt, Washington, April 15, 1938, Hopkins Papers, FDRL; Benjamine J. File, WPA Investigator to Howard O. Hunter, Deputy Commissioner, WPA, July 14, 1939, WPA, State Series, Pa., 610.2, WPA Records; Aubrey Williams, Washington, to J. E. Conzer, Labelle, Pennsylvania, July 28, 1938, WPA, State Series, Pa., 610, WPA Records.

23. Aubrey Williams, Washington, to Morris Sheppard, Philadelphia, October 24, 1938, WPA State Series, Pa., 610, WPA Records, Harrisburg *Evening News*, 13 September 1938; Philadelphia *Inquirer*, 4 November 1938; William H. Strong, Washington, D.C., to F. H. Dryden, Field Representative WPA, Philadelphia, January 30, 1939, State Series, Pa., 610, WPA Records.

24. William H. Strong, Washington, D.C., to F. H. Dryden, Field Representative WPA, Philadelphia, January 30, 1939, State Series, Pa., 610, WPA Records.

25. Hickok to Hopkins, July 24, 1935, Box 68, HP.

26. WPA Project Files, microfilmed, Record Projects T-935-938, Washington County, Pennsylvania, 1935-1939, WPA Records; report, "The Works Progress Administration—Washington County: From the Beginning of the Program to June 30, 1938," WPA, Division of Information, Appraisal Report File, Pa., WPA Records; report, "The Works Progress Administration—Fayette County . . . . ," ibid.

27. *Washington Reporter*, 15 October 1936; Federal Writers Project, Pa., *Homemaking Cottages* (Harrisburg, 1939), found in WPA Library, F/160/.E 35 A gd, WPA Records.

28. Madge Cruzon, Latrobe, Pennsylvania, to FDR, January 17, 1941, WPA, State Series, Pa., 651.321, WPA Records.

[8]
The City versus Relief: The Ordeal of Federal Works Programs in Philadelphia

The record of the Works Progress Administration in southwestern Pennsylvania is noteworthy. In Fayette, Washington, Greene, and Westmoreland counties, the agency left a legacy of paved roads, sanitary facilities, retaining walls, and public buildings. However, its achievements in Philadelphia are singularly unimpressive. To a great extent, this significant difference can be accounted for by examining the dynamics of the urban-federal relationship which appeared in its pristine form in the 1930s.

Historians impressed with the statistics on new streets, bridges, zoos, and public buildings have credited the New Deal with a needed face-lifting of urban America. Unquestionably, the New Deal's heritage of bridges, subways, and schools was significant, especially in cities such as New York and Chicago. However, whether in New York, Chicago, or, as in this case, Philadelphia, the federal programs of the 1930s left the massive pool of urban jobless undrained.

The New Deal's inability to achieve its goal of creating work for the mass unemployed was particularly egregious in Philadelphia. The problem stemmed in large part from Washington's failure to forge an urban policy capable of overcoming the kind of political obstructions which strangled its efforts in Philadelphia. The odyssey of the federal Works Progress Administration in Penn's city illustrates that, although informal federal-city relationships sufficed in pro-New Deal cities such as New York, in suspicious, conservative bastions such as Philadelphia, the barriers to effective cooperation were insurmountable.

In *A Nation of Cities* Mark Gelfand pointed out that by the 1930s the metropolis had long endured a distinctive form of isolation. Overlooked by the founding fathers, the city in America lacked any constitutional identity and existed merely as a creature of the states.[1] In the wake of the rapid urbanization of the late nineteenth century and as part of the Progressive movement, urban reformers launched home-rule campaigns to break the bonds fettering them to rurally dominated state governments. However, in practice Progressivism led more to civic boosterism than to an improvement of the city's questionable position in the federal system.[2] During the 1920s the subways, boulevards, skyscrapers, and other monuments of civic boosterism added billions of dollars to the bonded debt of cities such as Philadelphia, and weakened the tottering structure of urban finance.[3] The Great Depression exacerbated the economic and social woes of Philadelphia and other cities, and revealed the impotency of the voluntary relief structure that cities considered the first line of defense against mass misery.[4]

The city of brotherly love had not been alone in trusting in voluntarism; it was, however, one of the last cities to abandon it. When in desperation Detroit's Mayor Frank Murphy, seeking to force federal aid for urban jobless, convened in 1931 the first meeting of the United States Conference of Mayors, Philadelphia's chief executive, J. Hampton Moore, refused to attend. In fact, Philadelphia, headed in the early 1930s by the economically ultraconservative Moore, perhaps illustrates an extreme form of the urban provincialism into which the federal government intervened in 1933. As this chapter shows, Moore and Philadelphia's city council challenged the New Deal's ability to meet the needs of the city's ill-housed, ill-clothed, and ill-fed.[5]

Moore took office on January 1, 1932. The new major styled himself an independent Republican and an enemy of the political machine headed by boss William S. Vare.[6] In Philadelphia anti-Vareism meant that a politician drew his support, not from the historic river wards, but from the second- and third-generation ethnic American communities that comprised the outer zones of the city. Middle-class himself, Moore reveled in hobnobbing with the social and business elite and prided himself on his membership in exclusive Philadelphia clubs.[7] Yet, few envied the new mayor, for he had inherited from his predecessor, Harry Mackey, a mountain of unpaid debts. Like Chicago, Detroit, and other cities in 1932, Philadelphia was close to bankruptcy. In late 1931 the city government was regularly paying only a third of its employees and trying desperately to sell enough city bonds to pay nearly 26,000 city workers who had been without income for five weeks.[8]

After 1928, revenue from the city's main source of income — the property tax — declined sharply. The 9,000 sheriff's sales of 1928, followed by 12,000 in 1929 and 18,000 in 1931, helped lower by $300 million the assessed valuation of Philadelphia real estate between 1930 and 1932. Moreover, tax delinquency aggravated the effect of slashed assessed valuations. As early as 1928 uncollected taxes amounted to almost $7 million, by 1932 Philadelphia put the figure at well over $22 million. By refusing to take the necessary, if unpopular, course of fixing a higher tax rate to cover actual expenditures, the city council ignored the crisis as the city piled up annual deficits exceeding $7 million.[9]

Moore was elected in 1931 after a campaign in which he enjoyed the support of both independent Republicans and the Vare organization. Despite Vare's support, Moore pledged to fight for civic decency, to put an end to contractor steals, and to rid the city of bossism. Moore insisted that Philadelphia end graft and retrench. The city could not afford new City Hall annexes, subways, sesquicentennials, and $3-million stadiums. Under his administration, economy would reign.[10]

From the start, Moore rejected the need for big government. Like Herbert Hoover, he interpreted the job of government to be a supportive rather than a direct force in the nation's economic life. The government, according to Moore, should build canals, move commerce, keep the protective tariff, preserve the peace, and keep costs to a minimum. Primarily, Moore believed government should allow business the fullest opportunity to prosper and promote the general welfare.[11]

His faith that economy and retrenchment could unravel the Gordian knot of the city's financial crisis blinded Moore to the personal tragedy of mass unemployment and poverty caused by the depression. Moore's attitude toward poverty reflected his commitment to rugged individualism. According to Moore, the unemployed were spoiled by American plenty. If the poor would use their energies to work rather than to beg for relief, the depression would pass swiftly. Above all, Moore decried the idea already prevalent in 1932 that the city should provide relief or work for the unemployed. Despite the arguments of prominent Philadelphia social workers such as Karl deSchweinitz and Jacob Billikopf that voluntarism had reached the end of its resources, Moore continued to insist that voluntarism was the only way.[12] Moreover, he was convinced that relief represented a municipal expense the city could not afford. His plan was to restore public confidence in Philadelphia's bond issues by adopting an unyielding retrenchment policy. Thus, Moore dismissed half the employees of the city's Department of Public Works and slashed the salaries of other city employees by 23 percent. He exempted the already lowly paid police and firemen, but ordered policemen to take a two-week unpaid vacation.[13]

The city also stopped replacing broken lamps and halted the installation of new streetlights. More seriously, Moore decided to delay work on state-mandated sewerage and waterworks systems. The mayor recognized the need, but protested that, for the moment, the city could not afford these critical facilities.[14]

As Moore had planned, his retrenchment schemes brought timid investors back into the municipal bond market. By 1934 Philadelphia bonds were selling 21 points above par and at 5 percent interest instead of the 6 percent at which less cautious New York City was forced to sell its bonds.[15] Philadelphia's business organizations, the Chamber of Commerce, the Board of Trade, and the Real Estate Board all applauded the mayor. The Board of Trade resolved in December 1932 that "all employees unessential to the city and county administration . . . (should be) dropped from the payroll to insure a local tax rate at a minimum commensurate with thrift and good government, to the end that commerce and manufacturing of this city and port may be advanced and not retarded."[16] The Chamber of Commerce commended Moore for raising the value of city bonds and urged lower taxes to encourage the promotion of commercial enterprise.[17]

Whether public agencies disguised it as work, as food orders, or as cash, businessmen castigated relief as the "dole," a device that led straight to European socialism. "Once public funds are devoted to private relief . . .," warned the Board of Trade, "the slope becomes slippery and further declines are inevitable."[18]

Yet, despite all the rhetoric against socialistic experimenting and the "pork barrel," Philadelphia businessmen did not recoil from the "bold, persistent experimentation" of the New Deal. Most of them cheered Roosevelt's action of closing the nation's banks and commended him when he rushed legislation through Congress calling for government economy and a balanced budget.[19]

However, a dubious Mayor Moore remained adamantly opposed to the programs of the New Deal, particularly the Public Works Administration (PWA). The PWA fostered self-liquidating public works by granting cities 30 percent of the cost of projects and by making low-interest loans for the remaining 70 percent. In a June 1933 speech entitled "Imprudent Borrowing," Moore criticized the "political and finance engineers" who were coaxing the city to undertake $100 million in PWA projects. Moore accused the city comptroller, S. Davis Wilson, and Philadelphia's new Democratic party chairman, John B. Kelly, of heading this "new Band of Brothers."[20]

In 1933 Wilson ran for city comptroller as the candidate of the "Town Meeting Party," a fusion of Democrats and disgruntled Independent Republicans. Philadelphians could express their preference for works projects by voting for Wilson and for an item on the ballot calling for an increase in the city's debt limit. Naturally, Moore campaigned vigorously against both Wilson and the debt-increase item.[21]

The results of the 1933 election shattered Moore's expectations. Both Wilson and the debt increase won. "It may be," Moore reflected in a post-election statement to the press, "that the doling out at Washington of the money collected from all the people in aid of some of the people has become nationally popular and has found support in Philadelphia."[22]

The test of strength between Moore and the so-called reckless spenders came almost immediately. On November 9 the federal government dangled before the city $900 million in Civil Works Administration (CWA) funds. The offer unleashed a new feud over relief spending.[23]

Shortly after the creation of CWA, the Philadelphia city council was asked for $250,000 to provide materials for CWA projects to employ some 2,000 men. As December approached without council action on the CWA request Pennsylvania's Civil Works Administrator, Eric Biddle, threatened to make a public issue of the city's delay. Biddle avowed that the CWA had alloted Philadelphia $610,000 to employ 36,000 men and charged the city with spurning all responsibility for the destitute. "No economy program," he argued, "justifies the supreme disregard of Philadelphia's unemployed."[24]

Finally, in early January 1934, the council allocated over $500,000 for CWA materials. Then Moore astounded everyone by refusing to sign the necessary ordinances. At the time, state and federal projects in Philadelphia employed a little over 11,000 men, leaving unmet the largest part of the city's 36,000 man quota.[25]

With over 300,000 jobless Philadelphians registered at the state employment office, business conservatives now joined New Deal liberals in denouncing Moore's intransigence. CWA Administrator Harry Hopkins angrily threatened to transfer Philadelphia's CWA jobs outside the city, and the conservative *Philadelphia Inquirer* supported him. "Helpful Hampy," snarled one *Inquirer* editorial, "friend of the man who wants to work . . . who for five days let an ordinance approving money for CWA jobs rot on his desk."[26]

Pressure exerted upon Moore by business and the conservative press explains Philadelphia's even limited participation in the CWA program. By late 1933 Moore discovered himself alienated from the very people he had considered his constituency. The highly respected Bureau of Municipal Reserach contended that scrimping on money for recreation and streetlighting "simply short-changed" the city without saving much money. By 1934 evidence of this short-changing mounted. The Chamber of Commerce and the Board of Trade asked the city council to use federal monies to deepen Frankford Creek, whose rain-swollen, stench-burdened waters regularly spilled into surrounding commercial and residential districts. Owners of center-city property criticized Moore's cuts in police protection, especially when the press reported a crime wave of gambling, holdups, and murders. The Civic Club and the Board of Trade argued that federal funds could beautify the neglected banks of the Schuylkill River. Albert M. Greenfield, the city's real-estate giant, claimed that "Philadelphia should get its share" and demanded a massive slum-clearance project, while the Board of Trade trumpeted a plan to restore the Independence Hall area by replacing the adjoining slums with Curtis Mall.[27]

Unfortunately for the New Deal, which courted business support for both its relief and its recovery programs, the honeymoon in Philadelphia was all too brief. Criticism of Roosevelt followed the business sluggishness attending the spring of 1934. By October, Philadelphia businessmen were attacking the NRA vociferously. Charles Brinley, president of Philadelphia's American Pulley Company, blasted the NRA for failing to restrain cutthroat pricing and for recklessly adding to the federal debt. "The one crying need," he argued, "is to promote re-employment . . . in private, profit-making industry rather than in a variety of public and semi-public jobs of doubtful value and necessity."[28]

Loss of faith in the New Deal tempered business enthusiasm for projects of any kind. While the Chamber of Commerce and the Board of Trade still recognized the city's need for better sewage facilities, they advocated the most economical system available and observed that federal monies were encouraging other cities to "experiment" with "elaborate and fanciful sewage treatment plants." As far as Philadelphia businessmen were concerned, Moore had been right after all, and in 1935 they followed him in resisting Washington's next effort to bring federal funds to the city.[29]

To Moore and his cohorts, the Works Progress Administration (WPA) created in May 1935 epitomized feckless government. Dangling its $3,500,000 work-relief appropriation before American cities, the WPA enticed them, so sneered Moore, into extravagant spending sprees. Moreover, he suspected that the WPA would inundate the city and state with regiments of federal supervisors. Moore imagined "federal agents sneaking around establishing permanent bureaus here and there . . . and dictating how and where Philadelphia should spend its money."[30]

Bureaucratic tyranny notwithstanding, Moore stressed that Philadelphia could not contribute a cent toward WPA projects. He contended that the city welcomed federal money, but "not on the condition that federal authorities supervise the expenditures of sums within the confines of our municipality."[31] From time to time at Washington's behest, Moore even prepared long lists of possible projects, including sewage-disposal plants, transit facilities, underground concourses, and hospitals. However, Moore accompanied each list with a note affirming that the city had no borrowing capacity; therefore, only if the federal government made money available "as a free grant" could the city develop detailed plans.[32]

Moore now enjoyed substantial support for his stand. The business community, disillusioned with NRA and the mattressmaking-type projects of the Federal Emergency Relief Administration, defended the mayor's decision to withhold city funds from the WPA. In June 1935 the WPA allocated Philadelphia $60 million to employ 70,000 jobless people; however, by August fewer than 35,000 people had WPA work, and those who did toiled on non-city school, armory, and Navy Yard jobs.[33]

Washington hounded WPA state administrator Edward Jones to "get these men to work." And even after Jones had threatened to give the city's WPA workers jobs in the suburbs, Moore failed to act. To the horror of the *Philadelphia Bulletin,* which had ridiculed Jones's warning as a "dire threatening," a string of trains pulled out of Pennsylvania Station early in the morning on October 8 to transport city WPA workers to projects in Bucks and Montgomery counties. November 1 found 700 Philadelphia WPA workers laboring in the suburbs. By December there were 12,000.[34]

While Hopkins fretted over Jones's slow progress in finding WPA jobs in Philadelphia, he realized the problem. Lorena

Hickok had told Hopkins in July that Moore fought any effort to bring federal money into the city "except on leaf-raking terms." According to Hickok, Moore and his supporters were the "most completely Tory gang in the country, almost unbelievably bitter toward the President."[35] Jones fumed that "Philadelphia is the only city where both (the legislature and the administration) are not only unsympathetic, not only indifferent, but secretly desirous of seeing the program . . . fail on the grounds, as frankly stated by one influential person, that 'if these people were given work, Roosevelt would get the credit and we're against Roosevelt.'[36] Later, Jones excoriated Philadelphia's "callous" bosses and "financial dictators," who seemed more concerned about maintaining the selling price of the city's bonds above par than in cooperating to furnish employment for 68,000 unemployed men and women.[37]

The WPA's record in Philadelphia for the first year (June 1935 to June 1936) was deplorable. While in Pittsburgh the WPA built 156 miles of streets and roads, only thirty-three miles were laid in Philadelphia. Less than six miles of sewers were completed in the city, compared with the thirty-three miles in Pittsburgh and 85 miles in suburban Montgomery County.[38]

Yet, that for which Edward Jones had criticized Moore – the mayor's commitment to raising the value of city bonds rather than spending for work relief – many Philadelphians praised, especially the city's many tax-beleaguered homeowners and businessmen.[39] Despite the growing disenchantment with conservative rule in Philadelphia, as measured by the increasing size of the Democratic vote, the city in 1935 returned a Republican mayor. However, the new mayor, S. Davis Wilson, was a strange breed of Republican.

Despite his affiliation with the GOP, Wilson promised to be a welcome replacement for Moore, at least to federal relief officials. Prior to his election as mayor in 1935, Wilson had compiled an extraordinarily checkered career, which included serving as assistant to the United States Senate chaplain, Edward Everett Hale, operating an auto-body repair shop in New Jersey, and investigating Sunday blue-law violations at the

1927 Philadelphia Sesquicentennial. In 1932 Philadelphia voters elected Wilson city comptroller.[40]

As comptroller, Wilson's flair for concocting city budgets out of straw infuriated both Moore and the somber-faced accountants at the Bureau of Municipal Research. In 1934, for example, he based his budget estimates on "expected" income from the sale of city real estate and on the "expected" collection of delinquent taxes. Although Wilson's budgets balanced on paper, only the gullible believed they would balance in practice. Yet, the city council approved Wilson's "magical budgets," fully aware that, despite the inevitably larger deficits, Wilson had at least saved the council the chagrin of voting a tax increase.

Wilson's budget practices enhanced his image as the "tribune of the people." As the "kingfish" of Philadelphia, Wilson boisterously championed five-cent trolley fares, cheaper electricity, lower gas rates, and lower taxes. However, there was never dogmatism in his rhetoric; indeed, Wilson lacked any strong ideological bent. Aside from a fervid admiration for Woodrow Wilson—he named his first child Woodrow—Wilson avoided identifying himself strongly with any party, preferring to woo the city's large independent vote.[41]

In 1935, after the resurgent Democratic party rebuffed his overture to be their mayoral candidate, Wilson offered himself to the Republicans. Although oil millionaire J. Howard Pew donated $200,000 to assure City Treasurer WillB Hadley's nomination, the Republican party, fearing a Democratic victory, selected the popular Wilson. The Democrats chose party chairman John B. Kelly, who lost to Wilson after a hotly contested race in which city Republicans accused Roosevelt's postmaster general and political strategist, James A. Farley, of personally orchestrating Kelly's campaign.

The Republicans claimed victory in 1935, but few believed the chameleon Wilson stood for traditional Republican principles. Incredibly, his name was conspicuously absent from a list of prominent Republicans read at his own inaugural dinner. In no time at all Wilson vindicated his party's distrust, for within months after his election, he journeyed to Washington to shop for the Democratic convention for Philadelphia and to extoll Roosevelt as the nation's best choice in 1936.[42]

The Democrats, too, had no illusion about Wilson's politics. But, after Moore, the new mayor's enthusiasm for cooperation delighted New Dealers such as Hopkins. Arm in arm with prominent Philadelphia Democrats such as John B. Kelly, Wilson led the battle for a new work-relief program and committed the city to participate fully in the WPA. Wilson complained that, while the city's tax money was paying for work relief, thousands of unemployed Philadelphians were begging for jobs. He reasoned that work relief afforded an opportunity to rehabilitate the city's neglected public services, and maintained that the city could finance the cost of WPA projects by pawning its waterworks and subways. Because both were self-supporting, he considered these systems exempt from the city's state-imposed debt limit.[43]

During the first few months of Wilson's administration, the works program dominated the mayor's agenda. He launched his drive for federal works by announcing a $5-million bond issue for subway completion projects and then challenged his critics to block it in court. To speed the projects, Wilson cleared away WPA red tape, bypassed Harrisburg, and dispatched proposals directly to Washington.

By late January 1936, 45,000 Philadelphians were working for the WPA, and Wilson predicted that these would shortly be joined by another 40,000. His enthusiasm was heightened when he succeeded in bringing the 1936 Democratic convention to Philadelphia. Bolstered by the promise of the upcoming Joe Louis – Jim Braddock prizefight and by a $200,000 check —over half of it from Republican businessmen—Wilson outbid both Chicago and Los Angeles for the convention. As a result, Philadelphia received $600,000 in convention-related projects including the cleaning of the City Hall, the renovating of Independence Hall, the refurbishing of the Commercial Museum, the repairing and the remodeling of Convention Hall, and the repairing of city streets.

None of the work proceeded without difficulty. For example, because of union problems, the rehabilitation of City Hall started months after the conventioneers had departed; in fact, the WPA did not complete the City Hall project until 1938. The Democrats planned to stage the main activities of their June gala in Convention Hall and hold New Deal progress exhibits in the nearby Commercial Museum. Consequently, the renovation of these buildings was urgent. However, the WPA badly miscalculated the cost of all the projects, especially Independence Hall. In order to "pretty up" the shrine, WPA workers were called to paint the building inside and out and to repair the flagstone walks. The city estimated the cost at a little over $8,000; the final cost to the WPA was closer to $17,000.[44]

After the convention, Wilson regularly visited Washington. In August, he persuaded Hopkins to give the city $100 million in projects designed to employ 60,000 people over the coming winter. Naturally, Wilson welcomed Roosevelt's victory in November, especially since Philadelphia had overwhelmingly approved an item on the ballot permitting the city to "change the purpose" for which $10 million "in scattered and tag-end issues" had originally been authorized. Roosevelt's victory and this "green light" for spending moved Wilson to declare that "the city's future never appeared brighter." Within five weeks the mayor sat at the White House chatting with Roosevelt about filtration plants, sewage-disposal systems, and his other dreams for a federally financed transformation of Philadelphia.[45]

Shortly after the 1936 election, City Council voted Wilson thanks for his efforts in obtaining funds for "much needed improvements." Yet, despite this popular approval of WPA spending and the willingness of the city council to get at least "our share," by the end of 1938 Philadelphia had clearly failed to benefit significantly from New Deal largess. While cities such as New York, Cleveland, and Chicago could point to Triborough bridges, massive waterfront projects, new schools, city warehouses, zoos, and other projects, Philadelphia's record was disappointing. Wilson confessed as much in March 1938, when he admitted in an "Appraisal" that the WPA chiefly performed "routine tasks that could not have been done were it not for the assistance of the federal government." The WPA did paint fire hydrants, raze the walls of useless city buildings, improve pumping stations, renovate police stations, and perform chores in the city's parks and playgrounds. Unquestionably, the city benefited from the hundreds of "low-cost" WPA white-collar jobs. For example, workers prepared a comprehensive record of all delinquent taxes and water rents from 1883 to 1934. Other workers compiled a study of the city's bonds from 1929 to 1938.

But the city sponsored few large construction projects. It did, however, undertake a job at the Hog Island Airport. The project called for leveling one piece of land and filling in 200 acres of swampland. To keep as many people working as possible during the first few years, the men were compelled to use shovels and wheelbarrows rather than earth-moving equipment. By the spring of 1936 some use was being made of three gasoline locomotives, and in 1937 a steamshovel was employed. The manual-labor approach incited considerable criticism since the project lagged months behind schedule and was still unfinished in 1940.[46]

While the Philadelphia jobless cried for large projects employing hundreds of men, the city's need for sewerage and waterworks continued unmet. Although WPA repaired a number of cracked and collapsed sewer pipes, requests for sanitation projects were often returned to the city with the attached statement that "steps be taken to obtain . . . additional contributions . . . (to) reduce the federal man-month cost on non-labor items."[47]

Meanwhile, Dr. Haven Emerson, director of the Institute of Public Health of New York, called Philadelphia's water supply "worse than that of any other large city in the country."[48] After Wilson failed to get the city council to approve funds for a $70-million filtration plant, the mayor shocked many Philadelphians by describing the city's drinking water as "filtered filth." As late as 1940, *Time* magazine found a "bluish-black liquid stinking with chlorine, puckery and alum" gushing from Philadelphia taps.[49]

Although Philadelphia's need for public works was obvious and the city's jobless were numerous, the WPA never filled its quota. Wilson had promised to find 85,000 WPA jobs for the unemployed, but by the spring of 1938 the WPA employed fewer than 49,000—a sad commentary on the outcome of Wilson's ambitious program.

In truth the city had scraped together all the low-cost jobs it could find for which it had materials. Therefore, the WPA stamped many projects that had been approved for Philadelphia (such as destroying poison ivy in city parks) "No allocation involved; therefore, no warrant drawn or necessary." Although the city had thirty-seven sanitation projects between June 1935 and December 1938, only fifteen cost over $50,000. On the other hand, between those dates the city had fifty-four park projects which involved low-cost materials. Although twenty-one of these projects cost over $50,000, only eight fell under $10,000. Many WPA projects in Philadelphia fit into the white-collar category. Although they were modestly priced, white-collar jobs employed few people. While the city had ninety-seven such projects, forty-seven of them involved less than a $10,000 expenditure, and only thirteen cost over $50,000. Even the city's state-sponsored state street projects and federally sponsored shipyard and arsenal projects provided too few jobs to place a breadwinner in each of Philadelphia's 70,000 jobless families.[50]

In July 1938 Harry R. Halloran, WPA director in Philadelphia, lamented that "the failure of the city administration to appropriate its share of funds for WPA projects kept Philadelphia from full realization of the benefits of the government agency." Halloran correctly charged that in Philadelphia the WPA bore the brunt of city improvements. Yet, while the WPA allowed Philadelphia "a liberal and adequate program, the city failed to appropriate the comparatively small amount necessary for the purchase of material for a full program."[51]

There are several reasons for the WPA's poor showing in Philadelphia. In late 1936 the city's economic situation worsened. Wilson flamboyantly slashed the city budget from $83 million to $76 million and retrenched 1,300 city employees. But once again the mayor's budget proved unrealistic; by January 1937 he was forced to add $716,320 to it for "essential city services."[52] Wilson's critics once more scored the mayor for devising a "straw" budget, but he retorted that a realistic $90-million budget was politically unpalatable.

The city was impoverished. While most other city sanitation departments used trucks in 1938, Philadelphia still used horse-drawn trash wagons and sprinklers. By 1939 the municipal debt exceeded $40 million and, in order to meet operating expenses, the city was negotiating with a private firm to contract a loan on its $50 million gas works.[53]

The fiscal crisis taxed the capacity of the city council. Although most of the council resembled Moore in age and in social philosophy, they had initially embraced Wilson's budget "magic," including his plan to use the WPA to solve the city's ills. After 1937 Wilson's requests for funds to carry on the WPA met with little favor from an increasingly recalcitrant council. In 1937 the council budgeted a piddling $300,000 for WPA projects. When the WPA had exhausted that appropriation, Wilson ordered the council to transfer $770,000 from streetlighting funds over to WPA operations. However, the council delayed action until it was forced to act by the protests of labor unions, unemployed groups, and Wilson's threat to levy additional taxes to care for the 18,000 who had been thrown onto direct relief after they had lost their WPA jobs.[54]

The halting progress of the works program in the city disgusted WPA officials. In May 1938 WPA area-investigator Phillip Dryden reported that the council had tabled every request for funds needed to operate city projects. Without funds, only 9,000 WPA workers remained on the payroll; in a few weeks there would be only 5,000. Again labor and the unemployed protested. While the pro-New Deal press issued news releases showing the benefits of WPA employment and berated the city's refusal to provide sponsor's funds, 1,700 members of the AFL and the Congress of Industrial Organizations (CIO) gathered at City Hall Plaza to demand that the city council appropriate $5 million for a full WPA program.[55]

At the same time that Philadelphia's budget-conscious city council was withholding appropriations for WPA work, the WPA in Washington launched its own retrenchment. Throughout 1936 Hopkins periodically trimmed WPA spending. Unfortunately, as the Philadelphia County Relief Board pointed out, every cut in WPA rolls enlarged the city's direct relief load. Although WPA surveys demonstrated that furloughed WPA workers rarely found "real work," Washington accelerated the WPA retrenchment in late 1936.

The WPA eliminated workers from all projects, particularly from the white-collar programs. The agency's budget reductions in July 1937 led to a campaign to save the WPA. Project workers distributed cards to local merchants reading: "This money was earned on WPA: It is helping your business. If you want more of this money, write to President Roosevelt to stop all dismissals."[56] Despite the campaign, the layoffs continued. On July 30, 1937, delegates of the 5,000-member Philadelphia Joint Action Committee rushed to Washington to "vigorously protest the wholesale layoffs of WPA workers, creating a disastrously large pool of hungry, desperate, unorganized workers and a dangerous threat to trade union wages and working conditions."[57]

Amidst the 1937 recession, the WPA laid off 400 white-collar workers in Philadelphia and cut the wages on white-collar projects from $90 to $70 a month. By 1939 the WPA was eliminating all "undesirable," that is, "controversial," projects, such as theater projects and those having high labor or high supervisory costs. In addition, the WPA was firing personnel over forty-five years of age and furloughing others who had worked on projects for eighteen months. Some WPA officials openly admitted that the program had not succeeded in its mission. Aubrey Williams wrote in 1938 that the government was shirking its duty, "especially when the impression has been widely given that federal work relief would provide for all able-bodied unemployed." According to Williams, "It had never done so."[58]

The city council's obdurate position on relief in Philadelphia, as well as the WPA's toughened position, was in accord with America's post-1937 boredom with relief. Even Philadelphia labor moderated its concern for the unemployed. The jurisdictional conflicts between the AFL and the new and more aggressive Congress of Industrial Organizations, plus the unpopularity of the CIO's sit-down strikes, served to push the AFL into a more conservative stance on such issues as relief. The *Progressive Labor World*, which in early 1938 became the spokesman for Philadelphia's Central Labor Union, denounced the National Labor Relations Board as a tool of the CIO. In the latter part of 1938 even the once-militant hosiery union evidenced a new "willingness to play ball" with business. Under the "Philadelphia Plan" the hosiery union offered the industry a three-year guarantee against strikes and accepted a voluntary wage cut.[59] The *Progressive Labor World* welcomed the new year by attacking New Deal spending, calling for a general overhaul of relief, and expressing alarm that the WPA had become a "permanent federal construction company." Actually, union spokesmen feared that the depression had created a giant pool of jobless men which, if dumped onto the labor market, would endanger all of labor's gains. Labor demanded a permanent public-works program to keep these workers off the market.[60]

The strike activity of 1937 greatly alarmed business, while the subsequent recession convinced it that the depression would end only when the New Deal did. The Board of Trade viewed the 1937 recession as "the public's desire to escape the discouraging effects . . . (of) unwise legislative policies." According to the board, businessmen were "confused and discouraged by menacing, uncertain and repressive propaganda from Washington."[61]

Like labor, business accepted the inevitability of a large pool of unemployable labor. Rather than take needed money from business for expensive relief programs, business favored the cheapest possible solution to the welfare problem. The president of Curtis Publishing Company argued that heavy taxes of public assistance arrested potential business activity; therefore, the removal of the wall of welfare taxes would promote business and solve the relief problem.[62]

Social workers such as Gertrude Springer also expressed a nagging concern that America harbored a "shadowy valley of relief." Springer found "a growing willingness to accept (relief) as the inevitable, even the proper way of life for the unemployed."[63] Many people began to feel that WPA workers were just "reliefers" or bums. The song "WPA" portrayed the popular image of the WPA workers:

Dubya-pee-ay . . . Dubya-pee-ay . . .
Sleep while you work, while you rest,
While you play
Lean on your shovel to pass time
away . . .
Don't mind the boss if he's cross when
you're gay,
He'll get a pink slip next month anyway.
Three little letters that make life okay,
Dybya-pee-ay . . . Dubya-pee-ay . . .[64]

Not as easily sequestered as the poor client on the direct relief rolls, the WPA worker became a joke. It was all part of a process whereby America resigned itself to the harsh fact that the country sheltered a permanent class of unemployed and unemployable people.

Confronted by a sickly urban economy and massive unemployment, J. Hampton Moore had blatantly obstructed federal work-relief efforts. But even under S. Davis Wilson's friendly administration, federal work relief fared little better. In many respects the WPA's failure in Philadelphia was part of a greater failure of the New Deal to launch a frontal attack on the problems of urban-industrial America. Even when cities took full advantage of the WPA, relief remained a serious problem until late 1939 and 1940, when the armaments industry started to rehire large numbers of workers.

The New Deal concentrated its efforts not on cities, but on the cities' poor and jobless. The depression forced Democrats and Republicans alike to bend their rhetoric to the needs of the working class. Throughout the 1930s the AFL, the CIO, the Unemployed Councils and Workers' Alliances kept the grievances of the worker and the workless forcibly expressed. For many, the Democratic party became an effective sounding board, giving the hithertofore inarticulate American worker a national platform.

Nevertheless, by 1940 the urban point of view still lacked a strong advocate at the federal level. Despite the National Resources Board, the Federal Housing Administration, the United States Housing Administration, and Charles Merriam's

Urbanism Report, the federal government had not devised a plan to coordinate the development of urban America. Cities such as Philadelphia still floundered in an economic morass. Lacking a viable tax base and devoid of real borrowing power, Philadelphia had strained, even machinated, to scrape up funds for public-works projects. Moreover, by tying "work" to "relief," by constraining itself to pay "prevailing wages" pegged to a "budgetary deficiency," and by forbidding relief work to compete with "legitimate" labor, the WPA, like future federal programs, was chained to the frail economy of the city. At its best, the WPA operated as a beacon light that penetrated urban neighborhoods, segregated by class, race, and ethnicity, and marked the federal government as the primary architect and source of social welfare in the modern city. Therefore, for many of the working class and ethnic groups, the New Deal helped break down the worst isolation of city neighborhoods segregated by class and ethnicity. However, as the next chapter explains, the New Deal had less success in treating the isolation of the racial ghetto.[65]

NOTES

1. Mark I. Gelfand, *A Nation of Cities: The Federal Government and Urban America, 1933-1965* (New York, 1975); pp. 23-105; James T. Patterson, *The New Deal and the States: Federalism in Transition* (Princeton, 1969), passim.

2. Gelfand, *Nation of Cities*, pp. 18-22; Samuel Haber, *Efficiency and Uplift: Scientific Management in the Progressive Era, 1890-1920* (Chicago, 1964), passim; Zane Miller, *Boss Cox's Cincinnati: Urban Politics in the Progressive Era* (New York, 1968), pp. 147-60; Samuel P. Hays, "The Politics of Reform in Municipal Government in the Progressive Era," *Pacific Northwest Quarterly* 554 (October 1964): 157-69.

3. Hays, "Politics of Reform in Municipal Government; Roy Lubove, *Twentieth Century Pittsburgh: Government, Business and Environmental Change* (Pittsburgh, 1969), pp. 1-58; John F. Bauman, "The City, the Depression and Relief: The Philadelphia Experience, 1929-1939" (Ph.D. diss., Rutgers University, 1969), pp. 1-30.

4. Bauman, "*The City, the Depression and Reliefs*", pp. 114-54; Bonnie R. Fox, "Unemployment Relief in Philadelphia, 1930-1932: A Study of the Depression's Impact on Voluntarism, *The Pennsylvania Magazine of History and Biography*, 93, no. 1 (January 1969), 86-109.

5. Gelfand, *Nation of Cities*, pp. 35-40.

6. E. Eigby Baltzell, *Philadelphia Gentlemen: The Making of a National Upper Class* (Chicago, 1971), pp. 158-72; Marguis W. Childs and John Coburn Turner, "The

Real Philadelphia Story," *Forum and Century* 103 (June 1940): 289; the "Catalogue Main Line Hall of Fame, 1887-1937," found in the Samuel Matthew Vauclain Collection, Historical Society of Pennsylvania, Philadelphia, Pennsylvania.

7. Edward C. Banfield and James Q Wilson, *City Politics* (Cambridge, 1963), pp. 138-53; Samuel J. Astorino, "The Decline of the Republican Dynasty in Pennsylvania: 1929-1934" (Ph.D. diss., University of Pittsburgh, 1962); see numerous social-club membership cards, invitations to social and business clubs and organizations and adulatory correspondence from Philadelphia's social and business illustrious, in the J. Hampton Moore Collection, Historical Society of Pennsylvania, Philadelphia, Pennsylvania, hereinafter cited as MC.

8. Philadelphia *Public Ledger*, 19 December 1931; New York *Times*, 27 October 1931; William C. Beyer, "Financial Dictators Replace Political Boss," *National Municipal Review* 22 (April 1933): 163-64.

9. William C. Beyer, Philadelphia, to J. Ward Moffett, Philadelphia, Executive Secretary of the Philadelphia Realty Board, February 11, 1936, Bureau of Municipal Research Papers, Philadelphia, Pennsylvania, hereinafter cited as BMRP; Beyer, "Philadelphia – A Decade of Deficits," address before the meeting of the Philadelphia Conference on Government, 9 February 1934, BMRP; R. C. Atkinson, "Philadelphia's Dangerous Deficit," *National Municipal Review* 20 (November 1931): 679.

10. J. Hampton Moore "Statement for the Press," 15 October 1931 M.C.; Philadelphia *Public Ledger*, 14 September 1931; C. W. Carroll, president of Universal Publishing Syndicate, to Moore, Philadelphia, July 20, 1931, questioning Moore's link with Vare, M.C.

11. Robert Edward Drayer, "J. Hampton Moore, an Old Fashioned Republican" (Ph.D. diss., University of Pennsylvania, 1961), pp. 331-33; Herman Blum, Philadelphia, Pa., president of Craftex Mills, to Moore, Philadelphia, 29 January 1932, M.C.; "Thoughts and suggestions that could be used during the campaign of J. Hampton Moore for Mayor" (ca. June 1931), MC.

12. Moore speech on "Thrift and Its Virtues," n.d. (ca. October 1932), MC; Moore radio talk on William Penn, October 24, 1932, MC; Edmund J. Fitzmaurice, Philadelphia, to Moore, Philadelphia, November 19, 1931, MC; Moore, "Address to Republican State Committee," June 9, 1934, MC.

13. William C. Beyer, Philadelphia, to Albert S. Faught, Philadelphia, August 5, 1932, BMRP; Moore, Philadelphia, to Kern Dodge, Philadelphia, June 8, 1932, MC; Moore, "Statement for the Press," 10 June 1932, MC.

14. Moore, Philadelphia, to Dr. Theodore Appel, chairman of Sanitary Board, November 28, 1932, MC; news clipping, "Mayor Puts Budget Balancing Ahead of Building" (ca. June 2, 1932), MC.

15. Full-page advertisement placed by Corn Exchange Bank of Philadelphia, "LET'S PAY OUR TAXES AND STOP SHERIFF SALES," in the Philadelphia *Public Ledger*, 3 July 1933; S.C. Kelton, secretary of Rohm and Haas Company, Philadelphia, to Moore, November 8, 1933, MC; George Woodward, Congressman, 6th District, Philadelphia, to Moore, June 5, 1934, MC.

16. Minutes of the Philadelphia Board of Trade, December 19, 1932, in the Philadelphia Board of Trade Papers, Historical Society of Pennsylvania,

Philadelphia, Pennsylvania, hereinafter cited as Board of Trade Minutes; *Philadelphia* (magazine of the Philadelphia Chamber of Commerce), April 1932, pp. 8-9.

17. *Philadelphia* April 1932, pp. 8-9; Board of Trade Minutes, March 20, 1933.

18. Board of Trade Minutes, April 18, 1932, and February 20, 1933; C. W. Asbury to Henry Watson, January 14, 1932, Board of Trade Minutes; see *Federal Loans to Aid Unemployment, Hearings*, Senate Committee on Banking and Currency, Seventy-second Congress, 1st session, 1932.

19. Philadelphia Board of Trade, Philadelphia, to President Roosevelt, Washington, D.C., March 20, 1933, Board of Trade Minutes; Minutes of the Philadelphia Drug Exchange, May 10, 1933, Philadelphia Drug Exchange Papers, Historical Society of Pennsylvania, Philadelphia, Pa., Philadelphia Booster's Association and a number of other civic organizations in Philadelphia sponsored a prosperity parade to support FDR's plan for business recovery; see George G. Meade, Philadelphia Booster's Association, to Moore, April 8, 1933, MC.

20. Moore, "Imprudent Borrowing," June 20, 1933, MC.

21. Philadelphia *Public Ledger*, 21 June 1933; script of radio addresses by Moore on station WIP, 6 November 1933, MC.

22. Moore, "Statement from the Mayor's Office," November 8, 1933, MC.; George Hoffman, Philadelphia, to Moore, Philadelphia, November 10, 1933, MC.

23. Corrington Gill, *Wasted Manpower: The Challenge of Unemployment* (New York, 1939), pp. 163 ff.

24. Telegram, Eric Biddle, Philadelphia, to Moore, Philadelphia, 29 November 1933, MC; *Journal of City Council*, hereinafter JCC, Appendix 119 (November 1933, p. 395; memo, J. R. Blough, Philadelphia, to Harry Hopkins, Washington, November 24, 1933, in Record Group (RG) 69, FERA, State Series 610., Pa., Records of the Works Progress Administration, National Archives, Washington, D.C., hereinafter cited as WPA Records.

25. JCC (January-July, 1934), pp. 2-3; Philadelphia *Public Ledger*, 2 January 1934, and 7 January 1934; James M. Myles of the Central Labor Union, Philadelphia, to Edwin Cox, president of City Council, December 18, 1933, RG 69, FERA, State Series, 40, Pa., WPA Records.

26. *Philadelphia Inquirer*, 11 January 1934; Frank Burch, secretary of the CLU, Philadelphia, to Moore, October 20, 1933, MC; telegram, John A. Phillips, Harrisburg, to Harry Hopkins, Washington, August 24, 1934, RG 69, FERA, State Series, 460, Pa., WPA Records.

27. William C. Beyer, Philadelphia, to George Woodward, Philadelphia, January 19, 1933, BMRP; Walter Yoy and John E. Clemmons of the Citizens Civic League, Philadelphia, to Moore, January 10, 1933, MC; Board of Trade Minutes, November 16, 1934, and April 2, 1935, and February 1, 1935; Morris B. Levitt, Philadelphia, Counsel of the Vandalism Committee of the South Philadelphia Housing Association, "Report on Slum Clearance," June 20 1933, a memo found in Historical Society of Pennsylvania, Philadelphia.

28. Philadelphia *Public Ledger*, 4 April 1934; Charles E. Brinley, Philadelphia, chairman of Chamber of Commerce's Industrial Research and Development Committee and president of American Pulley Company, "Not Halfway Up the Business Hill," *Philadelphia*, October 1934, pp. 12-15.

29. Board of Trade Minutes, April 15, 1935, and June 17, 1935, and January 27, 1936; Drug Exchange Minutes, April 10, 1935, and May 8, 1935, and May 9, 1935.

30. Moore, untitled report on finance, n.d. (ca. April-May 1935). MC; Moore, "Bond Club Speech," February 19, 1935; MC; Philadelphia *Record*, 15 June 1935.

31. Moore, untitled report of federal grants and city finance, n.d. (ca. April-May 1935), MC; Moore, "Statement from the Mayor's Office," in response to a call from Mayor Phillip B. Fleming, acting administrator of FERA, for a list of projects, February 12, 1935, MC.

32. Moore, "Statement from the Mayor's Office," submitting further list of projects, February 14, 1935, MC; Moore, "Philadelphia Relief Projects Submitted to PWA, July 25, 1935," MC.

33. William C. Beyer, Philadelphia, to Newton, Abbe and Company, Philadelphia, March 22, 1935, BMRP; Harold Evans to President and Members of City Council introducing "A Balanced Program of Twelve Public Works Projects fo Philadelphia," Albert Smith Faught Papers, Historical Society of Pennsylvania, Philadelphia.

34. Philadelphia *Record*, 27 July 1935; *Philadelphia Inquirer*, 7 August 1935; transcript of telephone conversation between Edward N. Jones, Harrisburg, and Colonel Lawrence Westbrook, Washington, RG 69, August 14, 1935, WPA, State Series, 610, Pa., WPA Records.

35. Lorena Hickok, Philadelphia, to Harry Hopkins, Washington, July 14, 1935, in Harry Hopkins Papers, Franklin D. Roosevelt Library, Hyde Park, New York, hereinafter cited as Hopkins Papers.

36. Memo, Edward N. Jones, Harrisburg, to Hopkins, Washington, August 27, 1935, RG 69, WPA, State Series, 610, Pa., WPA Records.

37. Letter written by Edward N. Jones which he suggested Hopkins send to J. David Stern of the *Philadelphia Record*. It was not sent. Letter forwarded to Hopkins, September 13, 1935, RG 69, WPA State Series, 610, Pa., WPA Records.

38. Works Progress Administration, *One Year of W.P.A. in Pennsylvania* (Washington, 1936).

39. B. F. Kutchen, Philadelphia, to Moore, November 1, 1935, MC; Henry C. Miller to Moore, October 7, 1935, MC; A. Edward Newton, Philadelphia, to Moore, October 22, 1935, MC.

40. *Time*, 26, 16 September 1936, p. 16; Henry T. Walnut, "S. Davis Wilson," in J. T. Salter, ed., *Boss Rule: Portraits in City Politics* (New York, 1935) p. 191.

41. Walnut, "S. Davis Wilson," pp. 282-305; William C. Beyer, *Philadelphia Public Ledger*, 5 November 1935; for a chronicle of Philadelphia politics in the 1930s, see the newsclip file in the Papers of John B. Kelly, Free Library of Philadelphia, Philadelphia, Pennsylvania.

42. "A New Kind of Boss," *Time*, 35 (6 May 1940), 16; Philadelphia *Public Ledger*, 5 November 1935; for a chronicle of Philadelphia politics in the 1930's, see the newsclip file in the Papers of John B. Kelly, Free Library of Philadelphia, Philadelphia, Pennsylvania.

43. *JCC* (28 June 1933), pp. 231-32; *JCC* (18 January 1934), pp. 37, 102-03.

44. S. Davis Wilson, Philadelphia, to William H. Connell, Philadelphia, local FERA Administrator, RG 69, FERA, State Series, 451-53.1, Pa., WPA Records; Wilson, Philadelphia, to Joseph Baker, Washington, Assistant FERA Administrator, RG, 69, FERA, State Series, 451, Pa., WPA Records; *JCC* (14 June 1936), pp. 253-54.

45. *Philadelphia Inquirer*, 4 November 1936, 5 November 1936; *New York Times*, 5 November 1936; S. Davis Wilson, *First Annual Report* (Philadelphia, 1936), p. 7.

46. *JCC* (19 November 1936), p. 210; report of S. Davis Wilson in Brief of Pennsylvania Community Appraisal Committee Report, Division of Statistics, WPA records; Project Files, 3224, Reel, T. 935, WPA Records; draft of letter to the President regarding Philadelphia airport project (ca. 1937), RG 69, WPA State Series, 651.110, Pa., WPA records; Aubrey Williams, Washington, to Major Fitzpatrick, Philadelphia, February 25, 1936, regarding use of locomotives on the airport project, and F. C. Harrington, Washington, Assistant Administrator, to F. C. Dryden, Philadelphia, April 14, 1936, regarding inspection of the airport project, RG 69, WPA, State Series, 651.110, Pa., WPA Records.

47. F. C. Harrington, Washington, to Edward N. Jones, Harrisburg, December 11, 1936, RG 69, WPA, State Series, 51.108, Pa., WPA Records; records of the Division of Engineering and Construction, Offical Project 65-23-1775, Work Project 1883, which called for a sewage treatment plant for Philadelphia, WPA Records; Wilson, *First Annual Report*, p. 7.

48. Address given by Dr. Haven Emerson on "The Kind of Health Department Philadelphia Should Have," January 31, 1938, League of Women Voters Papers, Historical Society of Pennsylvania, Philadelphia, hereinafter cited as LWVP.

49. *Time*, 14 February 1938, p. 47; C. A. Little, Philadelphia, to Philadelphia League of Women Voters, LWVP.

50. Project Files, 1935-1936, 3424, T935, and 1938, 3571, T936, and 1939-1942, 4248, T937, WPA Records; Philadelphia *Record*, 15 October 1936; Works Progress Administration, *One Year of W.P.A.* (Washington, 1937), pp. 83-96.

51. *Philadelphia Inquirer*, 25 July 1938.

52. Philadelphia *Record*, 6 January 1937 and 30 January 1937; *Philadelphia Inquirer*, 16 November 1937; S. Davis Wilson, *Second Annual Report* (Philadelphia 1937), p. 4.

53. Philadelphia *Record*, 23 November 1937; William C. Beyer, Philadelphia, to American Fabricated Steel Company, Philadelphia, November 2, 1938, BMRP; *Philadelphia Inquirer*, 28 February 1939.

54. Telephone conversation, Banks Hudson, Washington, Deputy Administrator, with Colonel Mehaffey, Philadelphia, April 22, 1937, RG 69, WPA, State Series, 651.110, Pa., WPA Records; *JCC*, Appendix 308 (14 December 1937).

55. Telephone conversation, Aubrey Williams, Washington, with Dryden, Philadelphia, January 14, 1938, in Aubrey Williams Papers. Franklin D. Roosevelt Library, Hyde Park, New York, hereinafter cited as FDRL. Emerson Ross, Philadelphia, to Aubrey Williams, Washington, March 22, 1938, AWP; *JCC* (3 February 1938), p. 54; Wilson's address to the Council in *JCC*, Appendix 139 (14 July 1938).

56. Telephone conversation, J. David Stern, Philadelphia, with Williams, Washington, December 7, 1936, AWP; *Philadelphia Inquirer*, 4 March 1936; City Projects Council of Philadelphia, "Resolution," May 1936, sent to Hopkins, RG 69, WPA, State Series, 641, Pa., WPA Records; Philadelphia County Relief Board, "Monthly Report," November 1936, found in Free Library of Philadelphia.

57. Telegram, Milton Froner, Philadelphia, chairman of WPA Joint Action Com-

mittee, to Hopkins, Washington, July 1, 1937, RG 69, WPA State Series, 641, Pa., WPA Records; Dominic Pelusi, Philadelphia, Secretary of United Auto Workers Local 258, CIO, to F. D. Roosevelt, July 5, 1937, RG 69, WPA, State Series, 641, Pa., WPA Records.

58. John Edelman, Philadelphia, CIO regional director, to FDR, June 15, 1938, and Sylvia Stein, Philadelphia, American Federation of Teachers, to Hopkins, Washington, February 10, 1938, all in RG 69, WPA, State Series, 641, Pa., WPA Records; statement of U. S. Conference of Mayors, April 8, 1938, in President's Personal File, Box 1820, FDRL; Arthur W. MacMahon, John D. Millett, Gladys Ogden, *The Administration of Federal Work Relief* (New York, 1941, p. 170; draft of speech "To the Congress of the United States," n.d., Box 9, AWP.

59. *Philadelphia Inquirer*, 7 August 1937; *Progressive Labor World*, 23 December 1937, 2 February 1938, and 16 March 1939.

60. Testimony of William Green, U. S. Congress, House Subcommittee of Committee on Appropriations, *Hearings, Emergency Relief Appropriations Act of 1938*, and Public Works Appropriation Act of 1938, Seventy-fifth Congress, 3rd session, 1938, hereinafter cited as *Emergency Relief Appropriation Hearings*, 1948. Testimony of John L. Lewis, *Emergency Relief Appropriation Hearings*, 1938, pp. 767-70; *Progressive Labor World*, 22 December 1938.

61. Board of Trade Minutes, January 24, 1938.

62. *Philadelphia Inquirer*, 15 July 1938.

63. Gertrude Springer, "Relief in November 1938," *Survey* 74 (November 1938): 339.

64. "Unemployment in 1937," *Fortune* 16 (October 1937): 106; "Song Suppressed," *Time* 35 (June 1940): 60.

65. Gelfand, *Nation of Cities*, pp. 96-104.

[9]
The Great Depression and Black Housing in Philadelphia

In 1940, blacks comprised 39 percent of those Philadelphians on relief. Most of these blacks lived in the narrow streets and back alleys of the ghettoes of North and South Philadelphia. Slum housing as well as poverty plagued these neighborhoods. As part of its New Deal for urban America the Roosevelt administration envisioned public housing, like the WPA, not only as a stimulus to the urban economy, but also as a panacea for the cities' ill-housed. And like the WPA in Philadelphia, the New Deal housing program there operated against insuperable odds.

Philadelphia affords an interesting case study of the influence of race on the New Deal's public-housing experiment. During World War I and the decade following, Philadelphia and other Northern cities experienced a black in-migration which resulted in racial bitterness, rigid segregation patterns, and grinding poverty. And where very poor blacks jammed into aged hovels and seedy flats, there emerged a clearly recognizable "dark ghetto." Accordingly, urban America confronted the Great Depression gripped not only by a general decay of urban real estate, but also by an expanding core of decrepit black housing. While each city shaped its own distinctive black ghetto, recent studies of the New Deal in Pittsburgh and Boston suggest that the Philadelphia experience with "black housing" in the 1930s was, perhaps, not atypical.[1]

Block after block of overcrowded bandbox tenements and nests of back-alley and rear-court houses scarred Philadelphia in the late 1920s, and the ensuing depression brought a pall of joblessness and poverty to the city. Substandard housing spread rapidly and sapped inner cities of vitality. Spurred by reformers such as Edith Elmer Wood and Catherine Bauer, who for a decade had questioned the ability of private builders to serve the housing needs of the working class, and by the raspish demands of organized labor on behalf of the distressed building trades, the New Deal accepted the idea of public housing. Indeed, one of the first acts of the Public Works Administration was to inaugurate a program for urban slum clearance and low-cost housing construction.

Until 1939 only two projects comprised Philadelphia's share of the New Deal housing boom. The first, the Carl Mackley houses, was one of the nation's few Public Works Administration limited-dividend projects. In this case the PWA extended low interest funds to the American Federation of Full Fashioned Hosiery Workers' Union to build an attractive, park-ringed housing complex for the city's hosiery workers. An equally bucolic setting complemented a second PWA housing project, the Hill Creek homes, which opened in 1936. Both the Carl Mackley and the Hill Creek homes housed white families only, and to the dismay of planners and the vindication of finger-wagging critics, most of the project residents were middle-income, not low-income families.

The slow pace of the housing program in Philadelphia was set by the city's stubborn anti-New Deal mayor, J. Hampton Moore. From 1933 to 1935 Moore opposed all New Deal programs. Also, the housing program suffered from dwindling federal funds until the Wagner-Steagall Act revived federal housing activity in 1937. But another fact looms as large as or larger than either Moore's obduracy or the federal government's diminished outlays in explaining the problem of Philadelphia's housing program: racial considerations significantly slowed the pace of housing progress in Philadelphia.[2]

According to W. E. B. Dubois's *The Philadelphia Negro,* almost 40,000 Negroes lived in the city in 1890, approximately half of them in the century-old neighborhood around Lombard and South Streets. However, at the time DuBois described Philadelphia (1899), pressures in the South—low wages, Jim Crow discrimination, the boll weevil—were driving many young blacks toward Philadelphia. The city's black population rose from 40,000 in 1890 to over 84,000 in 1910, and World War I intensified the trend. Black migrants, seeking wartime jobs in Philadelphia's expanding shipbuilding, locomotive, and iron and steel works, had by 1920 swelled the number of Negro residents in the city to well over 134,000. Nor did the tide ebb during the following decade. By 1930 Philadelphia's black population had risen to 219,599—almost 13 percent of the total population.[3]

Prior to the 1930s, those black Philadelphians who were historically identified with the Lombard and South Streets community were a generally scattered, not a ghetto people. Black households in 1890 dotted many city wards, and nowhere did Negroes comprise a majority of the ward residents. Generally, city blocks included two or three black families who shared their working-class poverty with Irish, Jewish, or Italian neighbors. Instead of weakening this pattern, the turn-of-the-century migrations actually intensified the dispersion of the black population, so that Negroes lived in virtually every ward in the city by 1910.[4]

The migration of poor, uneducated, rural blacks exerted extraordinary pressure on the city's established black community. In 1900 blacks in Philadelphia had boasted a well-defined society with established ways of handling the limited social and economic opportunities afforded the race by the city; in addition, distinct lines of communication connected the black leadership to the white political power structure.[5] However, what Allan Spear, the historian of "black Chicago," has observed in Chicago was true of Philadelphia: the continued influx of thousands of "new settlers" constituted a demographic revolution which disrupted the ecological order of the old community. Black newcomers who crammed the old central city wards (the 2nd, 3rd, 4th, 13th, 14th, 15th) drove middle-class Negroes into the old but somewhat better housing of North Philadelphia, Germantown, and West Philadelphia. By 1927, over 30,000 Negroes lived in West Philadelphia, and a burgeoning community of some 26,539 blacks stretched along Broad Street and the smaller streets surrounding Temple University beyond Columbia Avenue.

Still, the largest black population huddled in the old central-city wards. During the early 1920s, when more than 10,000 black newcomers settled there yearly, Philadelphia, like the rest of urban America, faced a severe housing shortage. Although the shortage eased after 1923, housing for Negroes remained scarce. Out of necessity, migrants "doubled and tripled up" in a dwindling supply of horribly substandard homes. Frequently, every room of these rickety structures was converted into dingy quarters for migrants, and six-room houses in the dense 30th ward often accommodated nine black families. Of course, this overcrowding enriched the landlords. For example, houses renting for $14 a month in 1914 were converted into three-room apartments which brought $100 a month in the 1920s.

The migrants who congested the central-city wards and forced the middle-class Negroes to search for better housing undid the black-white accord which had prevailed when city wards had been sprinkled with black settlements. By 1924 white homeowners, fearful of being inundated by a black tidal wave, reacted violently. Real-estate agents conspired with white improvement societies, and white home buyers signed restrictive convenants promising not to sell their property to blacks. Where covenants failed to stay the onrush, stone-tossing demonstrators subjected their new neighbors to a dangerous reception.

Consequently, blacks were increasingly restricted to well-defined areas. As Sam Bass Warner was observed in *The Private City: Philadelphia in Three Periods of Its Growth,* by 1930 Negroes had become segregated by income and ethnicity—a clear contrast to the occupational clustering of the nineteenth century. The result, according to Warner, "was a core city of poverty, low skills, and low status surrounded by a ring of workingclass and middle-class homes."

The Philadelphia Negro in 1930 subsisted on the margins of the city's economy. The flickering hope that he would preserve some of his World War I economic gains faded as depression eclipsed the "normalcy" of the Harding-Coolidge years. As early as 1927 the city's entire economy—based on textiles and metal manufacturers—faltered and was sent skidding into depression.[6]

By adding to the Negro's economic woes, the Great Depression magnified the housing dilemma. During the 1920s both black and white Philadelphia burned with the fever of home ownership, so that by 1929 sixty-three Negro building and loan companies negotiated precarious second and third mortgages. The depression hacked unsparingly at these black mortgages. Sheriff's writs bedecked thousands of Philadelphia doorways in the 1930s (almost 19,000 in 1932 alone), and many of these lost homes were black. However, unlike the white Philadelphian, the typical Negro was a tenant, and in 1932 half of the black renting public lived in the shadow of eviction. Whether dumped onto the streets by the sheriff or constable, displaced black families herded more tightly into the city's already bulging roosts, thereby compounding the housing crisis.[7]

In 1936, conditions were at their worst in the old central-city wards, where 32,000 of the nearly 93,000 inhabitants were black. Some families occupied moldering bandbox tenements—encrusted three-room structures where the sweltering eleven-foot by eleven-foot cubicles sat "Father, Son, and Holy Ghost" atop one another. Others inhabited miserable shacks or nested in decrepit houses honeycombed with family rooms. Sixty-six percent of these ramshackle tenement structures were nearly a century old. In fact, 11 percent dated from the eighteenth or early nineteenth century. Incredibly, some residents still bucketed their water from yard hydrants, still poked about in murky rooms lit dimly by kerosene or oil lamps, and warmed unevenly by dangerous wood stoves. Over a quarter of the black occupants had to use foul-smelling outdoor water closets, sanitary artifacts frequently shared by three or four families. Of the 5,000 black residential structures in the area, fully 3,000 had neither bathtub nor shower, and close to 2,000 lacked electricity. Many houses were on a par with an aged three-and-a-half-story row dwelling on Lombard Street which had been divided into twenty-three apartments; here eighteen families shared twelve sinks, and twenty families used seven water closets.[8]

Despite these miserable conditions, most black Philadelphians endured in silence. Occasionally a group of tenants took to the streets to shake their fists at an unfair landlord, and the black press periodically denounced unsafe tenements; however, these outbursts were trifling releases of indignation and were not symptomatic of widespread protest. Outrage required a consensus on the matter of race, a consensus which did not exist. The great migration, dulling the edge of traditional black leadership, had sharpened class cleavage, making more difficult the advancement of race interests.

As the tide of black migration crested in the mid-1920s, more and more of the black elite—physicians, merchants, teachers, social workers—withdrew from the old black central-city neighborhoods to West Philadelphia. Aloof, incapable of identifying with the Negro peasant's adjustment problems, these black families blamed the migrant for the moral and physical disintegration of black society. Philadelphia's Armstrong Association and the local NAACP best expressed the qualms of these black bourgeois: both urged the newcomers to seek job training and moral rearmament, yet in the same breath flayed their crudeness and slothfulness. The depression, however, not only struck the penniless migrant but threatened equally to impoverish the entire black community. H. Viscount Nelson, a student of Philadelphia's black social structure, has noted that, while the recognition of a common plight forced outcroppings here and there of race consciousness, one set of beliefs bound all segments of the black community—a common hatred of discrimination and the conviction that the best society is integrated.

Despite this hatred of segregation, separate-race organizations had long been justified as "voluntary segregation" compelled by black exclusion from white institutions. Yet the existence of separate black churches, lodges, and YMCAs had never detracted from the goal of an integrated society. On the contrary, according to their spokesman, black organizations supplied the leverage necessary to lift the black lower classes into a condition of respectability. Understandably then, what interest there was in housing appeared principally among the ranks of these middle-class organizations. Like middle-class whites, bourgeois blacks subscribed to a housing rhetoric which identified disease, crime, delinquency, and other social problems with crowded, substandard housing.[9]

Accordingly, the PWA's first housing program granting federal loans for limited-dividend projects had hardly been announced in November 1933 when Cheney State College president Leslie Pinckney Hill, Wayne Hopkins of the Armstrong Association (affiliated with the National Urban Leauge), and Robert G. Taylor, the white Quaker president of the Whittier Center Housing Corporation, marched into Secretary of Commerce Dan Roper's office and extracted Roper's promise that the PWA not only would ignore racial lines in granting housing loans, but also would "not support local efforts to segregate Negroes or any foreign group." Shortly thereafter, PWA officials commissioned Taylor to establish a "Committee on De-Slumming," which, in one official's words, "would meet the needs of all Philadelphia." Taylor's Committee on De-Slumming produced a spate of housing proposals, a number of which were sponsored by black leaders to arrest blight in West Philadelphia. One of the most celebrated was the Park Court Apartments, designed by black architect Homer Jefferson. The Park Court plan envisioned a modern fourteen-unit complex located on a West Philadelphia slum tract which, in Wayne Hopkins' words, "was inhabited by a poor class of people who live in broken down shacks . . . (and created) an eyesore to the surrounding neighborhood near the new Martha Washington public school for colored children."

Neither Park Court nor Jefferson Terrace, nor the plans for the Blakiston Housing Corporation and the Whittier Center — all for black housing projects in West Philadelphia — were ever implemented. At the very moment these projects were being conceived, the PWA was phasing out its limited-dividend program and replacing it with a plan designed to grant state and local governments up to 30 percent of the cost of slum clearance and housing projects. Low-interest loans would be made on the balance.[10]

The PWA now earmarked $15 million for its housing program in Philadelphia, and in March 1934 authorized the city to form an advisory committee on housing (PACH) to "express preference for projects in certain sections of the city . . . and reach conclusions by considering the social and economic problems of each." The committee, which met for the first time in October 1934, embraced a who's who of Philadelphia civic luminaries, including James McDevit, a prominent city labor leader; J. David Stern, editor of the *Philadelphia Record;* and Bernard Newman, of the Philadelphia Housing Association. Despite the PWA's commitment to racial objectivity, Philadelphia's Advisory Committee lacked a delegate from the city's conspicuously ill-housed black community.[11]

The spring of 1935 witnessed only negligible progress toward ameliorating housing problems. While Mayor Moore's obstructionism raised one apparently insurmountable obstacle to better housing, the PWA itself added another, establishing for projects criteria which practically excluded action on inner-city housing. For example, projects could not be "influenced detrimentally by surrounding conditions" and had to be built on cheap land costing no more than $1.50 a square foot. These rules, as well as a federal court ruling prohibiting Washington from condemning land in Cincinnati for housing purposes, practically mandated that projects be built on the white fringes beyond the central city. Finally, when the nation's economy sagged again in late 1934, Roosevelt decided to buttress federal relief operations with housing funds, thereby slowing the already cautious public-housing program to a crawl.[12]

Housing progress was nearly at a standstill in March 1935 when the city's two black newspapers, the *Philadelphia Tribune* and the *Independent*, launched a series of scathing exposés of black housing conditions. Pictures of dangerously dilapidated tenements, of children playing in debris-strewn courtyards, and of ceilings threatening to collapse dramatized abominations which, according to the *Tribune*, both the federal government and the city heartlessly tolerated. Such squalid surroundings, charged the *Tribune*, encouraged black residents to pillage vacant buildings for firewood, a depression-born practice which rankled bourgeois blacks and whites alike.[13]

The *Tribune*'s campaign for black housing reflected the concerns of long-time reformers. Good housing, to follow the houser's line, was a key to social control. Raze the slums and build decent, park-ringed housing units, and crime, disease, alcoholism, and other hazards of slum living would vanish. Yet, "decent housing" did not necessarily mean "low-cost housing." Elitist Philadelphia blacks who spoke of "really significant neighborhood developments" for Negroes generally had in mind "fashionable housing" modeled after Harlem's Paul Lawrence Dunbar Apartments, an attractive Negro housing development constructed in the 1920s by the Metropolitan Life Insurance Company.

At least some poor black families on the relief rolls understood the nuances of black-housing rhetoric. A group of women employed on the WPA sewing projects insisted that, while they could see the advantages of such a "high-classed colored neighborhood as the Dunbar project," they staunchly opposed segregation "like they have in Baltimore." However, asserted the women, "Negroes in Philadelphia still need better houses made available." Whatever the motive, and however stated, this simple agreement on the need for improved housing launched the first housing campaign.[14]

Philadelphia's settlement houses and agencies such as the Armstrong Association enlisted the black press to lead the campaign for action on housing. The Southwest Belmont YMCA, located in the heart of the city's worst black neighborhood, hosted several groups who met to protest firetrap houses. Prodded by activist settlement workers, a number of slum residents, black and white, bombarded relief administrator Harold Ickes and President Roosevelt with letters and telegrams deploring ramshackle housing and beseeching federal aid. These letters were singular in the starkness of their often crudely scrawled descriptions. One black women, fr example, pleaded that conditions in her neighborhood were so bad "we would be very glad if there would be iny way for better houses for ous to live in we has damp wall and water in the cellar the toilet on the outside (sic)."[15]

Despite this letter-writing drive, the black-housing campaign was rooted in Negro professional, fraternal, and social-welfare organizations, not in the masses. Individuals such as architect Homer Jefferson and accountant Cornelius Garlick worked closely with the site-selection committee of the Philadelphia Advisory Committee on Housing. Another large contingent of black clergymen and other professionals concerned with housing fought the Negro housing battle as the "Committee of One Hundred." Never a group to ignore a worthy cause, the NAACP formed the Slum Clearance Committee, whose membership consisted exclusively of doctors, lawyers, clergymen, teachers, contractors, and other professionals. The National Negro Congress established a similar committee.

The letter-writing campaigns and the site-selection activities of the National Negro Congress and other groups kept alive interest in housing into 1936. In March of that year the Association of Philadelphia Settlements assembled 500 tenants to petition Washington for a government slum-clearance project. Then in October, the Philadelphia chapter of the National Negro Congress (NNC) visited Washington to demand action on housing. But the pleas of the NNC fell upon a New Deal already badgered by a budget-wary Congress. Harold Ickes claimed that there was no money; he told housing supporters that, if Congress would extend the Housing Division appropriation, black housing in Philadelphia would be improved. For now, he lamented, the administration could offer nothing.[16]

Yet the black-housing campaign, no matter how narrow its base or how weak Washington's reaction, registered an impact. Washington was alerted at last to black Philadelphia's enormous stake in the housing movement. Democratic politicians did not overlook the boost former Republican black voters gave to Democratic candidates in Pennsylvania's 1934 gubernatorial election. The housing issue offered the Democratic New Deal an opportunity to respond to its newest constituency. Evidence of the administration's new sensitivity emerged following the resignation in January 1935 of J. David Stern from his post on the Philadelphia Advisory Committee on Housing. In March — about the time of the letter-writing campaign — Washington began insisting that Stern's place be filled by a black representative.[17] Bernard Newman of the Philadelphia Housing Association was scarcely evasive about the absence of a black man on the committee. He confessed that, since a black project had not been considered, the committee had not seen a need for a black member. Newman's candor notwithstanding, Washington was goaded to act promptly. A high PWA official in Philadelphia hurriedly instructed Newman's Advisory Committee of its "entirely new enlarged function." The official apologized that "the thought had not originally been given to a Negro project when the committee was selected." However, he continued, now that a black project was being considered, "a site selection for such a project will probably be most difficult." And this difficulty, he concluded, "warrants the inclusion of at least two Negroes among the advisory committee membership."[18]

To fill Stern's place, Secretary Ickes assigned his advisor on Negro affairs, Robert C. Weaver, to compile a list of Philadelphia Negroes suitable for the post. On April 22, 1935, the Advisory Committee selected from that list Crystal Bird Fauset, field secretary of the UMCA and wife of Arthur Huff Fauset, a black sociologist and chairman of the Philadelphia area NNC. A month later, at Newman's behest, the committee chose a second black member, Mayor R. R. Wright, past president of the Georgia State Agriculture and Industrial Association and former special agent in the Department of Interior. At the time of his appointment, Wright was president of the Citizens' and Southern Bank and Trust Company. Although Wright's name had been absent from Weaver's list, Newman pressed for its inclusion, believing naïvely that the eighty-year-old Wright would appease the older Booker T. Washington faction, which was opposed to the younger DuBois element of the black community.[19]

As summer turned to fall there was every indication that the black leadership expected more than two blacks on a stalled housing committee. With the revival of a two-party system in Philadelphia, the black community asserted itself politically. In 1934, city blacks had elected a Negro, Marshall Shepard, to the state legislature. Emboldened by their newfound political independence, blacks demanded and won a generous slice of the city and state patronage pie. Even greater black expectations were aroused in 1935, when black Philadelphia helped elect S. Davis Wilson as mayor after Wilson had campaigned on a platform promising improved conditions, including better housing, for city blacks.

However, by late 1936 all housing promises looked questionable. Fauset's and Wright's initial flush of interest in the housing committee quickly lapsed. Possibly disillusioned by the inactivity of the committee and its cavalier treatment of black housing needs, Fauset and Wright lost interest in the committee's sessions. After they attended the first two meetings, their services were, in Newman's words, "practically nil."

In the fall of 1936 the undercurrent of restiveness with the sluggish pace of housing progress coursing beneath the black community began to surface. The September meeting of the Philadelphia area National Negro Congress gave housing top billing, and the meeting closed with a sharply worded petition to Ickes demanding at least $10 million to rehouse city Negroes. A revitalized letter-writing campaign in November and December underscored the NNC's million-dollar housing demand.[20]

Then, suddenly, in several horrifying minutes, the black housing problem in Philadelphia erupted into a grand cause. Just before midnight on December 19, 1936, Mrs. Alberta Richardson, a twenty-eight-year-old black housewife, felt her tenement trembling. Then, with a crackling sound, huge chunks of plaster broke loose from the ceiling and crashed to the floor. Within moments came a dreadful rumble, followed by a deafening roar as the walls teetered and the floor collapsed. Seconds later, the Richardson dwelling and the adjoining bandbox tenement crumbled into smoking rubble. Mrs. Richardson survived, but the tragedy took the lives of seven Negroes, including four children.

For two weeks the city seethed with indignation and thunderings against slums and slumlords monopolized politics and the press. Heartened by widespread public outrage, the *Tribune* pleaded that "indignation over the tragedy" not be allowed to die, and the paper summoned persons of all faiths to "rid the city of this menace to health, life, and property."[21]

Philadelphia's flamboyant Mayor S. Davis Wilson beat his

breast, gnashed his teeth, and promised to wreak full vengeance on slum housing. Overnight, Wilson created the Mayor's Housing Committee, which included the respected black physician Dr. Harry W. Barnes, who had handled Wilson's mayoralty campaign among black Philadelphians. The mayor also announced a spectacular assault on unfit housing, demanding the immediate demolition of 5,000 slum houses. To dramatize his determination, the mayor appeared two days later, crowbar in hand, to help demolish the first house.[22]

Unlike "proper" Philadelphians, the city's tenement inhabitants were too infuriated to be assuaged by crowbar gimmickry. A few days after the tragedy, a passionate National Negro Congress summoned hundreds of mourners to the Wesley AME church to honor the disaster victims and plan war against the slums. In the wake of that gathering a group of slum dwellers who lived near the site of the bandbox collapse formed the Tenants' League and less than a week later, the league held the first of many protest meetings at the Southwest Belmont YWCA. Present were representatives of the National Negro Congress, the Workers' Alliance, an activist organization of the unemployed, and the Communist-backed International Labor Defense. The protestors demanded that slum housing be razed forthwith and that displaced families be adequately housed at no added expense. At the same time, the group refused Wilson's offer to accommodate the homeless families in the city's National Guard Armories.

Soon after the Tenants' League protest, the NNC convoked a citywide forum on housing at which speaker after speaker decried the impotence of city housing ordinances and housing inspectors. The delegates demanded that the city enact strong ordinances to force landlords into making needed repairs. To bolster this denunciation of slum housing and city negligence, citizens deluged Mayor Wilson with letters and petitions demanding low-cost housing, as well as a list of housing vacancies for slum families frightened from their creaking homes or evicted by the mayor's crowbar.

Tenant strikes, housing meetings, and protests dominated 1937. The Tenants' League always stood in the vanguard of organizations actively battling for better housing conditions in Philadelphia. Unlike many other housing committees, the league boasted a grass-roots membership. Militantly and frequently, the league crusaded for "decent homes at low rent," while stridently opposing both Jim Crow practices in housing and the blacklisting of relief tenants. Street demonstrations, flyers, and protest meetings were among the tactics the league employed against belligerent landlords on behalf of better inner-city housing.

The Tenants' League was not alone in its campaign for better housing. On the first anniversary of the bandbox collapse, a council of housing groups hosted a citywide conference at which speaker after speaker, including Catherine Bauer and Langdon Post, the latter the head of the New York Housing Authority, attacked the evils of slum housing. In commenting on this meeting and others, the *Tribune* contended that, despite talk and petitions, the same housing menace existed (a year after the collapse): the city's black population still averaged 121 persons to an acre of crumbling rookeries.[23]

However, 1938 promised improvements. At the end of 1937 the new Wagner-Steagall Act authorized $20 million in housing funds for Philadelphia. The act also inaugurated the United States Housing Authority (USHA), under which a city housing authority was established to champion the cause of housing in Philadelphia.

From the first, Philadelphia's Housing Authority included as its black representative Dr. Harry Barnes, a surgeon who was president of the black National Medical Association and a member of Mayor Wilson's housing committee. Although Barnes, a spokesman for the conservative black elite, was suspected by some for his zealous support of Wilson, he enjoyed popular respect and took a sincere interest in Negro housing.

Blacks such as Barnes and Robert Weaver considered the new public-housing program the high point of the New Deal. Standing before the 1938 meeting of the National Negro Congress, Weaver extolled the USHA for ushering in a new era of black housing. Black Americans, exhorted Weaver, were the real heirs of the program. Previously, Weaver charged, the "very existence of segregated areas in which most of us are compelled to live . . . perilously circumscribed" black America's opportunity for decent housing. Several years earlier W. E. B. DuBois, in a different vein, used slum, poverty, and crime statistics to spice *Crisis* magazine editorials preaching the wisdom of voluntary segregation. While Weaver spoke for housing opportunity—never segregation—one finds it hard to believe he never foresaw that housing for Negroes could easily be read as "black housing."[24]

Yet, an important mission of Philadelphia's new housing authority was black housing; it was the unfinished business left by the defunct advisory committee, which for three years had grappled unsuccessfully with the problem. As early as 1935 the committee (and others interested in public housing) had proposed a "Negro project." Understandably, given the burgeoning segregation patterns of the 1920s, many white Philadelphians in the 1930s supported public housing for Negroes, not necessarily for humanitarian motives, but as more effective than restrictive covenants or improvement associations for controlling the expansion of the black community.

In 1935, Walter Thomas of the City Planning Commission briefed Housing Division head A. R. Clas on the possibility of low-cost housing for Negroes on slum-cleared land. According to Thomas, the area east of Broad Street around Girard Avenue was "heavily Negro and should remain so." He recommended, therefore, the development of a Negro area having a physical outlet into Fairmont and Girard Avenues, Broad Street, and the Girard Avenue business area. A Negro location so defined would contribute to the stability of the area, and, continued Thomas, "will have a wholesome effect on the values of Girard Avenue west of Broad Street."[25]

Thomas's point was expanded in a letter from a Philadelphia attorney to Bernard Newman. The writer was "delighted" to read that Newman was "contemplating the establishment of a Harlem section for Philadelphia . . . I have lived in this city my entire lifetime, and I have been shocked to observe . . . great belts of what used to be fine residential sections, now densely populated by colored people. This is a serious situation, and ought to be corrected, as it is resulting in large depreciation in the value of real estate in those sections."

Newman himself was blunt. When asked in 1935 about the city's plans for housing racial and ethnic minorities, the head of PACH argued that "we are ignoring racial matters entirely in our slum-clearance program, except, of course, we are seeking to promote a separate slum clearance in a Negro district, the new housing in which will be for Negroes." A few months earlier Newman wrote that "opposition of certain Negroes toward anything which appears to be segregated is unfortunate."[26]

In harmony with such thinking, the Philadelphia Housing Authority followed a simple formula for determining whether a project would be white or black: the racial composition of a project had to conform to the prevailing racial composition of the surrounding neighborhood. Therefore, a black project was a matter of site location, and criteria for locating a project were crucial.

Even with "Harlemization" as a goal, city housing officials wrestled vainly for years to determine a site. The Cincinnati decision of 1935, mentioned earlier, forbade the federal government's condemning land for housing purposes and encouraged the use of vacant parcels. Furthermore, housing officials declared that a Negro project had to be surrounded by a cordon of black or blight, lest property values be toppled.

These considerations forced the committee to find vacant sites for black housing on inner-city land. Despite the high cost of slum tracts, the advisory committee felt no alternative existed. In exasperation, Newman wrote in 1935 that "we (PACH) are finding great difficulty in locating an area suitable for Negro housing, our handicap being that we cannot recommend a Negro housing site in the heart of a white district." He might have inserted "near a white district," for when the committee suggested the Glenwood Cemetery site (a large triangular graveyard in North Philadelphia skirted on one side by railroad tracks and bordered on the remaining sides by a black neighborhood), an incensed Philadelphia architect protested that such a project would be "a great blow to West Philadelphia." The site, he argued, "could be used for white housing and not jeopardize adjacent institutions like the University of Pennsylvania and Convention Hall. The site is too valuable for black housing, as it might engender a feeling that anything is good enough for Negro housing."[27]

Every proposal for a site met with some objection. The historic Pennsylvania Hospital tract in the heart of the South Philadelphia ghetto, one likely location, proved too costly. A vacant field near the city's baseball stadium was too near an unblighted white middle-class neighborhood. The advisory committee finally selected the aforementioned twenty-acre Glenwood site, an abandoned cemetery whose 27,000 spectral residents had no objection to black housing. But the Glenwood proposal came too late; by 1936 federal housing was stalled.

The new Philadelphia Housing Authority turned elsewhere in 1937 to locate a black housing project and considered at first the infamous South Philadelphia bandbox area. Unfortunately for the city, Washington insisted that the first demonstration project be built on vacant land and that the cost per housing unit not exceed $6,000. Washington's stiff requirements clinched the defeat of slum clearance. Consequently, the Glenwood proposal was dusted off and found ideal for the first black project.

Great pomp and circumstance attended the May 1939 groundbreaking for a housing project named in honor of James Weldon Johnson, the black playwright and author. The decor of the ceremony was unmistakably black. The white police and fireman's band, USHA head Nathan Straus, and a scattering of white officials scarcely blurred the distinct blackness of the occasion. Virginia Lewis, described as a "young, colored soprano," sang "The Star Spangled Banner," and the Reverend D. W. Haywood of the black Mt. Carmel Baptist Church offered prayer. Surrounded by a crowd of black parents and gleeful black schoolchildren specially released from class to be present, Dr. Harry Barnes and Charles Lewis, president of the NNC, helped Straus turn the first spadeful of earth. When the $3-million housing complex opened on October 1, 1940, 1,800 people—well over 95 percent of them black—were housed in 535 units.

Work had no sooner begun at the Glenwood site than plans

were announced for a second black project, to be called the Richard Allen Homes. Unlike the Glenwood cemetery location, the Allen site necessitated the clearing of 27 acres of ramshackle slums around Fairmount and Poplar Streets—a heavily populated black area just below Temple University. In late October 1941, the first of 5,386 tenants moved into this project. As in the James Weldon Johnson homes, over 95 percent of the residents were black.[28]

Not until 1941 did Barnes question the housing authority's segregative policy of isolating blacks in all-Negro projects and, although Robert Weaver was sent to investigate, the federal government ultimately yielded to the city's neighborhood formula. By this time Philadelphia's housing program had in fact come to an end. In 1940 Mayor Robert E. Lamberton had refused further cooperation with a housing program he considered "a great public experiment whose value had not been proven." More importantly, by 1941 defense housing rather than public housing had become Philadelphia's major concern.[29]

In 1979 the James Weldon Johnson Homes and the Richard Allen Homes were as scarred by blight as the red-brick slums surrounding them. Their doom had been clearly sealed as a result of their misguided purpose. Initially, the architects of America's federal housing had never planned the projects for their present occupants. Public housing, whether for black or white, had been built originally for the hard-working but low-paid worker, the same individual who benefited from Social Security. Careful screening of the applicants for public housing assured that the families selected should profit from the experience. Places such as the Johnson project were designed to aid social adjustment and serve as rehabilitation centers for people temporarily sidetracked from the path of upward mobility. Accordingly, the housing units were deliberately bare, devoid, inside and out, of even a trace of what economy-cautious planners called "costly frills." The Housing Authority forbade the use of ceramic tile, and curtains replaced closet doors. In fact, only at the last minute did Raymond Rosen, a Philadelphia appliance dealer and member of the Housing

Authority, order the projects equipped with small 3.5-cubic-foot refrigerators to supplant the iceboxes specified in the original proposals.

Spartan living was only one feature of the regimen of the Johnson project. Units were laid out so that each family could learn responsibility and self-reliance by maintaining an assigned area. Workshops encouraged residents to practice frugality by decorating their units with salvaged furniture. Project community centers taught civic spirit, and project government promoted citizenship. Unseemly behavior, such as gambling on the premises, even for pennies, was strictly forbidden. It was hoped that those who had profited from the experience would outgrow the project and find more respectable accommodations elsewhere.[30]

But the black experience differed sharply from the expected pattern. The ghetto circumscribed black life. Moreover, the Philadelphia experience in public housing strengthened the segregation pattern of the city and thus narrowed the housing opportunities of the city's black population. Segregation had long severely limited black economic opportunity, and for many blacks joblessness rather than work characterized life in the black city. In fact, in 1939 Negroes comprised 60 percent of those eligible for public assistance or work relief. This swollen class of unskilled and often jobless blacks public housing failed to reach. Moreover, housing expert Edith Elmer Wood announced in 1939 in no uncertain terms that public housing should not foster "colonies of dependents."

Middle-class blacks were no more tolerant of failures than was Wood. They viewed public housing as a means of strengthening and enforcing traditional values, not as a receptacle for sickly human specimens. In their eyes, public housing increased the supply of decent housing for upwardly mobile blacks. Therefore, while the bandbox collapse of December 1936 heightened concern among blacks for decent housing, the resulting spate of interest in housing pointed to class, not race, goals. In addition, the very magnitude of middle-class blacks' concern over miserable housing conditions made them overlook the segregative consequences of the projects. Not surprisingly, the first black residents in the James Weldon Johnson project were middle-class employees of the Board of Education, hairdressers, and public-health workers. Less than 12 percent of the residents were on relief.[31]

There is some irony as well as pathos in the history of these black projects. Projects black Philadelphians eagerly sought as havens—ideal environments for child rearing and schools of good citizenship—were rife with narcotics and gang warfare in the 1960s and 1970s.

The James Weldon Johnson and the Richard Allen homes were inevitable victims of their misconceived purpose. Situated deliberately in the center of the city's black district, they were surrounded by crowded, substandard dwellings. The first easing of admission requirements in 1949 brought into the homes a new clientele who viewed the projects as anything but a way station. To these residents, the projects were just another lackluster place to live in the heart of the black ghetto.

NOTES

1. Robert Trout, "The New Deal in Boston," address delivered at Annual Meeting of the Organization of American Historians, Washington, D.C., April 7, 1972; Bruce Stave, *The New-Deal and the Last Hurrah: Pittsburgh Machine Politics* (Pittsburgh, 1970), passim; Gilbert Osofsky, *Harlem: The Making of a Ghetto* (New York, 1967); Allan Spear, *Black Ghetto: The Making of a Negro Ghetto, 1890-1920* (Chicago 1967).

2. By the early 1920s some housing experts such as Edith Elmer Wood and Catherine Bauer believed that only public housing would reach the lower income working class, see Edith E. Wood, *Recent Trends in American Housing* (New York, 1931); Helen Alfred, Washington, Secretary of the NPHC, to FDR, April 21, 1934, Franklin D. Roosevelt Library, Hyde Park, New York, hereinafter cited as FDRL; and Resolutions of 23rd Conference, National Federation of Settlements to FDR, June 10, 1935, FDRL; on the Carl Mackley project see "Housing in Philadelphia: Union-Sponsored Project Hailed as Model for U.S.," *Christian Science Monitor*, 2 November 1937, p. 2; and William McCloy, "Limited Dividend Projects Provide Housing for 11,000," Washington *Evening Star*, September 9, 1936; on public housing in Philadelphia from 1933 to May 1935, Housing Association Papers, Temple Urban Archives, Philadelphia, Pennsylvania, hereinafter sited as HAP; on Mayor Moore see Bernard Newman, Philadelphia, to A. R. Clas, Washington, D.C., PWA Director of Housing, July 8, 1935, HAP; Newman blamed bureaucratic lethargy for the lax pace of housing in Philadelphia, see Newman, "Recommendations on How to Stall on a Federal Housing Program," October 16, 1934, mimeographed, HAP.

3. William E. B. DuBois, *The Philadelphia Negro* (Benjamin Blom, 1967), pp.

46-65; Bernard Newman, "Philadelphia's Negro Population," June 10, 1930, mimeographed, HAP; Armstrong Association, "Report of Negro Population and Industries of Philadelphia," August 22, 1927, mimeographed, Armstrong Association Papers, Temple Urban Archives, Philadelphia, Pennsylvania, hereinafter cited as AAP; Blanche J. Paget, "The Plight of the Pennsylvania Negro," *Opportunity: The Journal of Negro Life*, December 1936, pp. 309-11; on the "Great Migration" of blacks into Philadelphia see Sadie Tanner Mossell, "The Standard of Living Among One Hundred Negro Migrant Families in Philadelphia, *The Annals*, 98 (November 1921): pp. 174-75.

4. Bernard Newman, "Philadelphia Negro Population," in T. J. Woofter and Madge Headly Priest, *Negro Housing in Philadelphia*, pamphlet (Friends Committee on Interests of the Colored Race, Whittier Center Housing Corporation, 1927), pp. 5, 14-15.

5. H. Viscount Nelson, Jr., "Race and Class Consciousness of Philadelphia Negroes with Special Emphasis on the Years Between 1927 and 1940." (Ph.D. diss., University of Pennsylvania, 1969), pp. 28-29, 40.

6. Spear, *Black Chicago*, pp. 11-27, 167-222; Bernard Newman, "Population Density by Wards; 1910 Census, 1930 Census," mimeographed, HAP; see too T. J. Woofter's report, *Negro Housing in Philadelphia* (Whittier Center Housing Corp., 1927), p. 5; Henry M. Miller, *Urban Home Ownership: A Socio-Economic Analysis with Emphasis on Philadelphia* (Philadelphia, 1927), 22-25; William Cowdery, Philadelphia, to a Mr. Johnson, Philadelphia, October 9, 1935, in Record Group 196, File H-3000, Records of the Housing Division of the Federal Emergency Administration of Public Works, National Archives, Washington, D. C., hereinafter, HDR.

7. Bernard Newman, "Housing of Negro Immigrants in Pennsylvania: An Address given January 3, 1924, before a conference held in Harrisburg, Pa." 3 January 1924, mimeographed, HAP; on housing discrimination, see Dorothy Weisner to Newman, Philadelphia, 13 May 1924, and Newman, Philadelphia, to Bruno Lasker, New York, 16 May 1924, both in HAP; see "Report of Negro Population and Industries of Philadelphia," mimeographed, AAP; Joseph H. Willets, "Some Impact of the Depression Upon the Negro in Philadelphia," *Opportunity*, July 1933, pp. 200-204; Sam Bass Warner, *The Private City: Philadelphia in Three Periods of Its Growth* (Philadelphia, 1968).

8. I. Maxmillian Martin, "Philadelphia's Building and Loan Association," *Crisis*, June 1937, pp. 173-74; on sheriff's sales and evictions, see John F. Bauman, "The City, the Depression, and Relief: The Philadelphia Experience, 1929-1939" (Ph.D. diss., Rutgers University, 19698), pp. 126, 186, 225.

9. Works Progress Administration, Philadelphia Real Property Survey, Philadelphia Surveys, Colored Housing, Bulletins 26 and 27, West and East Central Philadelphia Districts A-1 and A-2, April 10, 1936, R. G. 196, File H-3000, HDR; see also "Housing Conditions in Philadelphia: Extract from Complaints and Appeals for Help, Addressed to the Housing Division," n.d., mimeographed, R. G. 196, File H-30000.09, HDR; Woofter and Priest, *Negro Housing*, pp. 14-21; on problems on slum living, see Bernard Newman, "Fire Hazards," 20 September 1930, mimeographed, HAP; U. S., Bureau of the Census, *Fifteenth Census of the U.S.: 1930*, data taken from "Work Sheets," 47th, 30th, 40th, 27th, 14th, 20th and 7th wards.

10. See Nelson, "Race and Class Consciousness," pp. 2-15, 17-18, 95-99, 349-50; reports of Donald Wyatt, secretary of Industrial and Research Department of Armstrong Association, to Board of Managers of Armstrong Association, 1933 and December 1935 to January 1936; mimeographed, AAP.

11. Robert Gray Taylor, Philadelphia, to Bernard Newman, Philadelphia, 3 February 1934, HAP; Limited Dividend Applications for Park Court Housing Corporation, Jefferson Terrance, and Whittier Center Housing Corporation, R. G. 196, File H-3000, HDR; see in particular Henry Homer Jefferson, Philadelphia, to Horatio B. Hacket, Washington, D.C., PWA Director of Housing, 2 May 1935, R. G. 196, H-3000.09, HDR.

12. On the PACH see Robert Kohn, Washington, D.C., housing administrator of PWA Emergency Committee on Housing, to Morris L. Cooke, Philadelphia, 29 March 1934, R. G. 196, File H-3000.703, HDR; and Kohn, Washington D.C., to W. Logan MacCoy, Philadelphia, 28 April 1934, R. G. 196, File H-3000.703.

13. On J. Hampton Moore's attitude toward slums and federal projects, see Bauman, "The City, The Depression, and Relief," pp. 233-34.

14. Eustace Gay, Philadelphia, managing editor of the *Tribune*, to H. A. Gray, Washington, D.C., Division of Housing, PWA, 3 December 1936, R. G. 196, File H-3000.09, HDR.

15. Madge Headley Priest in T. S. Woofter's *Negro Problems in Cities* (New York, 1928), pp. 152-70; transcript of meeting between "Group of WPA women from 11th and York Streets" (a "Committee of twenty-two women mostly Negro"), and Bernard Newman, 5 August 1936, mimeographed, HAP.

16. See Janice Carp, Philadelphia of Neighborhood Center, 422-428 Bainbridge Ave., to FDR, 9 May 1935, R. G. 196, File H-3000.09, HDR; W.E.B. DuBois's views on race relations and segregation in the 1930s, see DuBois, "Postscript," *Crisis*, January 1933, pp. 140-41.

17. Abbie Johnson, Philadelphia, Grand Daughter Ruler, Protective Order of Elks, to Harold Ickes, Washington, 12 March 1935; and Robert Baskerville, Philadelphia, Omega Psi Phi Fraternity, to Ickes, Washington, 23 March 1935, all in R. G. 196, File H-3000.09, HDR; Arthur DuBois, Philadelphia, of PWA Housing Division, to Carrie Younker, Philadelphia Federation of Settlements, 4 April 1936, in response to telegram emanating from 27 March 1936 meeting of 500 tenants; and letter of Cornelius Garlick, secretary of Slum Clearance Committee of Philadelphia NAACP, to Horatio Hackett, Washington, 11 May 1935, all in R.G. 196, File H-3000.09, HDR; also transcript of conference with Negro group arranged by John Edelman, 21 May 1935, mimeographed, HAP; on housing committee of National Negro Congress, see H. A. Gray, Washington, D.C., to Newman, Philadelphia, 21 October 1936, in HAP.

18. Memorandum to Ickes from Horatio Hackett, director of housing, 15 April 1935, R. G. 48, File 1-276, Pennsylvania, HDR; Hyman Cunin, Washington, D.C., assistant architectural engineer, to B. M. Pettit, Washington, D. C., Initiation branch, 23 March 1935, R. G. 196, File H-3000.703, HDR.

19. On appointments of Major R. R. Wright and Crystal Bird Fauset, see Bernard Newman. Philadelphia, to Hackett, Washington, 3 May 1935, HAP; see also memorandum to Ickes from A. R. Clas, 23 May 1935, recommending appointment of Wright "as an outstanding citizen representing the older Negro interests in

Philadelphia," R. G. 48, File 1-276, Pennsylvania, HDR.

20. Nelson, "Race and Class Consciousness," pp. 10-11; E. Washington Rhodes, "Pennsylvania Politics as of the Year 1934," *Crisis*, July 1934, p. 212; on the role of Wright and Fauset on the PACH, see Philadelphia Advisory Committee on Housing, *Minutes*, 12 June 1935, pp. 102, HAP; Newman Philadelphia to J. A. MacCullum, president of Philadelphia Housing Association, 17 November 1936, HAP.

21. Eugene Pharo, "Philadelphia Named 'City of Homeless,' " *Washington Post*, 10 January 1937; Sec. B; *Philadelphia Inquirer*, 31 December 1936.

22. On Mayor S. D. Wilson's actions, see S. Davis Wilson, Philadelphia, to Arthur DuBois, Philadelphia, 14 February 1936, R. G. 196, File H-3000 (.2), HDR; also *Philadelphia Inquirer*, 31 December 1936.

23. On activities of the Tenants' League, see flyers entitled "For Decent Homes at Low Rents!!!," "Stop the Unfair Eviction of Mrs. Chandler," "Defend Your Neighbor!!!," all in HAP; on city-wide conference, see "Mass Action Sought on Local Housing," *Tribune*, 9 December 1937.

24. On the creation of the Philadelphia Housing Authority, see Newman, Philadelphia to H. A. Gray, Washington, D. C., director of Housing, PWA, 13 October 1937, HAP; Robert C. Weaver, "The Negro and Low Rent Housing," an address delivered before the Eastern Regional Conference of the National Negro Congress, Baltimore, Maryland, 7 October 1938, mimeographed, Temple Urban Archives Library.

25. Walter Thomas and Samuel Wetherhill, Philadelphia, both of City Planning Commission, to A. R. Clas, Washington, D.C., 28 May 1935, R. G. 196, File H-3000 (.2), HDR.

26. For Newman quotes, see Newman, Philadelphia, to Meta Herder, St. Paul, Minnesota, 1 June 1935, and Newman, Philadelphia, to Mrs. Allan F. Reith, Council of Social Agencies, Milwaukee, Wisconsin, 8 January 1934, HAP; on criteria for site selection, see Frank Smith, chairman of Philadelphia Housing Authority to Newman, 20 July 1935, HAP.

27. Philadelphia Committee on Public Affairs, "The Public Housing Program in Philadelphia," 15 March 1940, mimeographed, HAP; also Newman, Philadelphia, to J. A. MacCallum, Philadelphia, 26 July 1935, HAP; Newman, Philadelphia, to Clas, Washington, D.C., 31 May 1935, R. G. 196, File H-3000, HDR.

28. Philadelphia Housing Authority, *Minutes* [hereinafter, H. A., *Minutes*], 12 February 1938, found in Philadelphia Housing Authority offices, Philadelphia; H. A., *Minutes*, 27 September 1937, and 29 December 1937, and 11 March 1939 and 12 June 1939; see also *First Annual Report of the Philadelphia Housing Authority* (1937), HAP; on James Weldon Johnson project see Philadelphia Housing Authority, *Report, 1939-1941*, HAP.

29. HA, *Report, 1939-1941*, p. 28; on demise of housing program, see "Statement of Mayor Lamberton to Press," mimeographed, 13 May 1940, HAP; and Nathan Straus, "Statement before Members of the Philadelphia Housing Authority, 2:30 p.m., Monday," 1 July 1940, mimeographed, HAP.

30. U. S. Housing Authority, *Design of Low Rent Housing Projects: Planning Site* (U. S. Government P. O., 1939), pp. 7-14; the average monthly rent at the Glenwood and Richard Allen Homes was $18.94 including utilities. Since public housing was

restricted to families whose net income did not exceed five times the rental value of their unit, most clients were respectable, working-class people with incomes under $1,000 a year, see H. A., *Minutes*, 24 June 1940, and 8 April 1940; on absence of frills and project regimentation, see H. A., *Minutes*, 6 September 1939; Edith Elmer Wood, "One Third of a Nation," *Survey Graphic* 29 (February 1940): pp. 84-89; Dorothy Canfield, "I Visit a Housing Project," *Survey Graphic* 29 (February 1940): pp. 89-90.

31. On the first residents of the James Weldon Johnson homes, see Philadelphia *Tribune*, 18 July 1940, p. 1; a simple analysis of census tracts for the decennial years 1930 and 1940 shows that in census tract A of the 30th ward the black population rose from 90 percent of the tract in 1930 to over 96 percent in 1940; and in census tract B of the 20th ward the black population climbed from 64 percent of the tract in 1930 to 85 percent in 1940; Pennsylvania State Temporary committee on the Urban Colored Population, "Preliminary Report," May 1941, mimeographed Temple Urban Archives Library.

[10]
Democratic Politics in Pennsylvania, 1932-1938

As the preceding chapters suggest, the Great Depression and the New Deal profoundly affected Pennsylvania. The economic disaster so weakened existing institutions that New Deal programs broke through the barriers that had long isolated rural communities and urban ghettoes. In doing so, the Roosevelt administration—capitalizing on the new labor and social militancy—destroyed the industrial feudalism that had prevailed during the 1920s. In both coal fields and industrial centers, the New Deal enlivened dormant labor unions and encouraged the creation of new ones. Popular federal programs helped Pennsylvania's Democratic leaders win the allegiance of thousands of virtually disfranchised voters and brought new power and influence to the state's Democratic party. Ethnic and minority voters by the thousands switched from the Republicans to the Democrats, and in Pittsburgh and Philadelphia resurgent Democratic machines emerged to bring a new vitality to local and state political contests. In 1934 a Democrat was elected governor for the first time since 1890, and state Democrats now experienced the novelty of real political success.

On the eve of Franklin D. Roosevelt's election in 1932, the Democratic party in Pennsylvania barely existed. Between 1893 and 1931 Democrats lost 95 of 96 statewide elections; things were so grim that a Democratic gubernatorial candidate in 1928 withdrew from the race to campaign instead for Grand

Exalted Ruler of the Elks. In Philadelphia, Republican boss William S. Vare often decided who would be the Democratic candidates for the city's minority party officials; Vare even paid the rent for the Democrats' headquarters. Although in Pittsburgh the Democrats were perhaps not quite so subservient as in Philadelphia, only 5,200 of that city's 175,000 registered voters in 1929 were Democrats. Before the New Deal no industrial county and not a single region of the state normally voted Democratic. Not even organized labor felt allegiance to the Democrats, and both ethnic and black neighborhoods remained firmly loyal to the Republican party. Thus, in the years before Roosevelt, most political battles in Pennsylvania were waged within the Republican party, not between the GOP and the Democrats.[1]

However, the Great Depression and the failure of Herbert Hoover and the Republican party to respond adequately to its ravages rekindled Democratic aspirations in Pennsylvania. Headed by party stalwart Joseph F. Guffey of Pittsburgh, the Pennsylvania delegation at the party's national convention in Chicago in 1932 led all the states in supporting Roosevelt's nomination on the fourth ballot. The candidate visited Pennsylvania during the fall campaign and before an enthusiastic crowd at Pittsburgh's Forbes Field delivered his famous "fiscal responsibility" speech (later to prove rather embarrassing for him). Even though Pennsylvania remained true to its Republican tradition and voted for Hoover in 1932, resurgent Democrats had good reason to rejoice: among other things, Allegheny County had voted Democratic for the first time since 1856; in Philadelphia, the Republican majority was only one-fourth of its usually robust standard; the number of Democratic Congressmen was now the greatest since 1860; and over the state Hoover's vote was down from his 1928 total by over 600,000 ballots.

A few days after Roosevelt's inauguration in March of 1933, Congress convened in special session, and in the following 100 days passed an unprecedented array of recovery and reform measures. Abandoning the old concept of federalism which precluded positive federal intervention to relieve economic distress, the New Deal inaugurated a series of programs which provided for federal aid to the states for unemployment relief.

Pennsylvania's Republican Governor Gifford Pinchot moved deliberately to take advantage of Washington's new largesse. Although hampered by conservatives within his own party, Pinchot persuaded the General Assembly to provide some monies to enable the State Emergency Relief Board to administer relief. According to Pinchot, in 1933 and 1934 no governor in the country "pounded more consistently or vigorously on Washington's door to obtain the various kinds or relief which the federal government made available." However, Pinchot's entreaties for greater state funds produced more battles than money in the General Assembly. Only when Washington in 1934 threatened to stop the federal flow to Pennsylvania did the General Assembly agree to contribute a larger share of the relief burden.[3]

Of the early New Deal programs in Pennsylvania, the Civilian Conservation Corps (CCC) ranked among the most popular and successful. The state's CCC camps were among the first in operation. Men between the ages of eighteen and twenty-five were the initial enrollees. They were largely unmarried, were generally from urban relief families, and were paid $30.00 a month, $25.00 of which they were required to send home to dependents. By 1940, Pennsylvania's 160,000 CCC workers had planted thousands of trees, built over 6,000 miles of roads and woodland trails, constructed 100 small dams, scores of lookout towers and small bridges, and had spent innumerable days fighting forest fires. Although a bit more expensive than other New Deal relief programs, the CCC was a great success, not only for its conservation and reforestation projects, but, more importantly, for its reclamation of human lives.

Inexorably, politics intruded into Pennsylvania's CCC, though perhaps not quite so much as in other programs. Since the administrators at the camps, including project superintendents, foremen, and others, were appointive positions, politicans were aware of the CCC's patronage possibilities. Congressmen and other local politicians filled these positions, and more often than not, political persuasion rather than technical competence determined a candidate's success or failure in landing a position with the CCC. As usual, there were many complaints. Democratic Congressman John Buell Snyder of Fayette County often telephoned Washington officials his displeasure concerning CCC appointments; too many Republicans, he complained. Republican Congressman Benjamin Focht of Bloomfield cried that, although he "had voted for all these New Deal measures," he was not getting any appointments, and never dreamed, he said,that the (CCC projects) "would be administered so as to discriminate against Republicans." Despite these conflicts, most politicians enjoyed the patronage. In 1937 when Congress tried to place CCC administrators and supervisors under civil service, most Pennsylvania Congressmen helped defeat the move.[4]

Although through the Federal Emergency Relief Administration the New Deal was providing relief for many Pennsylvanians by the fall of 1933, thousands more desperately anticipated the hardships of the approaching winter months. Unemployment had reached staggering proportions, private relief funds were vitually nonexistent, and federal monies did not meet adequately the needs of the state.

In response to the obvious need for more federal aid, President Roosevelt established the Civil Works Administration (CWA) in November 1933. Charged with providing work for 4 million of the nation's idle workers, the CWA was granted $400 million to help the unemployed over the winter. From November through March 1934, the CWA undertook over 180,000 projects, and spent over $930 million. Pennsylvania had over 9,000 major projects which at one time employed as many as 320,000 people.

Although many Pennsylvanians claimed that the CWA kept them alive that winter, as with almost every federal relief program, criticism and complaints abounded. Workers grumbled about undue treatment, untimely discharges from work, discrimination in job selections, and pay cuts which affected some workers and not others. There were public charges of political interference with the agency's work, and disputes over personnel at supervisory levels.

Politicians, of course, eagerly sought the patronage of CWA and haggled endlessly over whether Republicans or Democrats were receiving the most help. The Democrats accused the Republicans of using the CWA to strengthen their county machines. Joseph F. Guffey, western Pennsylvania's Democratic overlord, bitterly charged Pinchot and the Republicans with receiving all the patronage from Democratically inspired relief measures, while the press insisted that only certain factions of both parties received jobs. Philadelphia's Democratic chieftain John B. Kelly later admitted that he had solicited, unsuccessfully, for CWA jobs. Failing, he then urged that politics be removed from CWA hiring practices.[5]

Along with aid for depressed groups, Roosevelt believed that his political well-being also demanded his cooperation with Democratic leaders in the nation's large cities. Patronage not only acted to seal the political troth between the president and his urban allies, and to attract thousands of city dwellers to the New Deal, but it also penetrated the barriers which had isolated them previously from federal support. Thus, the revivification of the Democratic party in cities such as Pittsburgh became crucial to the emergence of the party over the state.

Before the New Deal, Republicans in Pittsburgh outnumbered Democrats by huge majorities. But the Great Depression devastated highly industrialized Pittsburgh and changed the city's political configuration. While the jobless sold five-cent apples on street corners, Pittsburgh's employers cut wages for those fortunate enough to retain their jobs, and the city's Republican leadership—which had claimed credit for the good times—tried in vain to escape responsibility for the bad.[6]

The Democratic resurgence in the city began in 1932, probably the result more of economic conditions than political strategy. By the elections of that year 15 percent of Pittsburgh's white workers and over 43 percent of its Negroes were unemployed. For the city's black citizens, the Democratic party assumed a previously absent appeal.

In the presidential election of 1928, the great majority of the nation's black voters had continued their Republican ways and supported Herbert Hoover. However, leading Negro spokesmen over the country soon began to criticize certain features of the Hoover administration. In his appointments, Hoover had failed to reward his black political supporters. Then, too, the president's faint-hearted response to the plight of black Americans during the depression's early years further disenchanted many blacks. Negroes were, of course, among those hardest hit by the Great Depression. They constituted the majority of unskilled workers whose jobs were taken quickly by newly unemployed and equally hungry white workers. In the face of this economic distress, black leaders urged stronger federal action than Hoover was willing to propose.[7]

Among these leaders was Robert L. Vann of Pittsburgh. Publisher of one of the most influential Negro newspapers of the time, the *Pittsburgh Courier*, Vann led Pittsburgh's black exodus from the Republican party. Early in the campaign of 1932 Vann terminated his life-long Republican affiliation and joined Pennsylvania Democrats in supporting Roosevelt. Through the efforts of the president's close political advisor, James A. Farley, and Pennsylvania's Democratic leader, Joe Guffey, Vann became a manager of the Negro division of the Democratic Campaign Committee, a national publicity director of Negro newspapers, and state director of Negro Democrats in Pennsylvania. These appointments suggested not only the commitment of Vann and the influence of the *Courier,* they also indicated, Vann believed, that he would work with Guffey to dispense black patronage after the anticipated victory in the fall.[8]

Born in North Carolina in 1879, Vann, like thousands of sons and grandsons of former slaves, had migrated north. Attracted to the booming economic promise of Pittsburgh, Vann entered the Western University of Pennsylvania (later the University of Pittsburgh) from which he received a law degree in 1909. But his criminal law practice was modest at best, and like most of Pittsburgh's black attorneys, Vann had to supplement his income by other means. Thus, early in 1910 he and a few black associates launched the *Courier*, a weekly which was to enjoy a long and distinguished career.

Always interested in politics and especially the black role in the American political system, Vann intended to use the

Courier as a means of promoting his political views. According to his biographer, Vann became a highly influential spokesman for Pittsburgh's blacks. With the "power to speak to and for his race," he made the *Courier* "a vigorous advocate of social change," as well as a medium of news. An opportunist who believed in "accommodationist politics," Vann came to believe that the only way the Negro could obtain social and economic justice was to remain independent of any particular political allegiance. By 1932 he was convinced that unswerving loyalty to the Republican party had gained little for blacks; and, moreover, he contended that blacks were still isolated from any real political influence. He was ready—at least for the time being—to cast his lot with the Democrats. Outspoken and above reproach, Vann often changed his position on particular issues, but he remained always a political moderate and a crusader for civil rights.

Vann was often intolerant of others, even arrogant to some. With his light color, straight hair, and slim nose he probably could have disappeared across the color line. In fact, during his youth and early manhood, many urged him to do so; but the proud Vann always refused. Manicured, urbane, and well-tailored, the independent loner with his "elegant good looks and courtly manner" was recognized as perhaps the most prominent member of Pittsburgh's black community.[9]

When Vann beseeched Negroes to "turn Lincoln's picture to the wall (,) the debt has been paid in full," younger blacks, less bound by tradition than their parents, spread the word over Pittsburgh's Negro wards. In November, Roosevelt carried the third ward and won over 46 percent of the vote in the fifth. The nationwide shift of black Americans from the party of Lincoln to that of Roosevelt became one of the most significant political developments in the nation's history.[10]

At the other end of the state in Philadelphia, the Republicans had ruled with little opposition except when they fought among themselves. However, in 1931, the Democrats began to stir when J. David Stern, publisher of the *Philadelphia Record,* supported Governor Roosevelt's unofficial campaign for the presidency. Stern considered his support of Roosevelt not only as a means of getting behind the party's likely nominee, but also as a way to work with others to revive the party over the state.[11]

Of German Jewish ancestry, Stern as a youth worked as a cub reporter for a Philadelphia newspaper. Later he attended the University of Pennsylvania, where he was interested primarily in water polo, girls, and journalism, but did, however, take time to edit the journal of one of the university's oldest literary societies. Although Stern later wrote that he was "too busy to study," he managed to graduate from Penn's law school a year after his father, a Philadelphia garment manufacturer, died. Although he soon passed the bar exam, Stern had never intended to practice law, having pursued his legal studies only to fulfill his late father's wishes.

With his modest inheritance Stern purchased his first newspaper, the *New Brunswick* (N.J.) *Times*, in 1912, and owned at least a half dozen others in his thirty-five-year career in publishing. Small in physical stature, Stern employed a bit of bravado in his crusades for liberal causes, and often editorialized against racial and religious prejudice. He seemed always to be warring against transit interests and Pennsylvania's blue laws. An extrovert who enjoyed a drink or two with his friends, Stern later recalled numerous and lengthy celebrations of political and publishing victories.[12]

Besides the *Record*, Stern published newspapers in New York as well as in New Jersey and was a spearhead in the Democratic resurgence in Philadelphia. An outspoken reformer, Stern persistently badgered President Roosevelt to spend more money on relief and work programs. Often "completely confused and disheartened" by what he considered the New Deal's lack of vigor and direction in bringing about significant social and economic change, Stern nevertheless remained faithful. Although Roosevelt often called Stern his "hairshirt," and the "worst politician," the president found the publisher's editorials to be useful in reviving the party in Pennsylvania. After Roosevelt's victory in 1932, Stern brought wealthy Philadelphia contractors John B. Kelly and Matthew McCloskey into the Democratic camp and together this fledgling band of Democrats boosted the party in the city and began to prepare for the statewide elections of 1934.[13]

Despite Pennsylvania's Republican hegemony, the Democrats believed that the elections of 1934 offered them the best opportunity in years for a state victory. For one thing, the 1932 and 1934 elections in cities such as Philadelphia, Pittsburgh, and Scranton indicated a Democratic trend. Moreover, the Democrats could not count on the federal patronage engendered through various New Deal programs. Paradoxically, despite Democratic claims for economic improvements, in 1934 over 1,350,000 of the state's citizens remained dependent on some form of public assistance. While much of the relief was administered by the Republican administration of Gifford Pinchot, most people knew that the money came primarily from the Democrats in Washington. The number one Democrat was Franklin Roosevelt, and his popularity convinced state Democratic leaders that their hour had finally arrived.[14]

Among those Democratic leaders none was more important or more controversial than Pittsburgh's Joseph F. Guffey. Born in Westmoreland County in 1870, Guffey was reared in a Democratic tradition that stretched back to the age of Andrew Jackson. As a student at Princeton in the early 1890s, Guffey fell under the spell of Woodrow Wilson, who after World War I appointed him to the office of the Alien Property Custodian in Washington. In the meantime Guffey had organized several prosperous oil companies, and was on his way to becoming a millionaire.

After Wilson's election in 1912, Guffey won partial control of the party's meager holdings in western Pennsylvania. For years his suzerainty meant little. Guffey's organization repeatedly lost races to Republicans throughout the 1920s. Then, in 1931, Guffey publicly threw his organization behind Roosevelt, insisting that the New Yorker would not only win the nomination but in November carry both Pennsylvania and the nation.[15] When the New Deal came to power, Guffey wielded the federal patronage power in Pennsylvania. Along with David L. Lawrence of Pittsburgh, who became Democratic state chairman in 1934, Guffey built a powerful organization nurtured primarily on federal and state jobs.

In 1933 Guffey was a vigorous and intense sixty-three years

old, the only bachelor among the state's top Democratic leaders. Of medium height and chunky, his quiet but expensive clothes and heavy eyebrows gave Guffey a short, almost squat appearance, exaggerated by the habit of holding his hands together behind his back. He was very close to his brother Alexander and to his three sisters, one of whom was the irrepressible Emma Guffey Miller (the only one of the group to marry), a prominent figure in the Democratic party for many years. Guffey never claimed to be a statesman. He was interested in votes and jobs, in how pressure groups operated, in finding ways to get money for the party, and in keeping subordinates happy. A tireless worker who gave full attention to political matters, Guffey delivered very few speeches (he was not a very polished speaker), and did not view a colorful personality or extroverted charm as the means to political success.[16]

Guffey's subsequent career in the United States Senate was characterized by an almost servile devotion to President Roosevelt. No senator had a more pro-New Deal voting record. As one of his colleagues once remarked, "Guffey doesn't know what his position is on this bill because Roosevelt's line is busy."[17] Lawmaking was not his foremost political interest anyway, despite the attachment of his name to important coal legislation. For Guffey, patronage was the key in building and maintaining a political machine.

Nineteen years Guffey's junior, David Lawrence had been bred on politics as much as had his senior partner. Lawrence's father, a Democrat, always animated meal times with his lively political talk, and someone later wrote that Lawrence "(lived) politics twenty-four hours a day." Born in a home located at Greentree Alley and Penn Avenue (in the area of what became the Golden Triangle), Lawrence strongly identified with the city of Pittsburgh and lived there virtually all of his life.

He started young. At fourteen, after completing a high school commercial course, Lawrence went to work as a stenographer in the office of William J. (Billy) Brennan, a lawyer and Pittsburgh's Democratic party chairman. Within a handful of years Lawrence assumed the leadership of the skeletal organizaton. Although, defective vision kept him out of the draft in World War I, he did serve briefly in the wartime Judge Advocate General's Office in Washington.[18]

After the war Lawrence returned to Pittsburgh and to the insurance business. But he was primarily interested in politics, and became Allegheny County chairman in 1920—at the time when a Democrat in Pittsburgh was about as influential as a Republican in Georgia. Nevertheless, Lawrence persevered, taking Republican crumbs and whatever patronage he could get. Then in 1931, with Republican support, Lawrence received over 120,000 votes for county commissioner; although he lost, his vote total was about ten times greater than the Democrats usually polled.

Lawrence loved politics, he loved Pittsburgh, he loved dispensing patronage. Of Scotch-Irish descent, he persistently made a show of being Irish. Proud of his Catholicism, Lawrence, along with a few popular Catholic priests of Pittsburgh, doubtless brought many fellow Catholics into the Democratic party. Stocky, outspoken on issues, sometimes even brusque to subordinates and equals alike, Lawrence would later be aptly characterized as the "benevolent Irish despot of the wards."[19]

Called "Colonel Joe and Captain Davy'" Guffey and Lawrence beat a steady path to Washington and Hyde Park (the president's homestead) in search of jobs. While Guffey once exclaimed that it was "impossible to handle the patronage of a state . . . without offending some of the people," he worked at it diligently. When he complained that federal administrators did not give him "proper consideration," Roosevelt urged officials to cooperate with him. He made such demands upon the administration that one official complained that Guffey "(thinks) every job in Pennsylvania (is) Democratic patronage."[20]

A consummate politician, Guffey was among the first political bosses to fasten New Deal reforms to a political machine.[21] By organizing those who had been heretofore isolated from significant political influence in Pennsylvania—blacks, independent liberals, inner-city dwellers, and organized labor—Guffey put Pennsylvania's old bosses out of business and in 1934 he was ready to run for office himself.

But registered Republicans still outnumbered their Democratic counterparts by more than two to one. Despite Roosevelt's popularity among the people of Pennsylvania, the GOP confidently expected to carry the elections. In their gubernatorial primary of 1934 the Republicans selected Pinchot's attorney general, William A. Schnader, and renominated Senator David A. Reed, who defeated Governor Pinchot in the senatorial primary by 100,000 votes.

Democrats were determined to attach themselves to Roosevelt's coattails; at the same time they had to appeal to the state's Republican majorities. Thus, to the dismay of many Democrats, who since Woodrow Wilson had suffered through countless defeats, the party selected a former Republican, George H. Earle III of Philadelphia, as its gubernatorial candidate. Guffey won the nomination for the U. S. Senate, and Thomas Kennedy of Hazelton, a Guffey ally and an official of the United Mine Workers of America, was nominated for lieutenant governor.[22]

Earle was born in 1890 in Devon, Pennsylvania. His father, a successful businessman, had engaged in Philadelphia's Independent Republican politics. After being educated at Harvard, young Earle served in World War I, and was decorated for service in the Navy. He settled in Philadelphia, started his own business, the Flamingo Sugar Mills, became the director of several family businesses, and became somewhat of a figure in the city's social life.

Although a Republican like his forebears, Earle had contributed money to Roosevelt's campaign in 1932. To reward his financial help, the president named Earle minister to Austria, and the latter was in Vienna when Guffey, David Stern, and other party leaders asked him to come home and run for governor.

The party's selection of Earle made sense. For one thing, his was a rather fresh face in Pennsylvania politics. Not only could he attract independent voters, he could also contribute money to his own campaign. Closely identified with the president, Earle won the Democratic primary by almost four to one.[23]

In the fall campaign he promised a "Pennsylvania New Deal" by replacing Republican disinterest toward the unemployed and the hungry with Democratic concern. He outlined aid for farmers and miners, and proposed old-age pensions, unemployment insurance, and wages-and-hours legislation. Not only did Earle claim that a vote for him was a vote for Roosevelt, he insisted that a GOP victory in Pennsylvania would constitute a defeat for the president and mean the end of the New Deal.

Each party attacked the other's candidate for inexperience in government, for lies, for political and economic intimidation of employees, and for bribery, among other charges. Both parties picked up defectors from the opposition, with perhaps the Democrats doing better there. Both sides made special appeals to blacks and the Democrats' selection of Kennedy for lieutenant governor was an undisguised attempt to garner the labor vote.

Earle, Guffey, and Kennedy all won as Pennsylvania, the citadel of Republican strength, joined the nationwide Democratic sweep. The party also won in twenty-three of the state's thirty-four congressional elections, adding significantly to the Democrats' overwhelming majorities in Congress. Considering that the Democrats had a majority of registered voters in only eleven of the states' sixty-seven counties, Roosevelt's popularity and the New Deal's presence in Pennsylvania, especially in the cities and in the coal-mining areas, probably accounted for the party's victory. Earle later exclaimed: "They say we rode in on Roosevelt's coat tails. Hell, he carried us in piggyback." For the first time in over forty years, a Democrat was elected governor, and Guffey was Pennsylvania's first Democratic senator in sixty years. The elections transformed the perennial also-ran party into a winner, and the Democrats promised that the victory meant a friendly hand would be extended to the state's poorest and least-represented citizens.[24]

The new governor intended to "use the New Deal as a model and reproduce its image in Pennsylvania." Soon after his inauguration, friend and foe alike were calling Earle's administration the "Little New Deal." In translating a well-publicized promise into legislative and administrative reality, Earle had to contend with a Republican majority in the state senate, as well as face the persistence of hard times. As the legislative session of 1935 began, over 22 percent of the state's labor force was still unemployed, and within a few days all state relief funds would be exhausted. Washington filled the void with $68 million in relief monies, but warned that federal funds would end unless Pennsylvania provided $5 million a month for relief after April 15.

To pay for this and various state programs, Earle asked for $203 million in new and increased taxes. Specifically, he requested increases on utility, gasoline, and personal-property taxes, and asked for new taxes on corporate net incomes, chain stores, amusements, and cigarettes. Although there were the usual protests from vested interests, Earle won most of his tax battles.

Reforms were harder to come by, but Earle enjoyed some successes in 1935 and 1936. The legislature passed a new child-labor law, and an equal-rights bill. While the legislature also abolished the Coal and Iron Police, it refused to pass a proposal to prohibit employers from paying the salaries of deputies appointed by county sheriffs. Consequently, some strike breaking activities proceeded as usual.[25]

Midway through Earle's term, the presidential election of 1936 offered Pennsylvania Democrats an opportunity to capitalize on the president's popularity and win new majorities needed to continue the "Little New Deal." Pennsylvania also provided a perfect test for the New Deal's political cause nationwide. The state campaign would test the loyalty of the black vote, indicate the popularity of a state program modeled after the New Deal, measure the allegiance of both work-relief employees and organized labor, and generally weigh the New Deal's popularity in a large industrial-rural state.

Appropriately, the campaign started in Philadelphia with the Democratic national convention in June. For over a year Pennsylvania Democrats had urged Roosevelt and Farley to hold the convention in Philadelphia, and in early 1936 the city was selected. Philadelphia Democrats were ecstatic; not even the great electric sign of the Union League Club proclaiming "LANDON AND KNOX, 1936. LOVE OF COUNTRY LEADS" could diminish their optimism. John Kelly organized many of the convention's arrangements, distributed tickets for

Franklin Field, and even composed a convention song—a parody of the GOP. Guffey was in charge of things politically. Despite the usual intraparty struggles, Guffey had stayed out of most county battles and now led a state delegation united in support of Roosevelt. And the president's acceptance address—the famous "rendezvous with destiny" speech—climaxed a political orgy whose participants confidently looked toward the election in November.[26]

During the campaign the president traveled in Pennsylvania and was, of course, accompanied by state and local politicos. In late summer he visited the perennially flooded areas around Johnstown and subsequently visited both eastern and western areas of the state. Huge crowds applauded the campaigning president in Philadelphia and Pittsburgh. In the latter city Governor Earle compared the humane Roosevelt with the old order in Pennsylvania. Cries of contempt encouraged the governor's description of the state's plutocrats: the Mellons were wealthy "from the toil of the men of iron and steel"; Grundy's "sweatshop operators have been the shame and disgrace of Pennsylvania for a generation"; and J. Howard Pew wanted "a political and economic empire with himself as dictator."[27]

Democratic rhetoric could go only so far in promoting the cause of both the president and the party in traditionally Republican Pennsylvania. Patronage was necessary too. Besides the usual lengthening of job rolls before an election, the word was passed to Democratic leaders to organize the work-reliefers and win their votes. One Philadelphia leader wrote his "Dear Committeemen" to "get the names of all men on relief, also all those holding W.P.A. jobs." Then, the committeemen were told, "Urge them to register Democrat on March 25 or else lose their positions."[28]

Roosevelt won over 60 percent of the vote in Philadelphia and swept the rest of the state as well. By defeating his Republican opponent, Governor Alfred M. Landon of Kansas, by 2,353,987 votes to 1,690,20, the president won forty-one of the state's sixty-seven counties, and enjoyed the largest vote ever cast in Pennsylvania for the presidential candidate of any party.

Along with Roosevelt's victory the Democrats won greater majorities than before in the state house and also a two-thirds majority in the senate. Armed with these unprecedented numbers, Earle pushed through a reform program called by party leader David Lawrence "the most constructive, liberal and humane in generations." It included a new Department of Public Assistance, which replaced the system of poor boards; wages-and-hours laws for men and women; a new workmen's-compensation act; and an occupational-disease compensation act. Also in the interest of labor, the legislature passed the Little Wagner Act and abolished the system of privately paid deputy sheriffs. Further, the legislature replaced the Public Service Commission with the Public Utilities Commission, and enlarged the latter's powers. It passed the Little Agriculture Adjustment Act, and enacted the state's first tenure law for teachers.[29]

The relationship between Earle and Roosevelt seemed to be very close. The governor extended every conceivable courtesy to the president, soliciting his advice on political matters, sending numerous invitations to visit, and frequently presenting gifts to the president and his secretarial staff. Although not so independent or even so progressive as such reform governors as Floyd B. Olson of Minnesota or Philip LaFollette of Wisconsin, Earle was committed to change and cooperated fully with the New Deal.

In other large industrial-rural states, the situation was mixed.[30] In both New York and Illinois as well as in a few other states, intraparty dissension reflected distinct ethnic differences as well as upstate-downstate rivalries. At the same time, however, in New York and Illinois strong urban machines and active gubernatorial leadership had produced a strong state party long before the New Deal. In fact, New York's Democratic leaders, like Pennsylvania's, remained close to the New Deal throughout the era. Very few governors were closer to the president than was Herbert H. Lehman, Roosevelt's successor in Albany. However, despite the pair's warm friendship, Lehman sometimes protested New Deal rulings on relief eligibility and unemployables which he believed discriminated against New York. He might have wondered, too, why it was that, while New York's federal tax incidence per capita was $82 (third in the nation), the state received only $18 per capita (forty-seventh) in aid.

Despite Lehman's legitimate complaints, his liberal leadership reflected both the New Deal's spirit of reform as well as the governor's commitment to social justice. Progressivism in New York was equal to that in Pennsylvania; as one historian has written, reform under Lehman "was safe and unspectacular, but it was as humane as anywhere else in the nation."[31]

In many respects Massachusetts and Pennsylvania both faced difficulties with federal relief. In Massachusetts, where local and regional factors limited the thrust of the New Deal, there was an endless struggle between state and federal officials over relief and other federal programs. Democratic factionalism became a serious problem for the New Deal and strained relations between Washington and prominent Massachusetts Democrats persisted throughout the 1930s. Unlike Pennsylvania, where most all Democratic groups were pro-New Deal, in Massachusetts it seemed that Washington antagonized both the forces behind Governor James Michael Curley and those of his adversaries led by Governor Joseph B. Ely and Senator David I. Walsh. For a period Governor Curley lost all federal patronage, and when he was awarded a few jobs, it was only because his party rivals were also on the outs with the New Deal.[32]

In Ohio, state and local governments refused to provide relief proportionate to the state's resources. Although as hard hit by the depression as was Pennsylvania, Ohio averaged considerably less relief per individual than did the Keystone State. Less progressive than other industrial-farm states, Ohio officials left most relief responsibilities to local communities and provided little imaginative leadership at the state level. Further, there was great friction between Governor Martin Davey and the New Deal, as well as between Davey and other Ohio Democrats. However, though Davey and a number of other Ohio Democrats were ideologically opposed to the New Deal, they, along with Republican leaders led by Governor John Bricker—who succeeded Davey in 1939—accepted federal aid in the late 1930s. Indeed, the Works Progress Administration employed more people in Ohio in 1938–1939 than in any other state except one.[33]

Meanwhile, the New Deal continued to spread its influence in Pennsylvania, primarily by way of its work-relief programs. No matter how the programs were administered, they all promised patronage and they all became involved in local and state politics. For the most part, too, they all contributed generously to the popularity of the President among the laboring groups.

The Works Progress Administration (WPA), established by Roosevelt in 1935, involved direct federal relief. Perhaps the most significant of the New Deal's work programs, the WPA operated longer and spent more money than either of its two predecessors, the Federal Emergency Relief Administration and the Civil Works Administration. The WPA spent more than $10.5 billion between 1935 and 1943, and employed over 8 million people. Although the WPA faced serious political obstacles in Philadelphia, over the state the agency spent more money and employed more people than in any other state except New York. Since the WPA offered obvious patronage possibilities, especially at the supervisory levels, Pennsylvania's resurgent Democrats anxiously schemed to reap its rewards.[34]

Congress—with more Pennsylvania Democrats present than in recent memory—provided that any state or federal WPA administrator whose annual salary was $5,000 or more had to be appointed by the president with the approval of the Senate. Senatorial courtesy prompted the president to consult Democratic senators before selecting high-level WPA administrators. In Pennsylvania's case, this was Senator Guffey, who selected the first three men to serve as state administrator of the WPA.

Guffey and the first administrator, Edward N. Jones, fully intended to use the WPA to help build the Democratic party in Pennsylvania. Believing that state-administered relief had been a "Republican racket," Guffey resolved to make federal relief a "Democratic show." While over 90 percent of all WPA workers in Pennsylvania were project workers who had to be certified by state relief agents as in need of relief before being hired, there were around 3,000 WPA administrators who were political appointees. Even New Dealers confessed that in Pennsylvania most were Democrats. The importance to the party can be suggested by the fact that there were more WPA administrators in Pennsylvania than in any other state (New York City had more, but it was a separate WPA district), and more even than at the WPA headquarters in Washington.[35]

Republicans repeatedly complained that Guffey and Jones appointed only Democrats as WPA administrators and coerced rank and file WPA employees to vote Democratic. After former Governor Pinchot charged Guffey and Jones with "playing politics with relief," state Senator G. Mason Owlett of Tioga County launched a three-man Republican senate investigation into the charges of WPA intimidation and collusion, which heard a witness swear that WPA supervisors had to be approved by local Democrats before getting jobs. However, Washington ordered WPA officials to refuse to testify and the entire matter ended when a federal district court ruled that a state legislative committee had no jurisdiction over a federal agency.[36]

As Republicans suspected, relief exerted a major political impact on the state. Federal work-relief programs along with New Deal labor legislation brought the state's working class into the Democratic fold. By 1936 John L. Lewis, Philip Murray, and other labor leaders were committed to Roosevelt and the New Deal. The miners' victories in the coal fields were followed by labor success in other areas of the state's economy. In 1936 the Committee for Industrial Organization (later, the Congress of Industrial Organizations, CIO), formed the Steel Workers' Organizing Committee (SWOC), which began to organize the steel workers. Early the next year, United States Steel recognized the new union without a shot being fired. In May, Jones and Laughlin followed suit, and soon SWOC had 300,000 members. Although Little Steel (Bethlehem, Inland, Republic, Youngstown Sheet and Tube) held out until World War II, the march toward industrial unionism was in full force and the great majority of Pennsylvania workers credited the New Deal for much of the success.[37]

Other groups also added to the Democratic resurgence. For instance, Catholics such as David Lawrence and Father

Charles Owen Rice, the labor priest of Pittsburgh, capitalized on the large Catholic vote for Al Smith in 1928 by making Democrats of Pittsburgh's large Catholic vote.[38]

Much of the same occurred in Philadelphia, where local Democratic victories in 1934 persuaded Democrats to present the city's voters with a legitimate alternative to Republican rule. So in 1935 the party ran its city chairman, the handsome and athletic John B. Kelly, for mayor against the Independent Republican, S. Davis Wilson.

A Republican until Guffey, Stern, and the New Deal beckoned, Kelly had attended the Philadelphia public schools and served in France during World War I. After the war Kelly combined remarkable business and athletic careers that made him among the most well-known Philadelphians of his day. In the Olympic games of 1920 and 1924, he won medals in both single and double sculls and became an internationally famous oarsman. A daily handball player, Kelly rowed in Philadelphia's famous "Schuylkill Navy," and belonged to many boating clubs, social and athletic clubs, and the American Legion. Called the "Manayunk Adonis" (because the Kellys lived in the East Falls-Manayunk section of the city), the good-looking Irishman cut a dashing figure in Philadelphia society.

Meanwhile, Kelly became a successful contractor and owned one of the largest brickwork firms in the country. Besides his business reputation and physical attractiveness, Kelly had other personal features which added to his political potential. His organizational skills served him well, as did his interesting, witty, and engaging personality. As the "handsomest bricklayer in Philadelphia," Kelly sired an attractive brood of four children which, along with his attractive wife, made an excellent political photograph which Kelly displayed proudly and often in city newspapers. At Christmas, his annual greeting consisted of large playing cards with sketches of each family member smiling out at the recipient.

About a year before the inauguration of the New Deal, Kelly joined the Democratic party and soon his leadership enjoyed the votes of almost 350,000 Philadelphians. In 1934 he became the party's city chairman and was soon predicting that he would be the next mayor of Philadelphia. While his forty-five-inch chest protruded from his tall frame, Kelly towered above his fellow Democrats, and, when he rose to shake hands, one was "bound to take the Democrats seriously." While Kelly was never without foes within the party, he was nevertheless the party's obvious if ill-fated choice for mayor in 1935. City Comptroller S. Davis Wilson's subsequent victory reflected the enduring vitality of the Republican party's popularity among independent voters. Still, the resurgent Democrats did well; although the Republicans boasted 200,000 more registered voters than the Democrats, Kelly lost by only 45,000 votes.[39]

In 1936 Roosevelt carried forty-two of Philadelphia's fifty wards and won the city nearly 200,000 votes over Republican candidate Alf Landon. In the city elections of that year a Democrat won a city council seat for the first time in sixteen years. The results of 1936 left little doubt that the Democratic organization—buoyed by Roosevelt's popularity—had won a sizable constituency.

As in other large cities, Philadelphia Democrats made special appeals to organized labor, ethnic voters, and blacks. Labor leaders by 1936 had organized union workers by city wards and they campaigned for candidates friendly to labor and the New Deal. Unlike Philadelphia Republicans, Democrats not only courted black and ethnic voters, but after 1932 regularly ran Negroes and Italians on their city tickets. Besides, New Deal relief and work programs reached into black and Italian neighborhoods and won many over to local Democrats. Roosevelt was so popular among black Philadelphians that local Republican leaders in 1936 told their Negro constituents to go ahead and vote for him while at the same time asking their support for local Republicans.

The high point of Democratic popularity in Philadelphia came in the elections of 1937 when the party won sixteen of the seventeen minor city offices at stake. David Stern interpreted the outcome as proof that Philadelphia was "no longer a pocket borough of vested interests, . . . no longer corrupt and content."[40] Yet, the Democrats were already in the process of losing some of their newly won popularity not only in

Philadelphia, but also in the rest of the state, and over the nation as well.

After the mandate of 1936, unexpected national reversals for the New Deal in 1937 and 1938 reverberated throughout most of the states. In Pennsylvania, the euphoria of 1936 had hardly passed before the outbreak of bitter Democratic and labor feuds greatly weakened the party's leadership and its hold on the state's voters. By 1938 the intraparty battles had been brewing for at least a year, exacerbated by an ever-increasing number of willing candidates for any office. In Philadelphia John Kelly carried on an endless fight with Congressman Michael Stack over party matters. At the same time, Kelly, whose wife implored him to quit politics in order to spend more time with his growing family, openly resented the patronage policies of the Guffey-Lawrence duo. And the latter pair—with Guffey away in Washington—seemed to be drifting apart as the New Deal waned. In Harrisburg, an open struggle within Earle's Department of Public Assistance erupted over patronage and administrative policies and engendered ill feelings which remained long after the elections of 1938.

By that time, too, Pittsburgh's Robert Vann had become disenchanted with his new party. In 1933, Vann had gone to Washington as special assistant to the attorney general. But when he pressed the administration for jobs and special favor for blacks, he was counseled to "be patient." The Justice Department assigned Vann such trivial duties that before long he was spending only a few days a week in Washington; the rest of the time he attended to *Courier* business. Indeed, after the fall of 1935 he was rarely in Washington, and finally resigned his federal position the following January. His influence declined the more successful the New Deal became among black voters, especially after the presidential election of 1936. A quarrel over city patronage between Vann and Lawrence involved Guffey and helped fuel the fires of Democratic disunity. Vann supported the Republicans in 1938, all the while insisting that he was still loyal to Senator Guffey.[42]

If the embattled Guffey faced obstacles in his determination to control the party, his labor stalwarts were fighting, too. For a year, John L. Lewis, powerful head of the CIO, had been pushing the gubernatorial candidacy of Lieutenant Governor Thomas Kennedy, who was also the United Mine Workers secretary-treasurer. At the same time, leaders of the American Federation of Labor (AFL) demanded a voice within the party equal to that of Lewis. In the end, the national divisions within labor's house in 1938 were reflected in Pennsylvania politics, where labor leaders seemed more intent on routing each other than in electing Democratic candidates.

Thus, within the newly victorious but apparently unhappy party, political success and patronage disputes led to a Democratic factionalism which helped to produce a Republican victory in the statewide elections of 1938. In a fratricidal donnybrook unusual even for Democratic primaries, erstwhile western Pennsylvania allies Joe Guffey and David Lawrence led opposing factions in a bitter struggle for state control of the party. Pittsburgh's Lawrence and Philadelphia's John Kelly and Matthew McCloskey backed a relatively unknown Pittsburgh lawyer, Charles Alvin Jones, for governor, along with Governor Earle for the U. S. Senate. Guffey, whose desire to run for governor had been denied by a Democratic political summit, was joined by David Stern in supporting Thomas Kennedy for governor. Guffey and Kennedy than added S. Davis Wilson, nominal Republican and mayor of Philadelphia, as their candidate for the senate. The state's labor forces joined the battle when John L. Lewis and the CIO endorsed Kennedy and Wilson, while AFL forces backed the Earle-Jones ticket. Further complicating matters for the party was the gubernatorial candidacy of Charles Margiotti, a former Republican who had been fired as attorney general by Governor Earle.[43]

The primary turned into a free-for-all as all three groups bitterly attacked one another. The various charges included patronage dispensing, macing, and political corruption. The WPA was brought into the fray when John Kelly—who was never very friendly with Guffey—charged in a telegram to President Roosevelt that the senator was coercing WPA workers to work for his slate. Guffey denied the charge, and one of his supporters, Democratic Congressman Francis P.

Walter of Scranton, wrote Roosevelt that Kelly was bullying WPA workers to support his candidates. Margiotti charged both sides with macing, insisted that Lawrence and other Democratic leaders had accepted bribes to pass legislation, and charged Earle with so much assorted political corruption that a grand jury was called to investigate.[44]

Amidst charges from all sides, the Lawrence-Kelly-Earle-Jones group won the primary. But it was a Pyrrhic victory. In the general election the Margiotti charges still beclouded the party, and although the distraught Guffey agreed to serve as campaign manager for the ticket, the Democrats were demoralized. Even if Robert Vann's recent reversion to the Republicans did not hurt in the Negro wards, the serious rift in labor's ranks was not closed in the general election. Democrats stopped criticizing the WPA, but the Republicans made the agency an issue after Guffey and Earle sent letters to WPA workers in August asking them for political contributions and reminding them of the dark days before the New Deal. Shortly before the election, at the request of state Democrats, the WPA added 10,000 men to the relief rolls. (The rolls were reduced by 20,000 immediately after the election.) The GOP cried foul, and it must have been convincing because Republican Arthur James was elected governor and James J. Davis was returned to the Senate.[45]

In their post mortem, Democrats offered many explanations for their defeat. Some believed that the personal attacks of the primary were too great to overcome; others insisted that the charges of corruption alienated too many independent votes; many claimed that the patronage fight over the WPA cost the party thousands of votes, while still others blamed the defeat on labor's split and the lack of cooperation among party leaders on the local level. One incumbent Democrat who lost in the general election later wrote: "Perhaps, we had gained our strength in this Commonwealth too rapidly to build on the firmest possible foundations."[46]

Voter registration figures suggest that Democratic leaders failed to get out the vote in the general election of 1938, either among registered Democrats or those who had registered Republican.[47] In 1932 little more than 20 percent of the state's voters were registered Democrats; yet, Roosevelt received over 45 percent of the total vote. In 1934, 63 percent of the voters were registered as Republicans, but the GOP received only 48 percent of the vote. Two years later, 54 percent of the electorate were registered Republicans, but Landon received only 48 percent of the presidential vote. However, in1938, while 47.5 percent of the registered voters were listed as Democrats, the party's candidate for governor won only 45.8 percent of the votes.[48]

Furthermore, in the election of 1936, five southwestern Pennsylvania counties had led the state in percentage majorities for Roosevelt: Washington, 69-30 percent; Fayette, 68-31; Westmoreland, 66-32; Allegheny, 65-31; and Greene, 65-34. Yet in 1938, Earle won Washington County by only 2,000 votes, Fayette by 5,300, Allegheny by 1,624, and even lost Greene and Westmoreland counties, the latter by over 4,400 votes. In his race for governor four years earlier, Earle had won all these counties by comfortable margins. While it is to be expected that more voters show up in presidential election years than in off-years, the decline of the Democratic vote from 1936 to 1938 was dramatic. In 1938 in Allegheny County Earle received over 109,000 fewer votes than Roosevelt had won two years earlier. In Westmoreland County Earle's total was 28,000 less than Roosevelt's had been in 1936.[49]

It may be that Pennsylvania Democrats, through patronage and general New Deal favors, became too rich too soon. But the Democratic defeats in Pennsylvania were only part of a nationwide trend in 1938. In congressional elections over the country, for instancse, the Republicans gained eighty seats in the House and seven in the Senate, and won a majority of the gubernatorial races. The New Deal had come to an end, and so had the brief Democratic ascendency in Pennsylvania.

Nevertheless, no sweeping reversal of the New Deal or the Little New Deal ever took place. As Pennsylvania settled into a two-party state, it became apparent that the Republicans would retain great strength in the farm-rural-forest counties. Apart from the powerful force of habit and tradition, perhaps one of the reasons that the Republicans retained majorities in rural Pennsylvania was the unpopularity of certain New Deal

programs in the state. For instance, the Agricultural Adjustment Act of 1933 greatly infringed upon the farmer's freedom of operation and the Agricultural Adjustment Administration (AAA) received little support from a majority of Pennsylvania farmers, who were unsympathetic with its programs. Few Pennsylvania farmers participated in AAA crop reduction programs; for example, only about 5 percent of the state's wheat farmers signed contracts to reduce wheat acreage in the New Deal's first year. Total benefit payments to Pennsylvania farmers from the AAA in that period amounted to only $425,000, most of this going to tobacco farmers.

In the New Deal's early years Pennsylvania farmers complained of the inequities of the AAA as it applied to their state—while at the same time refusing to participate in the program. In 1934 Pennsylvanians paid an aggregate processing tax (a tax on all processors of farm products, which was used to pay AAA benefits) of over $8 million, but the state's farmers received benefit payments of only $866,000. Southern and Western states were the great beneficiaries of New Deal farm policy; Texas farmers, for example, received sixty-two times the amount of AAA payments that Pennsylvanians did.

Although later New Deal measures were a bit more palatable to Pennsylvania farmers, most of them still refused to vote in the various referenda held to determine the operation of various farm programs. In the wheat referendum of 1935, fewer than 4,000 of the 85,000 Pennsylvania wheat farmers bothered to vote. At the same time, however, many of the state's farmers took advantage of New Deal farm-credit programs, the tenant-purchase loan plan, and the federal government's purchase of surplus crops of apples, milk products, grapes, eggs, and potatoes.[50] Nevertheless, a majority of Pennsylvania farmers continued to register and vote Republican.

Among the blacks and nationality blocs in Pennsylvania's cities, the Democrats won lasting majorities. While the Republicans would continue to win most major elections in Philadelphia for over a decade, the Democrats remained strong there. In Pittsburgh, where New Deal relief created and nurtured the Democratic machine of David Lawrence, the party remained in power for over a generation, and it has remained

dominant in most of the state's coal and industrial regions outside of Philadelphia.

Irrespective of which political party won public office in Pennsylvania after the New Deal, the period reflected a new response to industrialism in the Keystone State. By responding to Democratic overtures, Pennsylvania's perennially slighted groups—poorer city dwellers, isolated coal miners, organized labor, Negroes, and others—served notice that there were options to traditional Republican control. The importance of the Roosevelt era is that it provided greater access to political power and governmental favors to these long isolated and neglected groups.

NOTES

1. For Philadelphia, see John F. Bauman, "The City, the Depression, and Relief: The Philadelphia Experience, 1929-1939" (Ph.D. diss., Rutgers University, 1969), chapter 4; for Pittsburgh, see Bruce M. Stave, *The New Deal and the Last Hurrah: Pittsburgh Machine Politics* (Pittsburgh, 1970), pp. 30-31.

2. *The Pennsylvania Manual,* 1933, p. 402. See also Charles E. Halt, "Joseph F. Guffey, New Deal Politician" (Ph.D. diss., Syracuse University, 1965), pp. 100-103; 112-114.

3. For studies of Pinchot, see M. Nelson McGeary, *Gifford Pinchot: Forester, Politician* (Princeton, 1960), and Samuel John Astorino, "The Decline of the Republican Dynasty in Pennsylvania, 1929-1934" (Ph.D. diss., University of Pittsburgh, 1962).

4. John A. Salmond, *The Civilian Conservation Corps, 1933-1942: A New Deal Case Study* (Durham, 1967), 4-24; Kenneth E. Hendrickson, Jr., "The Civilian Conservation Corps in Pennsylvania: A Case Study of a New Deal Relief Agency in Operation," *The Pennsylvania Magazine of History and Biography,* 100, no. 1 (January 1976), pp. 66-96.

5. James N. J. Henwood, "Experiment in Relief: The Civil Works Administration in Pennsylvania," *Pennsylvania History,* 39, no. 1 (January 1972), pp. 50-71; "Guffey, New Deal Politician," pp. 132-133, 155; *New York Times,* 21 January 1934.

6. Bette T. Krall, "Pittsburgh During the Great Depression" (unpublished seminar paper, California State College, 1969), pp. 4-9.

7. Elbert Lee Tatum, *The Changing Political Thought of the Negro, 1915-1940* (New York, 1951), pp. 75-80, 122 125; see also James A. Brewer, "Robert Lee Vann and the *Pittsburgh Courier*" (M.A. thesis, University of Pittsburgh, 1941).

8. John Dennis Korba, "The Editorial Policy of the *Pittsburgh Courier,* 1928-1940" (M.Ed. thesis, California State College, 1967), pp. 30-33.

9. Andrew Buni, *Robert L. Vann of the Pittsburgh Courier: Politics and Black Journalism* (Pittsburgh, 1974), pp. 13, 19, 39-40, xi-xii, 31, 124-25, 207.

10. Robert L. Vann, "The Patriot and the Partisan," copy in Robert L. Vann Papers, Carnegie Library, Pittsburgh, Pennsylvania; *Pittsburgh Courier*, 1 October 1932.

11. Columbia University Oral History Project, "The Reminiscences of J. David Stern" (New York, 1954), pp. 44-51.

12. J. David Stern, *Memoirs of a Maverick Publisher* (New York, 1962), pp. 56-61, 81, 10, 215.

13. J. David Stern, Philadelphia, Pa., to Franklin D. Roosevelt, Washington, D.C., December 8, 1933, November 1, 1936; Stern, Philadelphia, to Joseph F. Guffey, Washington, February 6, 1935; Stern, Philadelphia, to Marvin H. McIntyre, Washington, D.C., March 7, 1935, all in President's Personal File 1039, Franklin D. Roosevelt Library, Hyde Park, New York, hereinafter cited as PPF 1039, FDRL.

14. Edwin B. Bronner, "The New Deal Comes to Pennsylvania: The Gubernatorial Election of 1934," *Pennsylvania History* 27, no. 1 (January 1960), pp. 44-45; see also E. Jeffrey Ludwig, "Pennsylvania: The National Election of 1932," *Pennsylvania History* 21, no. 3 (July 1964), pp. 334-51.

15. Joseph F. Guffey, Pittsburgh, Pa., to Franklin D. Roosevelt, Albany, New York, July 20, 1931, PPF 451, FDRL; Joseph F. Guffey, *Seventy Years on the Red Fire Wagon* (Lebanon, Pa., 1952), pp. 18-30. As director of sales for the Alien Property Custodian Guffey once received the interest of $401,000 on money he had deposited in federal banks. An old precedent in some circles ruled that the interest on public deposits was a special gratuity of the official who deposited the funds. Nevertheless, the Harding administration—not particularly noted for its integrity—collected the entire amount from Guffey in 1921. Before the New Deal Guffey also had difficulties with internal revenue officials, who charged him with illegal tax avoidance of over $1 million. Guffey managed to overcome these and other financial difficulties.

16. For Guffey, see Halt, "Guffey, New Deal Politician"; Ray Sprigle, "Lord Guffey of Pennsylvania," *American Mercury*, November 1936; Charles J. Martoni, "Joseph F. Guffey and the Rise of the Democratic Party in Pennsylvania" (M.A. research paper, California State College, 1977).

17. Quoted in Alfred Steinberg, *Sam Rayburn* (New York, 1975), p. 137.

18. Frank Hawkins, "Lawrence of Pittsburgh: Boss of the Mellon Patch," *Harper's Magazine*, August 1956, pp. 55-61; *Pittsburgh Post-Gazette*, 22 November 1966. See also *The Pennsylvania Manual*, 1961-1962.

19. Quoted in Bruce Stave, *The New Deal and The Last Hurrah: Pittsburgh Machine Politics* (Pittsburgh, 1970), p. 183.

20. Telegram, General Stiles, Washington, D.C., to Joseph F. Guffey, Pittsburgh, Pa., November 8, 1933; Guffey, Pittsburgh, to Marvin McIntyre, Washington, D.C., August 8, 1933, both in PPF 451; Guffey, Pittsburgh, to L. M. Howe, Washington, D.C., August 7, 1934, Democratic National Committee-Pennsylvania, OF 300; FDR Memorandum to McIntyre, December 20, 1935, PPF 451, FDRL.

21. Joseph Alsop and Robert Kintner, "The Guffey, Biography of a Boss," *Saturday Evening Post*, 26 March 1938, pp. 16-17.

22. Bronner, "New Deal Comes to Pennsylvania," pp. 48-53; Joseph F. Guffey, Pittsburgh, Pa., to President Roosevelt, Washington, D.C., March 16, 1934, PPF 451, FDRL; Stern, *Memoirs of a Maverick Publisher*, pp. 208-10.

23. Alsop and Kintner, "Biography of a Boss," p. 6; Walter Davenport, "Pennsylvania — Of All Places," *Collier's*, 23 March 1935, p. 56; "Labor Governor," *Time*, 4 July 1937.

24. "Confidential," M. H. M., September 13, 1934, OF 300, FDRL; Raymond Clapper, "Political Parties of Tomorrow," *Review of Reviews*, December 1934, p. 28; *The Pennsylvania Manual, 1935-1936*, p. 422; Bronner, "New Deal Comes to Pennsylvania," pp. 55-58, 61-67.

25. Richard C. Keller, "Pennsylvania's Little New Deal," *Pennsylvania History*, 29, no. 4 (October 1962), p. 401-405.

26. Much of this description of the campaign of 1936 is based on hundreds of Philadelphia newspaper clippings in the John B. Kelly Scrapbook, Free Library of Philadelphia, Philadelphia, Pennsylvania, hereinafter cited as Kelly Scrapbooks.

27. David Lawrence, Pittsburgh, Pa., to Marvin McIntyre, Washington, D.C., April 14, 1936; Lawrence, Pittsburgh, to James A. Farley, New York, New York, July 17, 1936; Charles W. Carroll, (?), to M. R. Diggs, Washington, D.C., September 28, 1936; Lawrence, Pittsburgh, to McIntyre, Washington, October 6, 1936, all in OF 300, FDRL; George H. Earle, Harrisburg, Pa., to Roosevelt, Washington, September 7, 1936, PPF 1999, FDRL. See also Joseph F. Guffey Diary in Joseph F. Guffey Papers, Washington and Jefferson College, Washington, Pennsylvania, hereinafter cited as Guffey Papers. See also Thomas L. Stokes *Chip Off My Shoulder* (Princeton, N. J., 1940), pp. 447-61.

28. Letter from Charles McDonald, Philadelphia, Pa., to "Deal Committeemen," March 14, 1936, Kelly Scrapbooks.

29. For an excellent account of the Earle administration, see Richard Calvin Keller, "Pennsylvania's Little New Deal" (Ph.D. diss., Columbia University, 1960).

30. James T. Patterson, *The New Deal and the States: Federalism in Transition* (Princeton, N. J., 1969) describes the effect of the Roosevelt administration beyond Washington.

31. Ibid., pp. 22, 184, 198-99, 142-43, 145.

32. Harold Gorvine, "The New Deal in Massachusetts," in John Braeman, Robert H. Bremner, and David Brody, eds., *The New Deal: The State and Local Levels* (Columbus, Ohio, 1975), pp. 3-38.

33. David J. Maurer, "Relief Problems and Politics in Ohio," in ibid., pp. 77-99.

34. Priscilla Ferguson Clement, "The Works Progress Administration in Pennsylvania," *The Pennsylvania Magazine of History and Biography* 95, no. 2 (April 1971), pp. 244-45.

35. Ibid., pp. 245-46; Lorena Hickok, Washington, D.C., to Harry Hopkins, Washington, D.C., October 17, 1936, July 24, 1935, Harry Hopkins Papers, FDRL.

36. Clement, "WPA in Pennsylvania," pp. 248-53.

37. Irving Bernstein, *Turbulent Years: History of the American Worker, 1933-1941* (Boston, 1969), pp. 470-73.

38. For an account of the Catholic vote, see Neil Betten, "Charles Owen Rice: Pittsburgh Labor Priest, 1936-1940." *The Pennsylvania Magazine of History and Biography* 94, no. 4 (October 1970), pp. 518-32; also see Thomas H. Coode and John D. Petrarulo, "The Odyssey of Pittsburgh's Father Cox," *The Western Pennsylvania Historical Magazine* 55, no. 3 (July 1972), pp. 217-38.

39. Numerous news clippings, Kelly Scrapbooks.

40. Bauman, "City, Depression, and Relief," pp. 293-95, 305-307.

41. News clippings, Kelly Scrapbooks; Keller, "Little New Deal," pp. 291-293.

42. Buni, *Robert L. Vann*, 203-207, 221, 2ບ4, 291-292.

43. Keller, "Little New Deal," pp. 405-06.

44. Telegram, John B. Kelly, Philadelphia, Pa., to President Roosevelt, Washington, D.C., April 22, 1938; Francis P. Walter, Scranton, Pa., to President Roosevelt, Washington, D.C., April 23, 1928, PPF 451, FDRL.

45. Clement, "WPA in Pennsylvania," pp. 254-255.

46. Glen R. Shaw, Sharpsville, Pa., to James A. Farley, Washington, D.C., December 2, 1938, Democratic National Committee-Pennsylvania, OF 300, FDRL.

47. Voter registration increased significantly in Pennsylvania during the New Deal. In 1932 there were 3,912,671 registered voters, of whom almost 75 percent were Republicans. By 1938 registered voters numbered 4,647,507; the Republican share was now around 51 percent. In intervening elections Democratic candidates received the votes of thousands of registered Republicans.

48. H. F. Alderfer and Fannette H. Luhrs, *Registration in Pennsylvania Elections, 1926-1946* (State College, Pa., 1948), pp. 22-23, 44-47, 61-64. For a recent study of the elections of 1938, see Alfred L. Morgan, "The Significance of Pennsylvania's 1938 Gubernatorial Election," *The Pennsylvania Magazine of History and Biography* 102, no. 2 (April 1978), pp. 184-211.

49. *The Pennsylvania Manual*, 1935-1936, PP. 475, 519, 552, 585, 601, 606: also 1939, pp. 193, 236, 239, 302, 317, 322.

50. Stevenson Whitcomb Fletcher, *Pennsylvania Agriculture and Country Life, 1840-1940* (Harrisburg, Pa., 1955), pp. 391-404.

Conclusion: The New Deal and Isolation in Pennsylvania

Beneath the thick pall of economic depression overhanging Pennsylvania in the 1930s, great changes occurred. Mass poverty provided the catalyst which modernized basic social and political institutions. A revitalized Democratic party successfully challenged a once-invincible Republican dynasty, while bureaucratically structured state and federal welfare programs supplanted the quiltwork of ancient poor boards and voluntary relief societies. More importantly, for many Pennsylvanians living in either rural districts, industrial towns, or mill neighborhoods, the Great Depression and the New Deal ended years of isolation and connected these places physically and psychologically to the modernizing influences of extracommunity institutions. No doubt the jubilant Indiana County Democrat who in 1934 exclaimed that "Indiana County has come into civilization after 40 years in the wilderness" evinced some awareness of the dynamic nature of the transformation. Likewise, the political chicanery swirling about the activities of the Works Progress Administration in Pennsylvania during the late 1930s reflected the gestation of the state's social and political institutions as they were buffeted by the tide of modernization.

Each of the preceding chapters has revealed in some way the relationship between the Great Depression, the New Deal, and the process of modernization in Pennsylvania. Between 1890 and 1910 industrialization and urbanization had carved new contours in the socioeconomic and political landscape of America. Undoubtedly the configuration of those contours differed from state to state, for by 1929 Pennsylvania clearly lagged behind its Northeastern neighbors in its progressive response to industrialism. Where large ethnic populations clustered in inner-city neighborhoods as in New York, Massachusetts, Connecticut, and New Jersey, Democratic city politicians such as David I. Walsh, Frank Hague, and Charles Murphy worked independently or in tandem with settlement-house workers, labor organizers, and self-conscious middle-class reformers, to encourage immigrant participation in politics and enact state factory, wage, hour, and child-labor legislation.

Yet in Pennsylvania the edge of this urban liberalism was dulled. As several chapters explained, in the period between 1890 and 1930 one of America's most powerful Republican machines dominated Pennsylvania politics. Marshalled under the escutcheon of the Pennsylvania Manufacturer's Association, a cadre of entrenched and powerful state manufacturing and industrial interests exercised political hegemony over the state.

In effect this hegemony of Pennsylvania manufacturing tycoons effectively retarded the pace of modernization by regularly thwarting the passage of progressive social legislation, limiting popular political participation, and allowing industrial barons to wield social and political dominion over their employees. Pennsylvania's physical geography and social landscape confirmed the pattern. Although the state boasted large cities and an enormous industrial base, most of its new stock immigrant population avoided job competition with the old stock and black labor of cities such as Philadelphia, and nestled in widely scattered smaller industrial cities such as Allentown, Norristown, Steelton, and Williamsport, and in a myriad of little company towns such as Cokeburg, Vestaburg, and Daisytown.

Therefore, Pennsylvania did not produce large immigrant cities such as Boston, New York, or Jersey City. Although by the early twentieth century political machines had evolved in both Philadelphia and Pittsburgh and although these machines thrived on their ability to deliver political services to boss-ruled river wards, little evidence of "urban liberalism" appeared in either city. Neither a Martin Lomasney nor a Robert

Wagner nor a Franklin Roosevelt emerged from Philadelphia's Vare machine or the Chris Magee, Billy Flinn organizations in Pittsburgh.

According to Robert Wiebe twentieth-century progressivism strove to bridge the social and political distance separating the immigrant, racial, class, professional, and working-class groups which comprised America's "segmented society." Therefore, despite the continued proclivity of American groups to erect boundaries, modernization intensified the frequency of cross-country communication, thereby lessening isolation for many peoples.

But not for all. Spreading urban values stressed bureaucratic efficiency, technical proficiency, and organic solidarity; but these values were hardly diffused evenly throughout society. Mining towns, rural villages, and company-ruled mill communities were usually too isolated to experience fully the social transformations of the early twentieth century. Where people clung to tradition and where industrialists deliberately blocked contact with the outside world, broad regions and districts, including urban areas, often remained impervious to modern trends.

Pennsylvania illustrates this persistence of isolation. The many coal patches in Washington, Fayette, and Indiana counties described in the preceding chapters endured an especially severe form of isolation. Nineteenth- and early twentieth-century coal and steel industrialists imposed a feudal order upon their company-owned fiefdoms, a feudalism reinforced by local institutions of social control such as the constabulary and county poor boards, and abetted by the pre-modern settings of industrial communities and the ethnic traditions of the immigrants themselves.

A different form of isolation prevailed in urban mill districts such as Philadelphia's Kensington-Richmond. Nineteenth-century urban-industrialism fashioned cities segregated by class, race, and ethnicity. In cities such as Philadelphia, clearly demarked mill enclaves emerged, populated by hosiery workers, metal workers, and carpet workers. Mill districts such as Kensington-Richmond comprised a distinctive self-conscious neighborhood where workers nurtured fierce loyalties to family, work groups, and union. Shaped on the one hand by the potent social and political power of industrialism, and on the other by the assiduous boundary-building activities of both native and ethnic Americans, this working-class world clearly evinced the lineaments of an "island community."

Furthermore, by 1930 demographers and sociologists of Northern cities discovered that another distinctive urban social configuration was black. The northward and cityward migration of black Southern peasantry, underway since the late nineteenth century, produced in Philadelphia and elsewhere a segregated community marked by gnawing poverty and sequestered in horribly substandard housing.

Beyond this urban-industrial pale, modernization all but bypassed rural-farming regions such as Snyder County. Avidly individualistic, farmers and small-town merchants alike took pride in rural traditions best upheld by ancient institutions such as county poor boards. Consequently in 1930, although the last census had officially heralded the modern urban age, Pennsylvania harbored vast areas both urban and rural palpably insulated against the sweep of modernization.

It was the Great Depression which produced change in Pennsylvania. Several of the foregoing studies of Pennsylvania's coal baronies and textile neighborhoods revealed that long before October 1929 poverty stalked the state's industrial communities. Wall Street's debacle only exacerbated the misery suffered by miners, cokers, and hosiery workers. However, the economic cataclysm which befell the entire nation jarred loose the old ideological underpinnings of Pennsylvania's industrial hierarchy. Nostrums which had been at least partially effective in the earlier depressions of the 1870s, 1890s, and 1914 and 1921, proved futile against the mass misery of the 1930s. For example, the state's archaic public charity system, based on county poor boards, which doled out relief more from political expediency than necessity, buckled under the pressure of massive unemployment. This inadequacy of public relief overburdened private organization such as the Red Cross, Philadelphia's Union Benevolent Association, churches, family societies, and the host of local emergency agencies which traditionally mobilized to provide the "thin red line" of charity in periods of depression. However, the enormity of the Great Depression overwhelmed society's weak defenses against mass poverty. The experience of Philadelphia's celebrated Committee on Unemployment Relief proved conclusively that, despite professionalism and scientific efficiency, modern voluntary social casework was aimed too directly at particular segments of the fragmented metropolis to be marshalled effectively on behalf of the mass unemployed.

Ultimately, the formation of Communist- and Socialist-dominated unemployed councils and leagues, and the spectacle of hunger marches in Pittsburgh, Philadelphia, and Allentown compelled the denizens of Pennsylvania's Old Guard establishment to reconsider their hoary notions about the sanctity of laissez-faire. Although Philadelphia Mayor J. Hampton Moore never capitulated, in 1932 the city's conservative Chamber of Commerce joined social workers from Allentown and Pittsburgh and other apprehensive and concerned Pennsylvanians to demand that the state discard its antiquated welfare machinery and establish a modern, bureaucratically structured State Emergency Relief Board. The severity of the Great Depression had cut through the crusty cake of tradition and moved Pennsylvania in the direction of modernization.

Between 1931 and 1934 the growing militance of the jobless, the activism of social workers, and the dire poverty of the state's mine and textile working population formed the base for a dramatic social and political transformation. Together, the Great Depression and the "bold, persistent experimentation" of Franklin Delano Roosevelt and the New Deal combined to loosen the shackles of Republican state domination. Although Herbert Hoover's Emergency Committee on Employment, Organization on Unemployment Relief, and Reconstruction Finance Corporation reluctantly intervened to buttress the nation's sagging economy, Hoover's commitment to federal activism hardly matched the visible assault on the Great Depression which marked the New Deal.

Unlike Hoover, Roosevelt convinced Pennsylvania miners and textile workers that Washington, D.C. understood their plight and, moreover, meant to address their problems. New

Dealers capitalized on the frustration of destitute miners, steelworkers, poor farmers, jobless blacks and whites, the militant as well as those too emotionally depressed to be angry, and experimented with a variety of progressive social and economic measures that had been jelling in the minds of bureaucratic reformers and theoreticians since the early 1920s. Under the Federal Emergency Relief Administration (FERA) federal relief funds administered through the State Emergency Relief Board (SERA) and local relief boards helped fill the larders of needy jobless families throughout Pennsylvania. Civilian Conservation Corps (CCC) encampments in state parks employed Pennsylvania youth to plant trees, control floods, and build fire towers. Meanwhile, the National Youth Administration (NYA) helped young students finish college.

More importantly, the collective-bargaining provisions of the National Industrial Recovery Act enlisted the federal government on the side of the working class, elevating "big labor" as a massive countervailing force to big business. By energizing the union movement, affording a minimum of security to the poor and the jobless, and politicizing isolated miners, new-stock ethnics and inner-city blacks, the New Deal not only launched a revival of the Democratic party in Pennsylvania but also induced profound social change. In many ways, then, the New Deal brought within the framework of the new urban society the isolated peoples living in gray mining towns in Fayette and Washington counties, in blighted mill districts in Philadelphia, and small farms in Snyder County.

New Deal programs such as the FERA, the CCC, and the Works Progress Administration (WPA) reached out to bind segmented groups together into what John Higham has called a technical unity. The New Deal established a host of these translocal agencies, penetrating the barriers of isolation, and connecting places such as Daisytown, Vestaburg, Selingsgrove, and Kensington to the extracommunity. For example, as a centralized relief system FERA and SERA dissolved the poor board-corporation nexus which had made relief an awesome and pernicious instrument for social control and company domination. During the decade of the 1930s, Red Cross workers, Friends Service Committee people, FERA agents,

CCC, NYA, and WPA administrators swarmed into communities which for decades had been insulated against even the slightest outside influence. At first the National Recovery Administration and finally the National Labor Relations Board conducted federally supervised collective-bargaining elections. With federal backing, the union movement transformed once fiercely independent local unions such as John L. Lewis's United Mine Workers of America into large Washington, D.C.-based bureaucracies. In addition, under the Works Progress Administration storm sewers, water mains and paved roads introduced many backwash communities to modern sanitation, visibly linking them to the big city.

Naturally, the federal sponsorship of social welfare and union power unleashed a new era of political participation for working-class Pennsylvanians. In Indiana County as in Washington, Philadelphia, and Fayette Counties, the year 1934 witnessed the revival of the Democratic party. Joseph F. Guffey urged new-stock ethnic Americans to participate in Democratic politics, and with David Lawrence in Pittsburgh and John B. Kelly in Philadelphia identified the Democratic party not only as pro-labor, but as a house for all peoples in Pennsylvania. No doubt in Philadelphia Republican apprehension of the political potential of New Deal largesse greatly obstructed the works-relief programs. Nevertheless, although in the 1930s the Democratic party in Philadelphia failed to establish the kind of hegemony once enjoyed by Republicans, the new Democratic politicos, buttressed by the popularity of Roosevelt and the New Deal, won the allegiance of Philadelphia's Italians, Poles, Irish, and blacks. Blacks in particular played an important role in the Philadelphia New Deal arena. As elsewhere in urban America, Philadelphia's black population grew significantly in the 1930s; at the same time it became increasingly ill-housed and segregated. Philadelphia demonstrated that the planner's consciousness of this burgeoning black community germinated policy decisions regarding, for example, public housing. Yet, it was the leavening of black race and class consciousness during the depression which produced much greater black political participation and unleashed the black crusade for public housing. Paradoxically, in time public housing became a subtle vehicle for increased race segregation.

While the wafts of urban modernization invigorated the political and social life of mining and mill districts in the state, they also exercised a transforming effect on rural farming institutions in Pennsylvania. The Great Depression and the New Deal shattered the pre-industrial assumptions which had undergirded the highly personalized and inefficient system of poor-board relief. Yet, although SERA stood for bureaucratic efficiency, the case of Snyder County suggests that many pre-industrial values concerning the primacy of work and the social and psychological defectiveness of the jobless survived, entrenched in regulations governing client eligibility.

By the end of the depression decade, throughout Pennsylvania a bureaucratic scaffolding had been raised broad enough to reach into the most isolated regions of the state. Although New Deal-built highway, bridge, electrification, and other projects could bypass as well as connect isolated places, more significantly the new roads, dams, guidebooks, theater presentations, sewing projects, and homemaker cottages exposed isolated towns and regions to the greater scrutiny of society while availing miners, textile workers, and farmers alike of the values and appetites of the mass society. If problems such as poverty and racial segregation remained unsolved or overlooked by 1941, it was less because of isolation than the insufficiency of public funding, the persistence of a rural-urban clash, the malapportionment of the state legislature, and the failure of public policy to deal effectively with the income deficiencies of the aging, blacks, and migrant Americans. Like America, Pennsylvania society in 1941 remained fragmented in search of an always elusive unity whether primodial, ideological, or technical. However, during the 1930s Pennsylvanians watched federal and state programs end the most pernicious forms of isolation, leaving the state clearly more modern and clearly more urban.

Bibliographical Essay

I. General

Few histories adequately treat either the Great Depression or the New Deal in the states. Standard monographs such as Broadus Mitchell's *Depression Decade: From the New Era through the New Deal, 1929-1941* (New York, 1966), and Arthur Schlesinger, Jr.'s three-volume *The Age of Roosevelt* (Boston, 1957-1960) refer infrequently to events in particular states. Although William E. Leuchtenburg's *Franklin D. Roosevelt and the New Deal* (New York, 1963) focuses on the nation and not the states, it contains important insights into the New Deal's impact on American social and institutional life.

Of the few monographs examining the New Deal in the states, James T. Patterson's *The New Deal in the States: Federalism in Transition* (Princeton, N.J. 1969) is particularly useful. Mark I. Gelfand's *A Nation of Cities* (Oxford, 1975) covers the period 1920-1960, being most valuable for an understanding of how the New Deal launched a reshaping of the relationship between the city and the federal government.

There are several manuscript collections especially useful for the study of Pennsylvania in the 1930s. Among the most important are the records of the Federal Emergency Relief Administration, the Civil Works Administration and the Works Progress Administration, all in Record Group 69, National Archives, Washington, D.C. Although these records concern the relief activities of the New Deal, they also house reports, statistical data, newspaper clipping files, and correspondence illuminating every aspect of life in Pennsylvania in the 1930s.

The papers of the President's Emergency Committee for Employment and the President's Organization on Unemployment Relief covering the years 1930-1931, found in Record Group 73, National Archives, Washington, D.C., afford often penetrating descriptions of the relief crises affecting Pennsylvania communities in the early 1930s. Excellent field reports on Pennsylvania by Lorena Hickok and Henry Francis are found in the Harry L. Hopkins Papers, Franklin D. Roosevelt Library (FDRL), Hyde Park, New York. Members of Harry Hopkins' staff of roving reporters, Hickok and Francis supply exceedingly colorful, unvarnished, often spicy testimony on the political, social, and economic conditions in Pennsylvania's depression-ridden communities.

Other good general information on Pennsylvania during the 1930s can be found in the Gifford Pinchot Papers, Library of Congress, Washington, D.C. Less useful are the Papers of Joseph Guffey, Washington and Jefferson College, Washington, Pennsylvania.

II. Social Life

Jack Conroy's *The Disinherited* (New York, 1933) contains sections dealing with Pennsylvania society in the 1930s. The best general study of Pennsylvania mining communities during the Great Depression is Muriel Early Sheppard's *Cloud by Day: The Story of Coal and Coke and People* (Chapel Hill, N. C., 1947).

Several works written during the 1930s touch on relief activities in Pennsylvania during the period. Clinch Calkins's *Some Folks Won't Work* (New York, 1930) is excellent for unemployment and relief in the early depression. On the administrative history of federal relief Donald Howard's *The WPA and Federal Relief Policy* (New York, 1943), and Josephine Brown's *Public Relief, 1929-1939* (New York, 1940) are thorough and punctuated with references to state activities, although highly sympathetic to the Roosevelt administration.

Among the more recent studies which deal in part or wholly with social aspects of the depression in Pennsylvania is Bonnie

Fox's "Unemployment and Relief in Philadelphia, 1930-1932: A Study of the Depression's Impact on Voluntarism," *Pennsylvania Magazine of History and Biography* 93, no. 1 (January 1969), pp. 86-108. Searle Charles's *Minister of Relief: Harry Hopkins and the Depression* (Syracuse, 1963) contains skimpy material on the WPA in Pennsylvania. Priscilla F. Clement's study "The Works Progress Administration in Pennsylvania," *The Pennsylvania Magazine of History and Biography* 95 no. 2 (April 1971) and Kenneth E. Henrickson, Jr.'s. "The CCC in Pennsylvania: A Case Study of a New Deal Relief Agency in Operation," *The Pennsylvania Magazine of History and Biography* 100, no. 1 (January 1976) are two adequate studies of New Deal agencies in Pennsylvania. John F. Bauman's "The City, the Depression and Relief: The Philadelphia Experience, 1929-1939" (Ph.D. diss., Rutgers University, 1969) discusses the gamut of relief activities in Philadelphia during the 1930s, and concludes that New Deal relief failed to overcome the harsh Elizabethan view of the welfare client. Ernest B. Fricke stresses relief activities on the local front in his "The Impact of the Depression on Allentown, Pennsylvania: 1930-1940" (Ph.D. diss., New York University, 1974); York, Pennsylvania, in the 1930s, is examined in Carl E. Hatch, et. al., *York, Pennsylvania, in the Depression Thirties* (Martin Library Historical Series, no. 3, York, Pennsylvania; 1974).

Among the manuscript sources on relief in Pennsylvania the FERA, CWA, and WPA papers in Record Group 69, National Archives, are basic. In addition, the Hopkins Papers in the Roosevelt Library contain excellent information on relief including the aforementioned reports of Hickok and Francis. Unfortunately, the minutes of the State Emergency Relief Board in the State Archives of the Pennsylvania Historical and Museum Commission, Harrisburg, have only limited value.

Among the important studies of housing, Mabel Walker's *Urban Blight and Slums* (Cambridge, 1938), Nathan Straus's *The Seven Myths of Housing* (New York, 1941), Catherine Bauer's *Modern Housing* (New York, 1934), Lawrence Friedman's *Government and Slum Housing: A Century of Frustration* (Chicago, 1968), Roy Lubove's *Twentieth Century Pitts-*

burgh (Pittsburgh, 1969), and Mel Scott's *American City Planning* (Los Angeles, 1969), all refer at length or at least briefly to Pennsylvania, and are important for an understanding of the development of public housing in the 1930s. An article by John F. Bauman discusses housing in Philadelphia during the 1930s, "Safe and Sanitary Without the Costly Frills: The Evolution of Public Housing in Philadelphia, 1929-1939," *The Pennsylvania Magazine of History and Biography* 150, no. 1 (January 1977), pp. 114-28. For Pittsburgh, see David W. Lonich, "Pittsburgh's Black Community and Low Income Housing Ventures, 1928-1940" (M. A. thesis, California State College, 1974).

Several manuscript collections furnish information on public housing in Pennsylvania. The Housing Association of Delaware Valley Papers at Temple Urban Archives, Temple University, Philadelphia, help chronicle the extensive housing activities of the Philadelphia Housing Association. The Pittsburgh Housing Association Papers in the Archives of Industrial Society at the University of Pittsburgh elucidate the housing situation in the steel city. An invaluable body of information on New Deal housing is found in the Records of the Housing Division of the Public Works Administration, Record Group 196, National Archives, Washington, D. C.

For the general history of black America in the Great Depression with very limited reference to Pennsylvania, see Raymond Wolters, *The Negro in the Great Depression* (Westport, Conn., 1970). Pennsylvania's blacks in the 1930s are examined in James Erroll Miller's "The Negro in Pennsylvania Politics with Special Emphasis on the Years Between 1927-1940" (Ph.D. diss., University of Pennsylvania, 1969). H. Viscount Nelson's "Race and Class Consciousness of Philadelphia Negroes with Special Emphasis on the Years Between 1927 and 1940" (Ph.D. diss., University of Pennsylvania, 1969) emphasizes the travail of Philadelphia's black middle class during the Great Depression. Philadelphia's black community in the 1930s also comes alive in the Armstrong Association papers and the Philadelphia NAACP Papers, both found in the Temple Urban Archives, Temple University. Pittsburgh's black community is discussed in John Dennis Korba's "Robert Vann, The *Pittsburgh Courier* and the New Deal" (M.A. thesis, California State College, 1969). The experience of the black community in Pittsburgh during the Depression can be observed in Andrew Buni's *Robert L. Vann of the Pittsburgh Courier: Politics and Black Journalism* (Pittsburgh, 1974), and in the pages of Robert Vann's *Pittsburgh Courier.* Critical information on the Depression and the black community in Pennsylvania and the nation can be found in the 1930s issues of *Crisis Magazine* and *Opportunity: A Journal of Negro Life*.

III. Politics

The sources of information on Pennsylvania politics in the 1930s are fairly extensive. Bruce Stave's *The New Deal and the Last Hurrah: Pittsburgh Machine Politics* (Pittsburgh, 1970) traces the metamorphosis of Pittsburgh politics from Republican to Democratic domination. J. T. Salter's *Boss Rule: Portraits in City Politics* (Princeton, N.J., 1935) contains numerous vignettes on the struggle of Philadelphia Republican ward heelers to survive the New Deal social-welfare bonanza. Joseph Guffey's autobiographical *Seventy Years on the Red Fire Wagon* (Privately printed, 1952) explicates Guffey's key role in the revival of the Democratic party in Pennsylvania. In John L. Shover's "Emergence of a Two-Party System in Philadelphia," *Journal of American History* 60, No. 2 (April 1976) the author emphasizes the election of 1934 and the role of blacks and ethnic groups in the revival of the city's Democratic party.

A number of doctoral dissertations illuminate the politics of Pennsylvania in the New Deal era. Richard Keller's "Pennsylvania Little New Deal" (Ph.D. diss., Columbia University, 1960) is helpful; Samuel J. Astorino's "The Decline of Republican Dynasty in Pennsylvania, 1929-1934" (Ph.D. diss., University of Pittsburgh, 1962) concentrates almost exclusively on Philadelphia and Pittsburgh. Irwin F. Greenburg's "The Philadelphia Democratic Party, 1911-1934" (Ph.D. diss., Temple University, 1972) is an extensive treatment of Philadelphia depression politics. Guffey's political role is examined in Charles E. Halt's "Joseph F. Guffey, New Deal Politician from Pennsylvania" (Ph.D. diss., Syracuse University, 1965). On Pinchot, see M. Nelson McGreary's *Gifford Pinchot* (Princeton, 1960).

Among the manuscript sources for Pennsylvania's Depression politics are the extremely useful Franklin D. Roosevelt Papers in the Official File and the President's Personal File, FDRL, Hyde Park, New York. The aforementioned Records of the FERA, CWA and WPA in Record Group 69, National Archives, are equally important, especially the WPA news clipping files, which contain a running account of the political problems of the WPA in Pennsylvania. For an excellent picture of Philadelphia politics with glimpses of state politics, consult the albums of news clippings in the John B. Kelly Papers in the Free Library of Philadelphia. Philadelphia politics are prominently featured in the J. Hampton Moore Papers in the Historical Society of Pennsylvania, Philadelphia. The Joseph Guffey Papers at Washington and Jefferson College have limited value for state-wide politics while the Gifford Pinchot Papers in the Library of Congress, Washington, D.C., are particularly good.

IV. Labor

One of the best general works on labor during the Great Depression, but with very little on Pennsylvania in particular, is Milton Derber and Edwin Young, eds., *Labor and the New Deal* (Madison, 1957). Much more valuable for Pennsylvania are two volumes by Irving Bernstein, *The Lean Years: A History of the American Worker, 1920-1933* (Boston, 1960), and *Turbulent Years: A History of the American Worker, 1933-1941* (Boston, 1969). In both volumes Bernstein offers a definitive treatment of the struggles of both miners and steelworkers to gain union recognition. Both Sidney Lens's highly personal *Left, Right, and Center: Conflicting Forces in American Labor* (Chicago, 1949), and Daniel J. Leab's "United We Eat: The Creation and Organization of the Unemployed Councils in 1930," *Labor History* 8, no. 3 (Fall 1967) discuss the role of the unemployed councils of the early

1930s and both mention Philadelphia. On labor militance, see J. David Pivar "The Hosiery Workers and the Philadelphia Third Party Impulse, 1929-1935,"*Labor History* 5, no. 4 (Winter 1964), and also Richard Kelly, *Nine Lives for Labor* (New York, 1956). Pivar and Kelly provide a good perspective on the union activities in the textile industry in both Philadelphia and Reading, Pennsylvania. In her *Union Tactics and Economic Change: A Case Study of Three Philadelphia Textile Unions* (Philadelphia, 1932), and her University of Pennsylvania monographs such as *Trends in the Philadelphia Labor Market in 1934* (Philadelphia, 1935), Gladys Palmer provides indispensable material for an understanding of the Pennsylvania labor situation in the 1930s.

In addition to Muriel Sheppard's *Cloud by Day*, several studies provide insight into the union organizing activities in the Pennsylvania mine fields. John Brophy's *A Miner's Life* (Madison, 1964), is a sympathetic but very useful account of Brophy's life in the United Mine Workers of America. Lauren Gilfillan's dramatically written *I Went to Pit College* (New York, 1934) offers a vivid account of a young newspaper-woman's experiences among poor coal miners in southwestern Pennsylvania during the Depression. Among other important investigations of Pennsylvania miners are Morton S. Baratz's *The Union and the Coal Industry* (New Haven, 1955), J. P. Shalloo's *Private Police—With Special Reference to Pennsylvania* (Philadelphia, 1933), McAlister Coleman's *Men and Coal* (New York, 1934), and Homer L. Morris's *The Plight of the Bituminous Coal Miner* (Philadelphia, 1934).

Several articles by James P. Johnson afford a better understanding of the Great Depression and Pennsylvania miners, namely, "Reorganizing the United Mine Workers of America in Pennsylvania During the New Deal," *Pennsylvania History* 37, no. 2 (April 1970), "Drafting the NRA Code of Fair Competition for the Bituminous Coal Industry," *Journal of American History* 7, no. 3 (December 1966), and "Theories of Labor Union Development and the United Mine Workers, 1932-1933," *Register of the Kentucky Historical Society* 73, no. 2 (April 1975).

The labor history of Pennsylvania can be captured satisfactorily in the pages of labor publications such as *American Federationist, Labor Age, Labor Record, Progressive Labor World*, and *The United Mine Workers' Journal*, all available at the Free Library of Philadelphia and the labor archives, the University of Wisconsin, Madison, and in the American Federation of Labor Building Library, Washington, D.C.

Several manuscript collections offer good information on Pennsylvania labor in the Great Depression. The United Mine Workers of America Papers in Washington, D.C., are sketchy, but still useful. Father Charles Owen Rice's papers at the Pennsylvania State University shed some light on the labor situation in Pittsburgh. Phillip Murray's papers at George Washington University are often elliptical, suggesting more questions than answers.

Many of the unanswered questions concerning Pennsylvania in the Great Depression and particularly the state's labor history are being answered through ongoing oral-history projects. The extensive ethnic oral history project of the Pennsylvania Historical and Museum Commission represents a major resource for historians of Pennsylvania social life in the 1930s. The Pennsylvania Ethnic Heritage Studies Center at the University of Pittsburgh is endeavoring to use oral as well as census and other quantitative data to illuminate the history of the peoples of Pittsburgh. A similar major project is underway at the Center for Social History at the University of Pennsylvania. Elsewhere, the Pennsylvania State University Oral History Project collecting the oral reminiscences of Pennsylvania steelworkers has contributed greatly to the historians' knowledge about the role of the Steelworkers' Organizing Committee in Pennsylvania as well as the building of the Congress of Industrial Organizations. At California State College, California, Pennsylvania, the Oral History Project has collected over 400 tapes of the reminiscences of coal miners, making possible a more complete picture of miners' lives in the 1930s. The CSC tapes also highlight the role of the UMWA in producing change in the coal region. Using oral history in conjunction with such manuscript sources as the census, tax assessment records, and the payroll ledgers of the Vesta-Shannopin Mining Division of the Jones and Laughlin Steel Corporation and the Papers of the Bethlehem Mines Corporation affords crucial insights into the social, political, as well as the labor aspects of the Great Depression.

Index